A KING FOR ALL TIME

✴ D A V I D ✴

A Comprehensive Study

May David's Blessings Be Yours!

P.S.Snyder

Pamela Susanne Snyder

ISBN 978-1-64258-768-5 (paperback)
ISBN 978-1-64258-769-2 (digital)

Christian Faith Publishing, Inc.
832 Park Avenue
Meadville, PA 16335
www.christianfaithpublishing.com

Printed in the United States of America

Contents

Prologue

"For the Lord is great and greatly to be praised!" exclaimed David in Psalm 96:4. This was an exultation, like many other expressions that David offered to the Lord in his writings. David marveled at God's greatness and his goodness. David had experienced a lifetime of sin, sorrow, sanctuary, and salvation. He knew that he could go to God for help in times of trouble, and he journaled his experiences and relationship with God in the book of Psalms. Most of the account of his life, however, is recorded in the books of Samuel 1 and 2. There are examples of happiness, loss, friendship, family life, distress, privilege, poverty, love, lust, war, peace, distance from God, and fellowship with God. The purpose of this comprehensive study is to bring David's life to the reader in an easy-to-understand way, while still retaining the meaningful lessons. Because in the twenty-first century, we experience many of the same things that David experienced in 1,000 BC.

My journey as a Bible study leader began in 2002 with a small group of coworkers. For five years, I brought God's word to them with purchased Bible study guides. I wanted biblical truth and deep spiritual growth for my group. Then, in 2013, the Lord provided a different opportunity for me to lead a community Bible study. I began to think creatively and wrote a lesson on every topic the group wanted to study. Sometimes, the lesson became a series, such as the study of David. Its success was due to a researched description of the biblical account, personal applications, group participation, and prayer.

You will find that the unique elements of this study of David include the following:

- Text of the account
- Description of the text
- Commentary on historical background and interpretation
- Related references
- Special studies of David's diary in Psalms
- Contemporary questions and applications
- Appendix of timeline for David's life
- Appendix of characters in the account of David
- Group Leader Guide

How could the book be used? Besides being a really good read, it is valuable for personal devotion use or as a group study for both women and men. The most effective group studies are participative where thought and discussion initiate. Various members could successfully share roles with reading the text or references or even leading dialogue. The group leader might introduce and close the session, while incorporating the Study Guide tools. Since the book content is extensive, some preparatory reading will best utilize group time.

My desire is that this study of David be used to bring honor and glory to his successor—the Messiah, Christ Jesus. For David scribed God's words of the Messiah in Psalm 2:6: "Yet I have set My King on My holy hill of Zion." May Jesus Christ, through His servant, David, be praised.

Acknowledgements

My deep affection is extended to the dear ladies of
the David Series Bible study group.

Dottie Robe
Barbara May
Iris Chandler
Jan Henderson
Barbara Haglund
Carrie McCrohan
Charlotte Nusbaum

Special thanks to Marilyn Gnekow for suggesting a study of David's
life and to Beth Bohnsack for the creative book title.

Credits

The following public resources were consulted in writing this book:

Bible Hub
Got Questions?
Strong's Exhaustive Concordance
The Bible Knowledge Commentary
New Bible Dictionary
David by Charles Spurgeon
New Geneva Study Bible
Various Christian Websites
Jewish Virtual Library
A man after God's own heart by R.T. Kendall
Lumina Bible Study

All reference quotes have been taken from the New American Standard Bible.

Disclaimer: The information provided in this book was researched by an author who does not claim to be a theologian. Topics and concepts of theology may slightly differ from the reader's views. The resources that were referenced are considered to be fundamentally sound.

Estimated Chronological Timeline

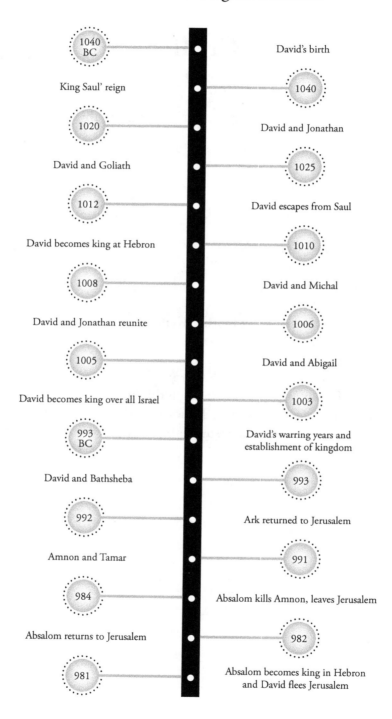

1040 BC — David's birth

King Saul' reign — 1040

1020 — David and Jonathan

David and Goliath — 1025

1012 — David escapes from Saul

David becomes king at Hebron — 1010

1008 — David and Michal

David and Jonathan reunite — 1006

1005 — David and Abigail

David becomes king over all Israel — 1003

993 BC — David's warring years and establishment of kingdom

David and Bathsheba — 993

992 — Ark returned to Jerusalem

Amnon and Tamar — 991

984 — Absalom kills Amnon, leaves Jerusalem

Absalom returns to Jerusalem — 982

981 — Absalom becomes king in Hebron and David flees Jerusalem

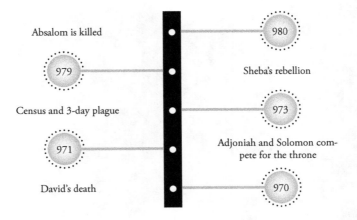

Absalom is killed — 980

979 — Sheba's rebellion

Census and 3-day plague — 973

971 — Adjoniah and Solomon compete for the throne

David's death — 970

Resources:

Life of David Discipleship Lessons www.jesuswalk.com

Chronology of King David's Life by William H. Gross www.livingstonesclass.org

David: Sought and Chosen

"The LORD has sought for himself a man after his own heart..."
—1 Samuel 13:14

David, sought and chosen by God, was a man of honorable character who possessed special spiritual stature. He lived 3,000 years after the creation of the world, 1,000 years before Christ, and 3,000 years prior to our current civilization. He is the only person in the Bible whom God called a man after his own heart. This is supported in both the Old Testament and the New Testament. It is important to know who David was as a person because it is clear that God enjoyed him and was deeply involved with David personally. If we were to quickly examine David's life, we would see that he had the unique ability to reflect upon his experiences and personality through poetry and music in the book of Psalms. He was Israel's greatest king and one of the most powerful military leaders in the Bible. Scripture certainly validates David's existence and experiences in the biblical timeline. Yet there is scant physical evidence of his life in the archaeological remnants.

According to the Jewish Virtual Library, until very recently there was no real evidence outside the Bible for the existence of King David. Egyptian, Syrian, and Assyrian historical documents fail to mention his name. Although there is plenty of evidence for an ancient Jerusalem, excavations had failed to uncover proof of David as a person or a king. Then, in 1993, a team of archaeologists led by Professor Avraham Biran found a section of a Syrian victory pillar at Tel Dan that had been nearly destroyed by an Israelite ruler. An inscription on the pillar states the words "Beit David" or house of David. This evidence strongly indicates that a king named David established a dynasty in Israel during the biblical timeline. Another archaeological survey led by Dr. Avi Ofer uncovered further evidence during the past decade. It shows that in the eleventh and tenth centuries BC, during David's dynasty, the population of the hill country of Judah doubled. The settlement size and positioning signifies an unusually strong and unified populace. This fact supports the biblical account of David's successful reign and kingdom.

Finding David (1 Samuel 16:1–13)

In Psalm 89:20-21 we read that God found David. David was a man that God was able to use and confide in. We read that God found David. Psalm 89:20-21 God sought out David. His choosing was not the result of David's actions. The predetermination was God's eternal plan for David to genetically propagate a royal line from which the Messiah would originate. The Psalm 89 passage further explains that God's unwavering help for this role would include support, strength, courage and success. David would be consecrated to his office by an anointing with holy oil. The oil was symbolic of God's endowment of the Holy Spirit in David's life. Other key verses that signify God's choice of David are found in 1 Samuel 13:14 and Acts 13:22.

First Samuel 13:14 uses the word sought, which means to search out or to strive after. It defines a completed action whereby God selected the right man for his plan; one who would be committed to his will and purposes. The end result would be search completed and choice made. Acts 13:22 references David's family. "I have found David, the son of Jesse". Children were often identified by name with their parents, which explains why David's father Jesse is named in this text. Jesse was Ruth and Boaz's grandson.

We cannot properly study David's life without first reviewing Israel's history dating to its first king. King Saul had deeply disappointed God. He was a defiant king who had trusted in his own authority and witchcraft rather than God. He also misconstrued God's requirements for sacrificial offerings by insisting that his worship practices were favorable. One day Samuel, the prophet, brought a message from God to Saul. I Samuel 15:22–23 The point Samuel made to Saul was that ritual performance is worthless if it is not accompanied by a sincere and submissive spirit. So, God would depose King Saul; in fact, He would eventually allow Saul's death. Samuel now searched for a new king, even while Saul remained on the throne. This was a very daring and dangerous thing to do…to anoint a new king while the reigning monarch was still alive. But Samuel was God's man. His confidence was in God and he stayed in touch with God, praying over every matter.

Now, as was the custom, Samuel wanted to please God by offering a sacrifice. However, this providentially gave Samuel an opportunity to evaluate each of Jesse's sons, one by one; allowing God the liberty to speak through him. God's only message was, "Go to Jesse's family." God often gives us part of the information so that we will trust Him more for the rest of the information. Trusting him to lead us is a great way to live and it brings us even closer in relationship to Him. Was there ever a time when you completely trusted in the LORD for the unknown future? Notice that in verse two, Samuel at first is fearful. He said, "How can I go? Saul will hear about it and kill me." We also read that the elders in the town of Bethlehem were fearful. They asked, "Do you come in peace?" And Samuel replied, "Yes." But God's plan was not to be deterred by fear.

Jesse brought forward the son who had made him most proud. Eliab was impressive in his appearance. According to verse seven the Lord refused to look upon David's eldest brother. He was not interested in Eliab's appealing figure. In fact, the context is one of God's awareness of the heart, not the physical appearance. Samuel also sensed that he was not the one. In fact, none of the sons Jesse presented was the one. Of interest is that Jesse's sons posed before Samuel. The word "presented" in verse eight means to pass in front of. There was still one son that Samuel needed to see and it was only upon his inquiring further that David appeared. As the youngest son, he had been tending the sheep. Probably all the sons had at one time tended sheep, but they had advanced to higher ambitions. Tending sheep was a simple occupation not to be compared to butchering animals, farming land, and selling or trading with other farmers. As David came before Samuel, Samuel knew in an instant that this was the future king of Israel. Although still a teenager; he was ready to be molded for the most important job imaginable. Verse twelve describes David as ruddy. He had reddish hair and skin; a healthy complexion sometimes associated with outdoor life. His eyes were bright and he was good looking. In fact, the Hebrew interpretation says he was a beautiful young man. But, again, did God care about the way he looked? No. God was looking for a man who had a heart for him. I Samuel 13:14 Another way of saying this is, a man of his own choosing.

A Good Choice

To be chosen of God must have a very special implication. God's choosing is not sourced in human plans or responses. The basis of God's choosing is due to his very good pleasure and his love for us. Ephesians 1:4 explains that God chose us before the foundation of the world. God knew that you, I, and even David would be born. I Corinthians 1:27-28 makes it clear that God does the unexpected. He chooses the foolish, the weak, the despised, and the least of us to accomplish his very special plan. God's choosing David over his talented and successful older brothers was a surprise, for David had few accomplishments. But as the New Testament points out, often it is the unlikely and unlovely that God chooses to change into a beautiful creation that will serve his purposes.

The reasons for God's choosing a man like David are, upon examination, extraordinarily relational.

- The choice involved God's direction for David's life. (John 15:16)
- The choice was intended to bring fulfillment and purpose to David for his God. John 15:16
- The choice signified a sacred position with God. (Ephesians 1:4)
- The choice resulted in a permanent alliance with God, as his special possession. (I Peter 2:9)
- The choice empowered David to proclaim God's character to others. (I Peter 2:9)
- The choice was initiated by God's love for David as he had loved the chosen people of Israel. (Deuteronomy 7:6-7)
- The choice was not predetermined by David's wisdom, power, or nobility. (I Corinthians 1:26-28)
- The choice means that we will receive divine direction.
- The choice means that we will live life fully with the satisfaction that God's purposes become our purposes.
- The choice allows God's holiness to permeate our being and determine our actions.
- The choice allows us to reside in the family of God who desires to call us his children.
- The choice enables us to be a light to others, with the ability to share the love of Christ.
- The choice proves God's complete and unconditional love.
- The choice does not require wisdom, power or nobility.

As evidenced in New Testament scripture, God's choice of us leads to a personal experience with him. The results are amazing, as his choice serves an immediate purpose but more importantly, an eternal purpose.

Man's Heart/God's Heart

In addition to being a man of God's own choosing, we read in Acts 13:22 that David was a man after God's own heart. What exactly does this mean? David was after God's heart in the sense of being committed to God's will and purposes. Thus, if David was a man after God's own heart, what type of heart did David have?

1. From his most humble beginnings we see that David was a person of integrity and David chose to serve the LORD. Psalm 78:70–72 That means, in

everything he did, from shepherding his flocks to shepherding his king-dom, David stayed in tune with God, listening to and obeying Him. I Kings 9:4

2. Psalm 51:1–4 tells us that David's heart was humble and repentant. He compared his own character to God's. God is loving, kind, merciful and just. David, on the other hand, acknowledged his sinfulness and his regret and sorrow for that sin. When we contrast God's holiness to our shortcomings, it helps us to have a clear picture of the truth about ourselves.

3. More insight into David's heart is found in Psalm 51:10–13. David valued God's presence in his life. He wanted more of Him. And in these verses, we get a sense that David thought God's Spirit might leave Him. As he saw his need for God because of his sinfulness, he made statements like "renew your Spirit within me" and "Don't leave me, Holy Spirit because you give me joy and confidence." Along with learning about David's heart, one that was honest, humble, repentant, obedient and seeking after God, we know that these are the characteristics God wants us to have. He desires for us to have:

- Hearts that take an honest look at our own actions and lives, and humbly admit the wrongs we have committed against others and Him.
- Hearts that do not hesitate to bring our sins to Him, lay them at His feet in prayer, plead for forgiveness and then realize that He has forgiven us.
- Hearts that seek after Him, and want more of him. This is what having a heart like God's is all about.

God's Will

Finally, give attention to the closing feature of Acts 13:22. "I have found David, the son of Jesse, a man after My own heart, who will do all My will." The last phrase of the verse is "who will do all My will." According to these words, doing God's will is the way to God's heart. To better know the depths of God's will, there are six actions we must take.

- Identify with God's will that results in His transformation of our minds. It is his power that instills in us a desire to not conform to the world around us, but to be separate unto God (Romans 12:2).
- Realize that this nonconformity with the world is the result of loving God more than the world. This is God's intentional and eternal will for us (1 John 2:15-17).

- Know that he who does the Father's will may enter into heaven (Matthew 7:21).
- Acknowledge God's goodness and be receptive to His instruction (Psalm 143:10).
- Know, live, and delight in God's word (Psalm 40:8).
- Have a full, deep understanding of God that is brought about by the Holy Spirit's ministry, thus fulfilling God's will for us (Colossians 1:9).

David was sought and chosen by Samuel, his earthly advisor, and God, his heavenly Father. At an early age, he already had a heart for God. And he fulfilled God's will through his responsiveness to Samuel, by realizing God had a special plan for his life. 1 Samuel 16:13 tells us that the Spirit of the LORD came upon David. This endowment from the LORD set him apart from Saul but promised to accompany him for the important role he would have as the future king.

Personal Applications

1. One might argue that in earlier civilizations, God had different or even more personal relationships with people. Are we at a disadvantage with people of that time because of God's decreased visibility and audibility? The Bible provides evidence that we can have easy access to God through his Son, Jesus Christ, and the Holy Spirit (Romans 5:1–2, 5).

2. Are you as loyal to God as your family, your job, or your comfort? (Jeremiah 16:17). Know that God is waiting for us to respond to his call, for he has sought us and chosen us.

3. Do you know if you have been chosen by God? If you knew that you had been selected by God, it might deepen your affection for Him. Who is actually called? The Bible plainly states that God has called all who will come to Christ. God calls through the gospel (2 Thessalonians 2:14), and the gospel is to be preached to every creature on earth. God calls every one that believes in Christ. God chose that person so that their faithfulness, their love, their service rests not in their actions but in his. God's choosing is not based on our response. The basis of God's choosing is due to his very good pleasure (Ephesians 1:4–5). These verses give further clarification. First, this choosing happened before the foundation of the world. God knew that you, I, and everyone would be born. Further, his action of choosing us to believe might only go so far, however, if we choose to exercise our own will to reject him. Because God is love and his love is evident in his choosing us, the end result of holiness is a reciprocating love for him.

David: Sought and Chosen
Chapter 1
References

Psalm 89:20–21 "I have found David My servant; with My holy oil I have anointed him, with whom My hand will be established; My arm also will strengthen him."

Acts 13:22 "After He had removed him, He raised up David to be their king, concerning whom He also testified and said, I have found David, the son of Jesse, a man after my heart, who will do all My will."

1 Samuel 13:14 "But now your kingdom shall not endure. The LORD has sought out for Himself a man after His own heart, and the LORD has appointed him as ruler over His people, because you have not kept what the LORD commanded you."

1 Samuel 15:22–23 "Samuel said, 'Has the LORD as much delight in burnt offerings and sacrifices as in obeying the voice of the LORD? Behold, to obey is better than sacrifice, and to heed than the fat of rams. For rebellion is as the sin of divination, and insubordination is as iniquity and idolatry. Because you have rejected the word of the LORD, He has also rejected you from being king."

1 Samuel 16:1–13

Ephesians 1:4 "Just as He chose us in Him before the foundation of the world, that we would be holy and blameless before Him in love."

1 Corinthians 1:27-28 "But God has chosen the foolish things of the world to shame the wise, and God has chosen the weak things of the world to shame the things which are strong, and the base things of the world and the despised God has chosen, the things that are not, so that He may nullify the things that are."

John 15:16 "You did not choose Me but I chose you, and appointed you that you would go and bear fruit . . ."

1 Peter 2:9 "But you are a chosen race, a royal priesthood, a holy nation, a people for God's own possession, so that you may proclaim the excellencies of Him who has called you out of darkness into His marvelous light."

Deuteronomy 7:6-7 "For you are a holy people to the LORD your God; the LORD your God has chosen you to be a people for His own possession out of all the peoples who are on the face of the earth. The LORD did not set His love on you nor choose you because you were more in number than any of the peoples, for you were the fewest of all peoples, but because the LORD loved you."

Psalm 78:70-72 "He also chose David His servant, and took him from the sheepfolds; from the care of the ewes with suckling lambs He brought him, to shepherd Jacob His people, and Israel His inheritance. So he shepherded them according to the integrity of his heart, and guided them with his skillful hands."

1 Kings 9:4 "As for you, if you will walk before Me as your father David walked, in integrity of heart and uprightness, doing according to all that I have commanded you and will keep My statutes and My ordinances."

Psalm 51:1-4 "Be gracious to me, O God, according to Your lovingkindness; according to the greatness of Your compassion blot out my transgressions. Wash me thoroughly from my iniquity and cleanse me from my sin. For I know my transgressions, and my sin is ever before me. Against You, You only, I have sinned, and done what is evil in Your sight, so that You are justified when You speak and blameless when You judge."

Psalm 51:10-13 "Create in me a clean heart, O God, and renew a steadfast spirit within me. Do not cast me away from Your presence and do not take Your Holy Spirit from me. Restore to me the joy of Your salvation and sustain me with a willing spirit. Then I will teach transgressors Your ways, and sinners will be converted to You."

Roman 12:2 "And do not be conformed to this world, but be transformed by the renewing of your mind, so that you may prove what the will of God is, that which is good and acceptable and perfect."

1 John 2:15 "Do not love the world nor the things in the world. If anyone loves the world, the love of the Father is not in him. For all that is in the world, the lust of the flesh and the lust of the eyes and the boastful pride of life, is not from the Father, but is from the world. The world is passing away, and also its lusts; but the one who does the will of God lives forever."

Matthew 7:21 "Not everyone who says to Me, 'LORD, LORD,' will enter the kingdom of heaven, but he who does the will of My Father who is in heaven will enter."

Psalm 40:8 "I delight to do Your will, O my God; your law is within my heart."

Colossians 1:9 "For this reason also, since the day we heard of it, we have not ceased to pray for you and to ask that you may be filled with the knowledge of His will in all spiritual wisdom and understanding."

1 Samuel 16:13 "Then Samuel took the horn of oil and anointed him in the midst of his brothers; and the Spirit of the LORD came mightily upon David from that day forward."

David: Psalm 23

"The Lord is my shepherd; I shall not want."

An important objective in studying David's life is to examine the Twenty-third Psalm, which is a description of his early years. Here we observe that David's energy came from God, as ours does. He is our loving shepherd who restores and reenergizes us. This psalm clearly expresses how a loving shepherd provides for *all* the needs of his sheep. It also describes God's supreme care for our souls in the way He leads us and provides rest. The metaphor of the shepherd caring for the sheep was often used in the near east culture because shepherding was a common occupation and a necessity as a food source. Kings compared themselves to shepherds in the capacity of leading people (Psalm 80:1). David used the language of a shepherd in reference to *his* king and father God. A picture of the coming Messiah used a similar description (Isaiah 40:10–11). These are prophetic verses that tell us that God will one day overcome all obstacles to Jesus's return. The Messiah will safely lead his people into his kingdom. With particular attention to verse 11, we see that the shepherd will feed the sheep (provide for needs), gather them into his arms (protect them), carry the sheep next to his heart (love them), and lead them. Many of the great men of the Old Testament were shepherds, including Abraham, Isaac, Jacob, and Moses. The most well-known example of a shepherd and his sheep, however, is found in John 10. This, of course, is describing Jesus and his relationship with people. So, as we study the Twenty-third Psalm, we will frequently compare Jesus's actions as the true shepherd with David's experiences as a shepherd boy. In respect to the study of David, the Twenty-third Psalm depicts clearly what David experienced as a boy and teen shepherd. These experiences prepared him for the role he would have as king. David worshipped God with his harp playing and singing in many of the psalms, so he may have very well worshipped God as the sheep grazed and rested. We do not know when the psalm was written. If it was a product of David's later years, he returns to contemplate those days of joy, peace, and communion with God. Preceding Psalm 23 is Psalm 22, called the psalm of the cross. In this psalm, there are no green pastures and no still waters, but instead, phrases like, "My God, my God, why have You forsaken Me?" These are the quotes and description of Jesus, as He died on the cross (good study would be comparing Psalm 22 and Psalm 23). Psalm 22 is a prophetic psalm written by David, and he may have been led to follow up with chapter 23. Because we must first have knowledge of the Savior's shedding of blood and sacrifice, before we truly experience the good shepherd's tender care. But David also used the image of a shepherd to recall the blessings he enjoyed from the Lord (Psalm 28:8–9).

Psalm 23

Verse 1. "*The Lord is my shepherd, I shall not want.*" Who is the good shepherd? It is one who goes out before the sheep and leads them. The sheep follow him because they know his voice (John 10:3–5). When sheep hear a strange voice, they lift their heads in alarm. They know it may be someone whom they cannot trust. Who is it that controls the door of the sheepfold? Their trusted shepherd! The sheepfold is a fenced enclosure with only one entrance. Thieves and predators might climb over the fence to steal and even kill the sheep. Furthermore, in verse 1, we see that David's shepherd is the Lord. We might compare the shepherd of psalms to the shepherd in the passage of John 10:3–5. It is the same shepherd, the Lord Jesus Christ! We can trust him completely and we can know him so intimately that we recognize his voice. Because the Lord was David's shepherd, his needs were met. Is he *your* shepherd?

Verse 2. "*He makes me to lie down in green pastures, He leads me beside the still waters.*" The first blessing David experienced was spiritual nourishment just as anyone who follows the Lord receives his strength. What is food for the soul? (Hebrews 5:12–14). These verses speak to the immature and mature Christian. With a newborn believer, one requires the milk of the word in small amounts. As one grows deeper in his/her Christian experience, more substantial food is necessary, comparative to meat. Green pastures are the scriptures of truth; always fresh, always rich, and never lacking. We not only find nourishment in God's word, but we find peace, rest, refreshment, calmness and satisfaction in studying the Bible, as a sheep does, while lying in the tall, lush, green grass. As a shepherd leads his sheep to placid waters for refreshment and cleansing, so the Lord refreshes the soul.

Verse 3a. "*The Lord restores my soul.*" This is a blessing that God brings to us—spiritual restoration. When the soul grows sorrowful, he revives it. When we are sinful, he sanctifies us. When we are weak, he strengthens us. *He* does it. Spiritual leaders are used of God, but it is he who accomplishes the work. Pray for that blessing of restoration of the soul in your life!

Verse 3b. "*He leads me in the paths of righteousness for His name's sake.*" The believer should delight in being obedient. At times, though, we want to obey some of God's commandments, but not all. *We* make that choice to either obey or disobey.

The paths of righteousness are the roads in life that the good shepherd picks for us. He knows the paths that are the best for us, the safest places for us. And he does this because of his reputation, "for His name's sake." It honors our great shepherd that we should be a holy people, walking in the narrow way of righteousness. It is narrow because it is a path most people do not take. But if we are led and guided, we cannot help but adore our shepherd's care.

Verse 4. "*Yea, though I walk through the valley of the shadow of death, I will fear no evil.*" Another blessing of the Lord's leading is protection. If we find ourselves in a valley of deep darkness, we need not fear. Think about the phrase, "Yea, though I walk." Walking indicates the steady advance of one who knows the road, knows its end, resolves to follow the path, feels quite safe, and is perfectly calm. Even though the road may seem life threatening. Do you have that calm resolution in your heart when you think about the end of your life, or even some difficult times ahead that you may have to go through? Notice, we walk *through* the valley, not around it. We have to go through valleys to get to our destination. And the valleys are often in the shadow of death. But think about this. Only a shadow is there, so we can still see the light. The light is the hope that we have in God's everlasting care for us. The next phrase tells us "we will fear no evil, for God is with us." We are not told that we will not face evil. But the key word is fear. When we think of the fears that overwhelm us, even imaginative fears, they take over, don't they? Fear is an enemy that needs to be destroyed. Why? Because of God's presence. The verse says, "You are with me." I have in You all that I want or need…perfect comfort and absolute security. David experienced fears in his shepherd years. Wild animals would come around for a meal, and David would have to ward them off or kill them (1 Samuel 17:34–36–37). The rod and staff are the shepherd's equipment to protect the sheep in such situations. David was comforted by the Lord's presence and protection. And we are never in situations where the Lord is not aware of all circumstances. He never leaves or forsakes his people (Hebrews 13:5–6).

Verse 5a. "*You prepare a table for me in the presence of my enemies.*" As David grew older he encountered enemies. Notice how the scene now changes to a banquet hall where a gracious host provides lavish hospitality. David rejoices that the Lord has provided for him. And yes, the enemy may be at the door, so to speak, yet God prepares a table and we can sit and eat in peace as if everything were okay. This is the kind of peace the Lord gives his people, even in the midst of the most trying circumstances.

Verse 5b. "*You anoint my head with oil.*" Pouring oil over a guest's head was a special and common practice that assigned honor to that person. Recall the story of the sinful woman who anointed Jesus's feet with oil. Interestingly, the common practice was to pour oil over Jesus's head, not his feet (Luke 7:46). This woman expressed the ultimate humility and worship as she poured out her affection for Jesus. Returning to Psalm 23:5, the oil was cooling, refreshing and soothing. In fact, to anoint in this verse means to refresh or to offer refreshment before extending hospitality at a feast.

Verse 5c. "*My cup runneth over*," The Hebrew meaning is to "fill up", to drink until one is full and completely satisfied. The spiritual implication is that the Lord wants to fill us with abundant blessings. Only He can provide what we best need and it will be sufficient for our needs and wants.

Verse 6a. "*Surely goodness and mercy will follow me all the days of my life.*" David realized that the Lord's gracious, loyal love would go with him everywhere throughout his life. This love is a deep and enduring commitment between two persons. The word mercy or faithfulness means devotion. This is what God promises to those who love Him. He is devoted to us. The phrase "will follow me" means to pursue, as an enemy would pursue or chase its prey. Therefore, this is a word picture of God chasing down the one whom he loves.

Verse 6b. "*And I will dwell in the house of the Lord forever.*" The house of the Lord refers to the tabernacle. We know that for the rest of his life, David would enjoy full and constant communion with the Lord. In fact, the phrase "I will dwell" conveys the idea of returning. So, as David meditated on the Lord's leading and provisions, he was prompted to recall his relationship with the Lord and return to the sanctuary for worship. The word *forever* does not mean for eternity, as one might think. But it means for the length of one's life.

Personal Application

How about you? Is the Twenty-third Psalm a reality in your life? Look at what it has to offer you today!

1. For the wandering person who does not have spiritual goals in his or her life and perhaps constantly takes a wrong path in life, the Lord as our shepherd, offers guidance, structure, and goals.

2. For the person who has everything; wisdom, maturity, stability, what can the Shepherd offer them?

    a. The shepherd offers a right way. Notice in John 10:7–10, there are ways that are not right. Thieves and robbers refer to anyone who falsely claims to be the way to God. There are many religions who claim to be the only way. But the Bible teaches there is one way and that way is through Jesus Christ. The result for those who trust in Christ, the good Shepherd, as the only way, is that they will be saved from eternal separation from God (John 14:6). A parallel meaning is that the sheep are saved from thieves and wolves who would keep them from following their shepherd.

b. The shepherd offers true freedom. John 10:9 speaks of the sheep entering and leaving by the door. The sheep leave and return in complete freedom. In comparison, we have complete freedom in Christ. What is meant by this? Jesus provides freedom from fundamental requirements that most religions deem as necessary (Galatians 5:1). His only requirement is to come to him. Think of the bondage that accompanies ritualistic worship. This type of worship may involve heightened expectations and usually results in human satisfaction that is gained by meeting all the requirements. But what happens when it is no longer possible to meet the expectations? This is when we realize that good works truly have us in bondage. What matters most is a simple commitment of trust in Jesus Christ's good work on the cross, which satisfied God's requirement of us. Placing our trust in Jesus is a genuine act of faith, unrelated to good works.

c. In contrast to the good shepherd's care, the hireling, or paid worker, may not give the sheep special attention (John 10:13). We know that the Lord lovingly provides for his sheep—those who know and love him.

- Verse 1. The Lord lifts us up with his encouraging words.
- Verse 2a. The Lord gives us guidance and nurtures us.
- Verse 2b. The Lord provides emotional and relational healing.
- Verse 3a. The Lord teaches us and helps us to grow spiritually.
- Verse 3b. The Lord encourages and protects us when things become frightening.
- Verse 4a. The Lord stays with us and stands with us during hard times.
- Verse 4b. The Lord provides comfort when we need it.
- Verse 4c. The Lord grants us peace.
- Verse 5a. The Lord gives hope.
- Verse 5b. The Lord provides satisfaction.
- Verse 5c. The Lord shows his goodness and grants forgiveness.
- Verse 6. The Lord holds onto us, loves us, and plans for our future.

d. The shepherd offers personal communication with him. We have 24/7 access to God (Ephesians 3:11–12). Through faith in Christ, we have the right of address, which means freedom, courage and boldness. We can personally communicate with God freely and confidently.

e. Finally, the shepherd offers us his love. His love is demonstrated by Christ's love for us. The good shepherd demonstrated his love for the sheep by being willing to give his life for them (Mark 6:34). In this verse, you truly see the heart of God. You see humanity's condition and you see God, in human form; in action. Jesus took action to tell the people the good news of God and his love for them.

3. How can we not love him because of his care for us? David expounded on his love of God's perfect care in Psalm 145. He wrote:

a. "The Lord is gracious and full of compassion, slow to anger and great in mercy" (verse 8).

b. "The Lord is good to all, and his tender mercies are over all His works" (verse 9).

c. "The Lord upholds all who fall, and raises up all who are bowed down" (verse 14).

d. "The Lord is righteous in all His ways, gracious in all His works" (verse 17).

e. "The Lord is near to all who call upon Him, to all who call upon Him in truth" (verse 18).

f. "The Lord preserves all who love Him" (verse 20).

David: Psalm 23
Chapter 2
References

Psalm 23 "Give ear, O Shepherd of Israel, Thou, that leads Joseph like a flock; Thou that sits above the cherubim, shine forth."

Isaiah 40:10–11 "Behold, the Lord GOD will come with might, with His arm ruling for Him. Behold, His reward is with Him, and His recompense before Him. Like a shepherd He will tend His flock, in His arm He will gather the lambs and carry them in His bosom; He will gently lead the nursing ewes."

Psalm 22 "The LORD is their strength, and He is a saving defense to His anointed. Save Your people and bless Your inheritance; be their shepherd also, and carry them forever."

John 10:3–5 "To him the doorkeeper opens, and the sheep hear his voice, and he calls his own sheep by name and leads them out. When he puts forth all his own, he goes ahead of them, and the sheep follow him because they know his voice. A stranger they simply will not follow, but will flee from him, because they do not know the voice of strangers."

Hebrews 5:12–14 "For when by reason of the time you ought to be teachers, you have need again that someone teach you the rudiments of the first principles of the oracles of God; and are become such as have need of milk, and not of solid food. For every one that partakes of milk is without experience of the word of righteousness; for he is a babe. But solid food is for full-grown men, even those who by reason of use have their senses exercised to discern good and evil."

1 Samuel 17:34–37 "And David said unto Saul, 'Your servant was keeping his father's sheep; and when there came a lion, or a bear, and took a lamb out of the flock, I went out after him, and smote him, and delivered it out of his mouth; and when he arose against me, I caught him by his beard, and smote him, and slew him. Your servant smote both the lion and the bear...' And David said, 'Jehovah that delivered me out of the paw of the lion, and out of the paw of the bear, he will deliver me out of the hand of this Philistine.'"

Hebrews 13:5–6 "He hath said, I will in no wise fail you, neither will I in any wise forsake you. So that with good courage we say, The Lord is my helper; I will not fear: What shall man do unto me?"

Luke 7:46 "My head with oil thou didst not anoint: but she hath anointed my feet with ointment."

John 10:7–10 "Jesus therefore said unto them again, Verily, verily, I say unto you, I am the door of the sheep. All that came before me are thieves and robbers: but the sheep did not hear them. I am the door; by me if any man enter in, he shall be saved, and shall go in and go out, and shall find pasture. The thief cometh not, but that he may steal, and kill, and destroy: I came that they may have life, and may have it abundantly."

John 14:6 "Jesus said unto him, I am the way, and the truth, and the life: no one cometh unto the Father, but by me"

Galatians 5:1 "For freedom did Christ set us free: stand fast therefore, and be not entangled again in a yoke of bondage."

"He flees because he is a hireling, and cares not for the sheep" (John 10:13). Ephesians 3:11–12 "According to the eternal purpose which he purposed in Christ Jesus our Lord: in whom we have boldness and access in confidence through our faith in him."

Mark 6:34 "And he came forth and saw a great multitude, and he had compassion on them, because they were as sheep not having a shepherd: and he began to teach them many things."

Psalm 145:8, 9, 14, 17, 18, 20

David: Anointed and Appointed

"Then Samuel took the horn of oil and anointed him in the midst of his brothers; and the Spirit of the LORD came mightily upon David from that day forward."

—1 Samuel 16:13

The term "anointed" may not be a familiar word or activity in twenty-first century culture. But, according to Hebrew history, there came a day when Samuel was commissioned to anoint David. The word "anoint" is a translation from the Greek word "chrisma". Chrisma is derived from the root "chrio" with the associated word "Christ". Jesus, as we know to be the Son of God, was called Christ, meaning Messiah or anointed one. The word anoint also indicates an action: to smear or rub with oil or to pour oil over. Anointing is a ritual performed in religious ceremonies to consecrate, bless, or in this case, ordain. Its origin actually came from the practice of shepherds. Lice and other insects would get into the wool of the sheep and when the insects got near the sheep's head, they would burrow in the sheep's ears and kill the sheep. So, the shepherd would pour the oil on the sheep's head to stop the progress of the lice. From this, came the symbol of blessing, protection and empowerment.

Anointment: A Special Blessing

The practice of anointing with oil is found over 20 times in the Bible. Curiously, the exercise of anointing was used for various purposes. To gain a closer look at the usage of this word, we find the following examples in the Bible.

- In the account of Samuel anointing David as king, David was authorized to fill the role of king; a high calling of God indeed (1 Samuel 16:1, 13).

- Aaron, Moses's brother, and his sons were anointed to go into their special roles as priests (Exodus 29:7–9).
- David recalls and writes about the anointing of Aaron (Psalm 133:1–2).
- The practice of anointing was used as a symbol of dedication of the tabernacle and its utensils and altar (Exodus 40:9–10). The tabernacle of worship was dedicated as a place of holiness unto God.
- Jeru was anointed to serve as king of Israel—after David's time (2 Kings 9:1–3).
- Written by Solomon, David's son, this verse provides a different example of anointing (Ecclesiastes 9:8). Solomon refers to anointing as continual favor and approval from God.
- In the NT, we learn that olive oil was commonly used as a medicinal treatment in the ancient world (James 5:14). It had a symbolic reference to the healing power of God.
- Often, we observe Jesus opening the scriptures and reading to the people (Luke 4:18). On this occasion, he read a prophetic section from Isaiah 61:1 regarding his anointing. The texts are not identical since one is Hebrew and the other is Greek, but they hold the same message. The "Me" in the Isaiah reference is referring to the Messiah. Isaiah simply wrote what God told him to write and not necessarily in first person narrative. The poor, the brokenhearted, the captives, and the prisoners needed to hear Isaiah's message, as they did in Jesus's time. As Isaiah was authorized and directed to proclaim liberty to the Jews in Babylon; so was Christ, God's anointed messenger, commissioned to publish the message to a lost world. It is important to note that Isaiah's Lord (God Jehovah) anointed the Lord (the Messiah, Jesus Christ). Isaiah speaks of someone else, not himself. But Jesus speaks of himself because he is the Messiah and the OT quote confirms this. Jesus came to preach the gospel, give spiritual liberty and heal the sick; and he could do this because he is anointed with the Spirit of God.
- God himself anointed Jesus. Notice the result of this anointing (Acts 10:38):

  - Doing good things
  - Healing
  - Power
  - Presence of God

- We who believe in and trust in Jesus Christ are also anointed (2 Corinthians 1:21–22). The three persons of the trinity are all involved in our anointment. God establishes us in Christ—this means to strengthen. The anointment in this passage is reference of consecration to God. It involves a sealing. God places a seal on us as a sign of ownership and he places his Spirit within us as a guarantee of his presence. Truthfully, the Holy Spirit is the secret power of God.

David's anointing as king was similar to that of Jesus. David would a good king, a powerful king, and most important of all, the presence of God would be evident in his life. First Samuel 16:13 says that Samuel poured the horn of oil over David's head. But, also accompanying this act was the Spirit of the Lord that came upon David from that day forward (Ps. 89:20). What does it mean for the Spirit of the Lord to come upon a person?

- In David's case, this endowment with the Spirit of God was permanent, because, note that 1 Samuel 16:13 says, "From this day forward." Frequently in the Old Testament, however, the bestowment of the Spirit is an empowerment by God of an individual for a particular task. So, the effect of God's Spirit in these situations are temporary. Samson's empowerment is a good example of the temporary work of the Holy Spirit (Judges 14:6, 19).
- The emphasis of the anointing is inward. The most important aspect of David's anointing is that it was the real reason for his success. David was not born with a supernatural ability to do things any better than anyone else. He recognized that he was nothing more than a mere man, shaped in iniquity and conceived in sin (Psalm 51:5–6). David wrote that he began his life as a sinner in need of God and in verse 6, we see that God, indeed is the answer. Verse 10 reveals that David initiated God's intervention. He asked for forgiveness and he asked for God to renew his Spirit within him. We must remember that God's presence in our life depends on our response to his prompting. Part of acknowledging God's power is the fact that it was his holy oil that anointed David. Thus the anointing depended on God and not on any external factors. What factors might those be? RT Kendall, in his book, "A man after God's own heart," provides further insight.

Factor 1: David's anointing did not depend on the circumstances in his kingdom. During the period of the judges, "everyone did as he saw fit" (Judges 21:25). The nation of Israel was spiritually bankrupt and rebelling against God. Thus, they demanded a king (1 Samuel 8:4–5). We are reminded of the world around us today. Does everyone do as they see fit in their own eyes? Yes, for the most part. Would you say that society as a whole is becoming more moral or immoral (difficulty with truth telling, stealing of ideas and financial funds, government and corporate takeovers, hate and disrespect)? Is there an increase in rebelliousness (civil lawlessness, refusal to obey the laws of the country, refusal to submit to God's authority, parental authority, and the government's authority)? Would you say that decreased sensitivity to or exposure to the God of the Bible is increasing or waning? As we continue to study David's life, we will find that we are living in David's world! But with all that was happening back then, it did not prevent David from accepting his anointing.

Factor 2: The anointing did not depend upon parental authority. Had it been left to Jesse, he might not have been anointed! David could not say, "My father chose me to be king of Israel." The same is true for us. If the Holy Spirit comes to indwell us, it will not depend on our parent's wish for our life. It is quite possible for God to step in and overrule a parent's influence on their child. On the other hand, if one has believing parents, their salvation cannot be passed on to their child. A parent can baptize a child and encourage church attendance; but in the end, the individual is personally responsible for him/herself (Ephesians 2:8–9). So, here we see that it is God's grace that saves us. It is not anything in ourselves, or anything we or others might do. Why? We would have the tendency to boast in it—to take pride in it.

Factor 3: David's anointing did not depend on Samuel, who poured oil over his head. This is evident because shortly after the anointing, the prophet traveled to the nearby town of Ramah. Samuel left, trusting that the Holy Spirit would work in David's life (1 Samuel 16:13). Comparatively, what God will do in your life will not depend on the spiritual leader who gives you the message. It is entirely the work of the Holy Spirit in one's life that deserves the credit.

Factor 4: David's anointing did not depend on him, but completely on God's grace. It is God who regenerates a person. With David's anointing, God planted a root that we read about in Isaiah 11:1. Jesse and David were part of an ancestral root system from which the Messiah would come (Revelation 22:16). David's anointing was so significant that not only would it affect the whole of Israel, but it would be deeply significant to the greater kingdom of God. The anointing of God's presence in David's life was so great, it determined all decisions he made as king. Did this mean he became perfect? Absolutely not. As future studies will reveal, David would always be tempted to sin, and even fall to that sin. He admitted that his heart had not always determined to do what was right (Psalm 51:10). David requested a clean heart from God and spiritual renewal. This is how David lived—with a faith in God that held him accountable for his actions.

David wrote about the Holy Spirit's presence in his life in the book of Psalms. New Testament verses are also provided for comparison.

- The Holy Spirit guided him (Psalm 31:3, Romans 8:14).
- The Holy Spirit taught him, opening his understanding. (Psalm 25:4, Luke 12:2, John 14:26).
- The Holy Spirit counseled him (Psalm 73:23–24).
- The Holy Spirit probes the depths of divine knowledge for our benefit (1 Corinthians 2:10).
- The Holy Spirit rescued him (Psalm 35:17, Romans 8:26).
- The Holy Spirit influenced his responses to daily circumstances (Psalm 101:2).

David was not perfect, as we know, but we read that it is possible to obey God's commandments and live in holiness (Galatians 5:16–17, 22–23).

The New King (1 Samuel 16:14–23)

The final part of this study will examine the beginning of David's career. It is useful to recognize the importance of developing talent at an early age. David was still a very young man because he continued to tend the sheep. We read that King Saul was a man with big problems. He had disobeyed God and was unrepentant. If only he had listened to the prophet Samuel when he warned Saul about God's wrath (1 Samuel 15:23). Often in the Old Testament when God told someone, "You are finished!" and the person repented; God forgave and extended the person's privileges. But not so with King Saul. We might compare him with David, who later wrote Psalm 51:17. God removed his Spirit from Saul. Has your heart and spirit ever been humbled, broken, and crushed? These are the words that David uses to describe himself and his people as they came before God in worship. God will show us our sin if we ask him. He will give us the remorse that is needed for forgiveness, and he eagerly waits to extend his grace (2 Chronicles 7:14). What was this evil spirit that came upon Saul? In a subsequent chapter, we can read that God allowed this evil spirit (1 Samuel 18:10a). It was not evil in the sense that it came from Satan. Instead, it was a tormenting spirit. Saul felt restless, bothered and troubled. Saul's hired help tried very hard to give Saul good advice. They suggested a harpist for him. There is nothing like harp music to bring peace to your soul! It is therapeutic! But we might look at this another way. What if Saul's servants had instead encouraged him to seek after God for that peace? This would have certainly made for a different ending to the account!

Consider the scripture we have just read (1 Samuel 16). David did not approach Saul, but Saul's people came to David. David had not advertised his talent. But God used his talent because David had God's anointing on him. The servant's description of David is of interest. He is but a young man and yet he is described as a mighty man of valor and a man of war. This is a clear exaggeration by the servant. And yet we see God paving the way for David's future role. These words will return to Saul in the next account of David and Goliath.

The big question arises; did Saul know who his replacement as king would be? No. But based on the servant's recommendation, Saul sent messengers to Jesse requesting that David come to him. He was recruiting for a young man who had harpist skills and played soothingly so as to alleviate his bad mood. Jesse received word of Saul's request and his first action was to prepare a gift for King Saul.

David walked into the king's court, leading a donkey. The donkey was overloaded with long loaves of bread, a wine flask and a live, young goat. This brought a smile to Saul's face. In fact, the scripture says he loved David (the Hebrew word for *love* means "affection"). And Saul gave him his first real job apart from family responsibility. David became his armor bearer. An armor bearer was a servant who carried extra weapons for the commanders. Their additional responsibility was to kill enemies that were wounded by the commander. So, in this case, the enemy soldier might be wounded with a javelin or an arrow and the armor bearer would finish the person off with a club or a sword. After David's time, armor bearers are no longer mentioned in the Bible. Probably because the chariot was developed for use in battle, bringing armies in closer proximity to each other. What perfect training for David! He not only learned about weaponry but also war tactics. No doubt this helped him develop into a mature man.

We have just learned that God was not only preparing David to be king, but he used David in Saul's life to influence him and alleviate his distress. David was learning about people and even difficult people. Yet, he did not forget his roots (1 Samuel 17:15). David certainly had a busy life in those early years. So, while continuing to serve his father and brothers and King Saul, David learned true servanthood.

Personal Application

1. Give examples of how God's anointing in your life has empowered you or resulted in special blessings.

2. Does God ever remove his spirit from us, as he did with King Saul? We must remember that God's spirit enabled Saul to accomplish his specific assignment for a temporary period of time. It was not an endowment initiated by faith in God. Ephesians 1:13-14 aptly describes God's permanent action of indwelling the believer. *GotQuestions.org* succinctly explains

the impossibility that one could lose the Holy Spirit or salvation. "For a Christian to lose salvation, God would have to erase the mark, withdraw the spirit, cancel the deposit, break his promise, revoke the guarantee, keep the inheritance, forego the praise, and lessen his glory."

David: Anointed and Appointed
Chapter 3
References

1 Samuel 16:1, 13 "Now the LORD said to Samuel, 'Fill your horn with oil and go; I will send you to Jesse the Bethlehemite, for I have selected a king for Myself among his sons.' Then Samuel took the horn of oil and anointed him in the midst of his brothers; and the Spirit of the Lord came mightily upon David from that day forward."

Exodus 29:7–9 "Then you shall take the anointing oil and pour it on his head and anoint him. You shall bring his sons and put tunics on them. You shall gird them with sashes, Aaron and his sons, and bind caps on them, and they shall have the priesthood by a perpetual statute. So you shall ordain Aaron and his sons."

Psalm 133:1–2 "Behold, how good and how pleasant it is for brothers to dwell together in unity! It is like the precious oil upon the head, coming down upon the beard, even Aaron's beard, coming down upon the edge of his robes."

Exodus 40:9–10 "And you shall take the anointing oil, and anoint the tabernacle, and all that is in it, and you shall sanctify it, and all the furniture in it: and it shall be holy. And you shall anoint the altar of burnt-offering, and all its vessels, and sanctify the altar: and the altar shall be most holy."

2 Kings 9:1–3 "And Elisha the prophet called one of the sons of the prophets, and said unto him, Gird up your loins, and take this vial of oil in your hand, and go to Ramoth-Gilead. And when you come near, look there for Jehu the son of Jehoshaphat the son of Nimshi, and go in, and make him arise up from among his brethren, and carry him to an inner chamber. Then take the vial of oil, and pour it on his head, and say, Thus, says Jehovah, I have anointed you king over Israel. Then open the door, and flee, and tarry not."

Ecclesiastes 9:8 "Let your clothes be white all the time, and let not oil be lacking on your head, for God has accepted your works."

James 5:14 "Is anyone among you sick? Then he must call for the elders of the church and they are to pray over him, anointing him with oil in the name of the Lord"

Luke 4:18 "The Spirit of the Lord is upon Me, because He anointed Me to preach the gospel to the poor. He has sent Me to proclaim release to the captives, and recovery of the sight to the blind; to set free those who are oppressed."

Isaiah 61:1 "The Spirit of the Lord GOD is upon me, because the LORD has anointed me, to bring good news to the afflicted; He has sent me to bind up the broken-hearted, to proclaim liberty to captives and freedom to prisoners."

"You know of Jesus of Nazareth, how God anointed Him with the Holy Spirit and with power, and how He went about doing good and healing all who were oppressed by the devil, for God was with Him" (Acts 10:38).

2 Corinthians 1:21–22 "Now He who establishes us with you in Christ and anointed us is God, who also sealed us and gave us the Spirit in our hearts as a pledge."

1 Samuel 16:13 "Then Samuel took the horn of oil and anointed him in the midst of his brothers; and the Spirit of the LORD came mightily upon David from that day forward."

Psalm 89:20 "I have found David My servant; with My holy oil I have anointed him."

Judges 14:6, 19 "The Spirit of the LORD came upon him mightily, so that he tore him as one tears a young goat though he had nothing in his hand; but he did not tell his father or mother what he had done. Then the Spirit of the Lord came upon him mightily, and he went down to Ashkelon and killed thirty of them."

Psalm 51:5–6 "Behold, I was brought forth in iniquity, and in sin my mother conceived me. Behold, You desire truth in the innermost being, and in the hidden part You will make me know wisdom."

Psalm 51:10 "Create in me a clean heart, O God, and renew a steadfast spirit within me."

Judges 21:25 "In those days there was no king in Israel; everyone did what was right in his own eyes."

1 Samuel 8:4–5 "Then all the elders of Israel gathered together and came to Samuel at Ramah; and they said to him, 'Behold, you have grown old, and your sons do not walk in your ways. Now appoint a king for us to judge us like all the nations.'"

Ephesians 2:8–9 "For by grace you have been saved through faith; and that not of yourselves, it is the gift of God; not as a result of works, so that no one may boast."

1 Samuel 16:13 "And Samuel arose and went to Ramah."

Isaiah 11:1 "Then a shoot will spring from the stem of Jesse, and a branch from his roots will bear fruit."

Revelations 22:16 "I, Jesus, have sent My angel to testify to you these things for the churches. I am the root and the descendant of David, the bright morning star."

Psalm 51:10 "Create in me a clean heart, O God, and renew a steadfast spirit within me."

Psalm 31:3 "For You are my rock and my fortress; for Your name's sake, You will lead me and guide me."

Romans 8:14 "For all who are being led by the Spirit of God, these are sons of God"

Psalm 25:4 "Make me know Your ways, O LORD; teach me Your paths."

Luke 12:2 "But there is nothing covered up that will not be revealed, and hidden that will not be known."

John 14:26 "But the Helper, the Holy Spirit, whom the Father will send in My name, He will teach you all things, and bring to your remembrance all that I said to you."

Psalm 73:23–24 "Nevertheless I am continually with You; You have taken hold of my right hand. With Your counsel, You will guide me, and afterward receive me to glory."

1 Corinthians 2:10 "For to us God revealed them through the Spirit; for the Spirit searches all things, even the depths of God."

Psalm 35:17 "Lord, how long will You look on? Rescue my soul from their ravages; my only life from the lions."

Romans 8:26 "In the same way the Spirit also helps our weakness; for we do not know how to pray as we should, but the Spirit Himself intercedes for us with groaning's too deep for words."

Psalm 101:2 "I will give heed to the blameless way. When will You come to me? I will walk within my house in the integrity of my heart."

Galatians 5:16–17, 23 "But I say, walk by the Spirit, and you will not carry out the desire of the flesh. For the flesh sets its desire against the Spirit, and the Spirit against the flesh; for these are in opposition to one another, so that you may not do the things that you please. If we live by the Spirit, let us also walk by the Spirit."

1 Samuel 16:14–23

1 Samuel 15:23 "For rebellion is as the sin of divination, and insubordination is as iniquity and idolatry. Because you have rejected the word of the LORD, He has also rejected you from being king."

Psalm 51:17 "The sacrifices of God are a broken spirit; a broken and a contrite heart, O God, You will not despise."

2 Chronicles 7:14 "If My people who are called by My name humble themselves and pray and seek My face and turn from their wicked ways, then I will hear from heaven, will forgive their sin and will heal their land."

1 Samuel 18:10 "Now it came about on the next day that an evil spirit from God came mightily upon Saul."

1 Samuel 17:15, 17–18 "But David went back and forth from Saul to tend his father's flock at Bethlehem. The Philistine came forward morning and evening for forty days and took his stand. Then Jesse said to David his son, 'Take now for your brothers an ephah of this roasted grain and these ten loaves and run to the camp to your brothers. Bring also these ten cuts of cheese to the commander of their thousand, and look into the welfare of your brothers, and bring back news of them.'"

Ephesians 1:13-14 "In Him, you also, after listening to the message of truth, the gospel of your salvation—having also believed, you were sealed in Him with the Holy Spirit of promise, who is given as a pledge of our inheritance, with a view to the redemption of God's own possession, to the praise of His glory."

David and Goliath

"The Lord...he will deliver me from the hand of this Philistine."
—1 Samuel 17:37

Philistine History (1 Samuel 17:1–3)

This account examines the Philistine civilization. Who were they? History provides a lot of information. They were an aggressive, warmongering people who occupied a part of southwest Palestine between the Mediterranean Sea and the Jordan River. They are first recorded in scripture as the patriarchal founders of seventy nations descended from Noah. They had migrated to the Mediterranean coast and Gaza and were known as sea people. From the very beginning, the Philistines were archenemies of God's people. For nearly two hundred years, they had harassed and oppressed the Israelites after invading Israel's territory. And the Israelites simply could not withstand the Philistine's overwhelming military might. Their advanced work with iron—that is, tools, weapons, machinery—gave them this military advantage. The Philistines worshipped three gods: Ashtoreth, Dagon, and Baal-Zebub (Matthew 12:24). Here we see different forms of the name Baal-Zebub, but it should gain our attention to know that the Philistines were involved in devil worship. Their gods were enshrined throughout the land and the soldiers even carried images of their gods into battle (2 Samuel 5:21). We read that the Philistines whom David just defeated, had left their images or idols behind, as they ran in defeat. The Israelites frequently referred to the Philistines as "uncircumcised", as we shall read in this account. This meant at that time, those who had no relationship with God Jehovah. They were not God's chosen people and were to be strictly avoided as a contaminating evil (Genesis 17:10–11). Today, the word Philistine is used to refer to an unsophisticated, dull, or unrefined person. This probably goes back to the giant, Goliath, whom, along with his genetic aberration, projected a repulsive presence. In the end, the Philistines were assimilated into Canaanite (now called Palestinian) culture and that distinct group has disappeared altogether.

Goliath the Giant (1 Samuel 17:4–11)

Picture the two armies facing each other across a wide valley. The valley of Elah was several miles southwest of Jerusalem. The man Goliath was designated as a champion for the Philistines. Apparently, the armies were intimidated by each other and decided the outcome should be determined by a contest of champions. Goliath was nine feet nine inches tall. The fact that he was double the height of men at that time, though unusual, was not an impossible phenomenon. Human skeletons of similar stature at roughly the same time period have been discovered in Palestine. Genesis 6:1–4 speaks of another kind of giant. The Nephilim were the evil race of giants that were the offspring of demons. "Fallen angels" are those who followed after Satan when he rebelled and was thrown from his dwelling in heaven. They do not care about God's created order and throughout history have actively sought ways to disrupt and twist God's plan. We know that Matthew 22:30 states that angels do not marry. But the Matthew angels in heaven distinguish themselves from fallen angels (Hebrews 13:2). Angels, while spiritual beings, can appear in human form and perform even to the point of reproduction. Why has this practice not continued, you may ask? (Jude 1:6). God imprisoned the fallen angels who committed the sin of fathering humans so that others would not do the same. Gigantisim exists today. It is caused from an excessive amount of growth hormone in childhood. It is usually related to adenoma, a tumor of the pituitary gland, which secretes too much growth hormone (GH), leading to many changes in the body. Gigantism is known to be a genetic disorder, which explains why Goliath's brothers were also giants.

We read that Goliath wore a bronze helmet on his head and a coat of armor weighing 125 pounds. He had a large javelin and a long spear with a fifteen-pound iron tip. Daily, Goliath would walk out in the valley and taunt the armies of Israel. When Goliath referred to the servants of Saul, the likely choice for an opponent would have been King Saul. He was a man of large stature and a force not to be reckoned with. We read that the contest was all about servanthood—"if you lose, you will be our servants, if we lose, we will be your servants." But what was Saul's reaction? He and all his army were amazed and afraid. Goliath struck terror into their hearts, and no one dared to accept his challenge. Now, David, on the other hand, was armed with the confidence of God.

David the Boy (1 Samuel 17:12–37)

There are many stories of countries going to war and young men from every family joining the forces to serve. This was also the case in Jesse's family. The three oldest sons went to follow King Saul in battle. David, however, was tasked with split duties between serving his brothers and his father. He carried food to his brothers, specifically grain, cheese and bread. But Jesse also had another reason for his son, David's excursions. He wanted news of his eldest sons who were in battle and reassurance that they were safe. When David arrived at the camp, he saw that the two armies were facing each other in battle readiness. They were lined up and the battle cry had gone out. David was an opportunist and his curiosity took him right into the soldier's line of formation. Curiously, in his excitement to get to the front line, he left the food with the equipment specialist. Can you picture this? David was casually talking with his brothers when Goliath walked out onto the field for his daily exposition and challenge. So, David did not hesitate to ask if there was a reward for the Israelite who would take Goliath down. "Yes", answered the men. The king would reward the giant slayer with great riches, his daughter's hand in marriage, and his family's exemption from paying taxes. So, the fact that there was a bounty on Goliath tells us that Saul had to incentivize his army, which included David's three brothers. Now, Eliab, his oldest brother, had taken about as much as he could from David's curiosity. He saw him as an intrusive pest. But, even deeper, Eliab's sudden outburst reflects the resentment and jealousy he had for David.

- David, who is probably seventeen to eighteen years old, was positioned on a dangerous battlefield, where he had no formal approval to be. Remember that his assignment was only to deliver food to his brothers.
- David asked the questions that perhaps his brothers should have been asking. He networked, which perhaps they were not doing.
- David, the youngest, had, prior to this time, been anointed king. It was he, instead of the oldest brother, who, according to custom, would have been chosen to be king.

Eliab was jealous and he became angry with David. He said, "I know your pride and the insolence of your heart." Another way of describing Eliab's attitude is arrogant, disdainful, presumptive. But let's contrast Eliab's judgment of David with God's observation of David. God had said back in 1 Samuel 13:14 that David's heart was after his own. God achieved his plan when he favored David over Eliab to lead Israel.

Word soon spread around camp and King Saul heard about David and sent for him. We now have a situation where David seemed to give King Saul advice; a highly unusual conversation that one presumes displayed disregard for King Saul's position.

David said to him, "We should not be afraid to engage with this enemy. I will fight him." In view of David's God-given confidence and lack of fear, his assertiveness should not be viewed as incorrect or disrespectful.

Israel

Now, Israel had some principles concerning warfare that they had forgotten about (Deuteronomy 20:1–4). First of all, the priests were to comfort and encourage the people to trust in the Lord. There is no mention in this account that the priests offered encouragement to the troops. Second, the people were to look to God to be their deliverer. What was their response? In verse 11 of our chapter we find that they were dismayed. To be dismayed in the Hebrew means to break down with confusion. What usually results from confusion? Fear. The army was not trusting in the Lord, but instead, they let Goliath's words intimidate them. King Saul did not take the higher approach to trusting God either. Instead, he listed reasons why David should not engage with Goliath. King Saul rationalized that David was too young and lacked training. In 1 Timothy 4:12, we see that God does not discredit youthfulness. But David acknowledged the Lord's power—the same power that gave him the ability to kill lions and bears that attacked his sheep. This same Lord would empower him to defeat Goliath. We know of another Bible character who was faced with a similar situation. That was Samson (Judges 14:5–6). There was also a New Testament character who experienced a lion attack, the apostle Paul (2 Timothy 4:17–18). The actual meaning of the word lion here is the animal, not people whose attacks are like lions. And, as we see in this context, Paul gives God the glory for saving his life.

Saul is now convinced that David, who operates in the Lord's might, should be taken seriously. He said, "Well, go and the Lord be with you!" This is a type of benediction that separates David from the rest of the men. Remember the description of David in 1 Samuel 16:18? He is described as having the Lord with him. So, Saul simply acknowledged what he knew to be true.

The Battle (1 Samuel 17:38–54)

The armor that Saul gave to David was so heavy and large for him that he could not walk. Did David need armor to kill the lion and the bear? No, and he did not need it now. This is a sign that Saul still does not trust in the Lord's might and protection. But what David did need were five smooth stones and a slingshot. Archeologists have found evidence that sling stones were important weapons in an ancient army's arsenal. The stones have been found at many excavation sites in Israel. Interestingly, the tribe of Benjamin (King Saul's family) known as an elite corps of slingers, were mostly left handed! (Judges 20:15–16). The stones would have been the size of a golf ball or a tennis ball and the throw would have been one underhanded wind up. Slingers were known to hurl their stones as far as a quarter of a mile and would aim them at the head of the enemy. Experiments demonstrate the stones traveled in excess of sixty miles per hour. Entire armies used these stones as a primary weapon. Undoubtedly, it resulted in many casualties. Minimally armed David advanced toward Goliath, who carried his sword and shield. Goliath was really a coward at heart. He applied his commonly used technique of intimidation, making fun of David because he was young and good looking. He made note that David wore no protection and had no sword. Goliath then took his pagan god's names in vain. This informs us of several things about Goliath.

- He was not able to trust in his gods for help.
- He responded emotionally. Emotional reactions take over the situation, leaving one with less control and less prepared to respond in a rational and measured way.
- Goliath also said, "Am I a dog, that you come to me without military armor?" The Hebrew name for dog means a male, homosexual prostitute. Goliath felt that sending David to fight him was an insult to his manhood; similarly, as homosexuality was an insult to manhood.

So, why five stones? History tells us that Goliath had four brothers, and it may be that David was preparing for the possibility they would come to Goliath's rescue. However, we know that David's faith was not in his stones but in the Lord of hosts. David was not intimidated by Goliath's taunts that he would feed David to the birds of the air and wild animals. Birds of prey are frequently mentioned in the Bible in reference to their eating the carcasses of those who had been killed. The birds were probably vultures, who reside in Israel in large numbers. David then compared Goliath's strength to God's strength. Notice in verses 45–47 that his response was God-centered and that David admitted there was nothing exceptional about his physical strength, strategy, or success.

David then ran toward the Philistine army. It took only one stone, which sank into Goliath's skull. The text says it hit him in the forehead. The frontal lobes of the brain contain the mental faculty of a person. The stone knocked out Goliath so that he fell down. But that stone did not kill him! So, as David approached Goliath, he stabbed him to kill him and cut off his head. The Bible emphasizes that David did not have a sword, thus contrasting the fact that Goliath had all the advantages. David was able to triumph without any advantage but his God. In the meantime, the Philistine army was watching from the sidelines. They ran and were immediately pursued by the men of Israel and Judah. The Philistines refused to submit themselves as servants to Israel, as was their promise. They ran back to their Philistine cities,

Ekron and Gath (Goliath's hometown), and many were killed along the way. The account does not give details about Goliath's head. It was not until many years later that David brought Goliath's head into Jerusalem. Because, at the time of this slaying, the city of Jerusalem was under Jebusite rule when Jerusalem had earlier been conquered by the hill country Canaanites (Jebusites) around the city.

Post Battle (1 Samuel 17:55–58)

We read that Saul asked a question about David. "Abner, whose son is this youth?" It is apparent that Saul's question and Abner's response are in chronological conflict with the events described in 1 Samuel 16:18–22 and 1 Samuel 17:31–37. However, Saul's question may have been prompted by his concern about his future son-in-law who would gain his riches. In verse 25, Saul was most interested in David's father. In other words, what family would his daughter be marrying into? It seems odd that Saul does not remember David nor Jesse. Quite possibly, Saul was indirectly involved in the everyday events such as choosing a harp player and dressing David in armor for battle. It may be that he assigned someone else to do these things. We may never have an explanation for Saul's incomprehension of David.

There are several lessons we can learn from in this account of David and Goliath.

1. Defeating Goliath was a spiritual battle. Goliath represented a pagan culture and pagan gods. We read that he cursed his gods. Yet David came in the name of the Lord, operating in his strength. He represented God. David knew the outcome before others did because he trusted in God so completely. This account should help us realize that we have spiritual battles to fight. We may not see them as such, but Satan is constantly accusing us before God. He takes advantage of all situations to destroy that which is good (Revelation 12:10). So, if we want to operate in the strength of the Lord, like David, we will need the spiritual armor he had. The New Testament provides the weaponry available to us in Ephesians 6:16. The courage and initiative that comes only from God through prayer and communion with him. Today, we have an advantage over David in that we can read God's words, transcribed over thousands of years (Hebrews 4:12). These verses speak to the power of the word of God, sharper than any sword could be. The scriptures cut into our thoughts and intentions, and help us make the right life decisions.

2. The killing of Goliath defied natural explanations. Some have tried to explain away the miracle of a small boy killing a giant. Because Goliath was a giant, he probably had associated anomalies related to *giantism*. Two disorders would be deafness and visual disturbances like blurred vision and

lack of peripheral vision. These physical impairments, according to some, may have been the reason he had so easily been killed. Why don't we want to give credit to God for his ability to act? People from the beginning of time have been lacking in faith. It is common practice for man to look to science for the unexplainable answers. However, in verse forty-seven we are informed that the Lord does not need science nor military might to perform his miracles. We read the profound statement that the battle belonged to the Lord. This indicates he controlled the action and the outcomes for one of history's most puzzling wartime victories.

Personal Applications

1. How is your faith today? Are you defeating spiritual Goliaths? What techniques have you used successfully? Are you willing to trust in David's God, who proved to be completely trustworthy?

2. People have always claimed to have visions of angels. Do you think this is possible? Even though the presence of angels is a distinct possibility, their importance should be minimally valued. God emphasizes the importance of his Son, Jesus Christ, over angels and we should also (Hebrews 1:1–4).

3. What about the aggressors in our lives that seem to attack or destroy us? Each circumstance that David faced and overcame strengthened him to handle the next challenge. And they were actually preparing him to be king. It is the same with our lives. We should not fear what lies ahead. Our success in conquering the challenges depends on how much reliance we have on the holy spirit to empower us. If we have the advantage of hearing from God, why wouldn't we wait to hear from him first? Possibly we believe he is not listening or that he does not have the desire to help us. But if we truly believe this great God of the universe listens intently to our problems and the cry of our hearts, there should never be any circumstance that is too great for God or that we should not bring to him. Here is a process we can follow to initiate our communion with God (Micah 7:7, Isaiah 59:1–2).

    *   Look to the Lord
    *   Wait for the Lord
    *   Listen for the Lord

The only thing that can separate us from God's communication is a heart that does not know him or that is not in a healthy relationship with him.

David and Goliath
Chapter 4
References

1 Samuel 17:1–3 "Now the Philistines gathered their armies for battle; and they were gathered at Socoh which belongs to Judah, and they camped between Socoh and Azekah, in Ephes-dammim. Saul and the men of Israel were gathered and camped in the valley of Elah, and drew up in battle array to encounter the Philistines. The Philistines stood on the mountain on one side while Israel stood on the mountain on the other side, with the valley between them."

Matthew 12:24 "But when the Pharisees heard this, they said, "This man casts out demons only by Beelzebul the ruler of the demons."

2 Samuel 5:21 "They abandoned their idols there, so David and his men carried them away"

Genesis 17:10–11 "This is My covenant, which you shall keep, between Me and you and your descendants after you: every male among you shall be circumcised. And you shall be circumcised in the flesh of your foreskin, and it shall be the sign of the covenant between Me and you."

1 Samuel 17:4–11

Genesis 6:1–4 "Now it came about, when men began to multiply on the face of the land, and daughters were born to them, that the sons of God saw that the daughters of men were beautiful; and they took wives for themselves, whomever they chose. Then the LORD said, 'My Spirit shall not strive with man forever, because he also is flesh; nevertheless, his days shall be one hundred and twenty years.' The Nephilim were on the earth in those days, and also afterward, when the sons of God came in to the daughters of men, and they bore children to them. Those were the mighty men who were of old, men of renown."

Matthew 22:30 "For in the resurrection they neither marry nor are given in marriage, but are like angels in heaven"

Heb. 13:2 "Do not neglect to show hospitality to strangers, for by this some have entertained angels without knowing it."

Jude 6 "And angels who did not keep their own domain, but abandoned their proper abode, He has kept in eternal bonds under darkness for the judgment of the great day."

1 Samuel. 17:12–37

1 Samuel 13:14 "The LORD has sought out for Himself a man after His own heart, and the LORD has appointed him as ruler over His people."

Deuteronomy 20:1–4 "When you go out to battle against your enemies and see horses and chariots and people more numerous than you, do not be afraid of them; for the LORD your God, who brought you up from the land of Egypt, is with you. When you are approaching the battle, the priest shall come near and speak to the people. He shall say to them, 'Hear, O Israel, you are approaching the battle against your enemies today. Do not be fainthearted. Do not be afraid, or panic, or tremble before them, for the LORD your God is the one who goes with you, to fight for you against your enemies, to save you'"

1 Samuel 17:11 "When Saul and all Israel heard these words of the Philistine, they were dismayed and greatly afraid."

1 Timothy 4:12 "Let no one look down on your youthfulness, but rather in speech, conduct, love, faith and purity, show yourself an example of those who believe."

Judges 14:5–6 "Then Samson went down to Timnah with his father and mother, and came as far as the vineyards of Timnah; and behold, a young lion came roaring toward him. The Spirit of the LORD came upon him mightily, so that he tore him as one tears a young goat though he had nothing in his hand; but he did not tell his father or mother what he had done."

2 Timothy 4:17–18 "But the Lord stood with me and strengthened me, so that through me the proclamation might be fully accomplished, and that all the Gentiles might hear; and I was rescued out of the lion's mouth. The Lord will rescue me from every evil deed, and will bring me safely to His heavenly kingdom; to Him be the glory forever and ever."

1 Samuel 16:18 "Then one of the young men said, "Behold, I have seen a son of Jesse the Bethlehemite who is a skillful musician, a mighty man of valor, a warrior, one prudent in speech, and a handsome man; and the LORD is with him."

1 Samuel 17:38–54

Judges 20:15–16 "From the cities on that day the sons of Benjamin were numbered, 26,000 men who draw the sword, besides the inhabitants of Gibeah who were numbered, 700 choice men. Out of all these people 700 choice men were left-handed; each one could sling a stone at a hair and not miss."

1 Samuel 17:55–58 "Now when Saul saw David going out against the Philistine, he said to Abner the commander of the army, "Abner, whose son is this young man?" And Abner said, "By your life, O king, I do not know." The king said, "You inquire whose son the youth is." So when David returned from killing the Philistine, Abner took him and brought him before Saul with the Philistine's head in his hand. Saul said to him, "Whose son are you, young man?" And David answered, "I am the son of your servant Jesse the Bethlehemite."

1 Samuel 16:18–22 "Then one of the young men said, Behold, I have seen a son of Jesse the Bethlehemite who is a skillful musician, a mighty man of valor, a warrior, one prudent in speech, and a handsome man; and the LORD is with him. So Saul sent messengers to Jesse and said, Send me your son David who is with the flock. Jesse took a donkey loaded with bread and a jug of wine and a young goat, and sent them to Saul by David his son. Then David came to Saul and attended him; and Saul loved him greatly, and he became his armor bearer. Saul

sent to Jesse, saying, Let David now stand before me, for he has found favor in my sight."

1 Samuel 17:31–37

1 Samuel 17:25 "The men of Israel said, 'Have you seen this man who is coming up? Surely he is coming up to defy Israel. And it will be that the king will enrich the man who kills him with great riches and will give him his daughter and make his father's house free in Israel.'"

Revelation 12:10 "Then I heard a loud voice in heaven, saying, 'Now the salvation, and the power, and the kingdom of our God and the authority of His Christ have come, for the accuser of our brethren has been thrown down, he who accuses them before our God day and night.'"

Hebrews 4:12 "For the word of God is living and active and sharper than any two-edged sword, and piercing as far as the division of soul and spirit, of both joints and marrow, and able to judge the thoughts and intentions of the heart."

Deuteronomy 32:20 "Then He said, 'I will hide My face from them, I will see what their end shall be; For they are a perverse generation, sons in whom is no faithfulness."

Ephesians 6:16 "Take up the shield of faith with which you will be able to extinguish all the flaming arrows of the evil one."

Hebrews 1:1–4 "God, after He spoke long ago to the fathers in the prophets in many portions and in many ways, in these last days has spoken to us in His Son, whom He appointed heir of all things, through whom also He made the world. And He is the radiance of His glory and the exact representation of His nature, and upholds all things by the word of His power. When He had made purification of sins, He sat down at the right hand of the Majesty on high, having become as much better than the angels, as He has inherited a more excellent name than they. For to which of the angels did He ever say, 'You are my son, today I have begotten you?' And again, 'I will be a father to him and he shall be a son to me?'"

Micah 7:7 "But as for me, I will watch expectantly for the LORD; I will wait for the God of my salvation. My God will hear me."

Isaiah 59:1–2 "Behold, the LORD's hand is not so short that it cannot save; nor is His ear so dull that it cannot hear. But your iniquities have made a separation between you and your God, and your sins have hidden His face from you so that He does not hear."

David: Friends for Life

"Jonathan made David vow again because of his love for him, because he loved him as he loved his own life."
—1 Samuel 20:17

Have you ever had a friend for life? What would you say were characteristics of that friendship? Familiar verses from Proverbs, like "A friend loves at all times," "A friend sticks closer than a brother," and "Do not forsake your own friend," are welcome reminders of the value of friendship. In this chapter, we will study one of the great friendships of the Bible. The friendship between David and Jonathan. Immediately following the slaying of Goliath, King Saul brought David before him to question him and to get to know his future son-in-law. The passage is found in 1 Samuel 18:1–15. The first verse in this chapter is key. "The soul of Jonathan was knit to the soul of David." This verse says that Jonathan loved David as he did his own self. Have you ever loved a friend that much? It seems that friendships often change, based on extenuating circumstances. But it was not so with these two men. Consider some factual observation about their friendship.

1. Their friendship was covenantal. In verse 3, we read that David and Jonathan formed an agreement. Jonathan was to be second in command in David's kingdom, even though Jonathan was the heir apparent (1 Samuel 23:16–18).
2. Their friendship was ancestral. As a result of this covenant, their families would be knit together physically and spiritually (1 Samuel 20:42).
3. Their friendship was giving and sacrificial. Jonathan gave David his clothes and military garb...and this time, the apparel fit! (1 Samuel 18:4). His display of generosity was significant because it showed that Jonathan recognized and accepted that David would one day be king of Israel. Rather

than being envious or jealous, Jonathan submitted to God's will and relinquished his right to the throne.

4. Their friendship was rooted in truehearted devotion. Jonathan exhibited a loyal defense of David. He protected David and in order to do this, he worked around his father's plans (1 Samuel 19:3).

A Troublesome Relationship (1 Samuel 20:1–42)

In the years leading up to his kingship, David experienced a lot of persecution from King Saul. Saul did not attempt to hide his hatred and jealousy for David, and he made many attempts to take his life. As we read in verse 1, David did not understand Saul's hostility toward him and he sought to learn the reasons, hoping it would bring them to reconciliation. The test would be, Saul's response to David's absence from the new moon feast, held on the first day of every month. The festival brought a time of rejoicing, marked by the sound of trumpets Numbers 10:10, Psalm 81:3, and special sacrifices (Numbers 28:11–15). It was an expectation that one be present for this ceremony. If Saul became angry over David's absence, then David would know that there was no hope of patching up their differences. However, if the king was amenable, then their relationship could be salvaged. The plan was that Jonathan would approach his father on the matter and communicate the results to David by signaling with arrows. At first, Saul thought David to be absent because he was ceremonially unclean. If one was unclean, they were unfit to worship God (Leviticus 5:1–4). So, an unclean offense could be touching a dead person or animal, or touching excretion waste, or something even more foul to God such as swearing. But then, Saul's response was what David had feared. Saul became filled with rage toward David and also toward his own son, Jonathan. In verse 30, we hear strange responses from Saul. "You son of a perverse, rebellious woman" and "To the shame of your mother's nakedness." This kind of speech is similar to modern expressions and the insult was meant for Jonathan, not necessarily his mother. Next, we read in verse 31 that Saul disagreed with or wanted to deny the covenant between David and Jonathan. Even after Saul heard from Samuel that his kingdom would not continue, Saul still clung to hope for his dynasty (1 Samuel 13:14). We know that Saul had an anger management problem and its evidence is seen in verse 33 when he attempted to kill Jonathan by throwing a spear at him! It is now that Jonathan realizes how serious a situation this is for David. For, if Saul tried to kill his own son, certainly he would do the same to David. We know that he had already tried to kill David three previous times (1 Samuel 18:11, 19:10). Jonathan was deeply affected by his father's behavior. So much so that he lost his appetite and grieved for David.

Bow and Arrow

It was with heavy heart the next morning that Jonathan went to the rock of Ezel, a place where David would be hiding. The word *Ezel* means "mound or stone heap," signifying that it was a large rocky hill. Jonathan took a young boy with him who was probably a servant (verse 38 refers to Jonathan as his master). There had been a predetermined plan between the two friends. If the situation was safe for David, Jonathan's arrows would fall short of the boy, who was out in the field. If it was unsafe, the arrows would go beyond the boy. Jonathan began to bow the arrows, and one by one, they landed far beyond the boy. As soon as the boy was dismissed, David came out of hiding. He fell on his face to the ground and bowed three times. It is unclear who he was bowing to, but he probably was thanking God for sparing his life through his friend's help. It certainly shows the gratefulness and humility of his heart. As the friends exchange affection, they acknowledge the name of the Lord, saying that the Lord was the reason for their friendship. According to scripture, after this account, they only saw each another once again in their lives. The account is found in 1 Samuel 23:14–18. David was residing in the wilderness, in different locations and mostly in the forest Ziph. Saul ordered daily search parties to find David but all had been unsuccessful up to this point. Jonathan then made a purposeful effort to see David. The purpose was to strengthen David's hand in God. What is meant by this? He aided David in finding strength where only true strength can be found (1 Samuel 30:6b). His strength came from God! The word *strong* in this text means to encourage. It is highly probable that Jonathan and David prayed together. We know that our prayers are very affective when two or more are praying together (Matthew 18:20). In what other ways did Jonathan encourage David? Verse 17 of I Samuel 23 tells us several things.

- To not be afraid
- That David wouldn't be captured by King Saul
- That David would be king over Israel
- That Jonathan would be by his side

The Covenant

Next, we read in verse 18 that they renewed their covenant with each other. It is likely that David prayed a prayer like that which is in Psalm 27:1–3. Here is the word strength again…the Lord is strengthening David. In fact, he is the strength of David's life. Saul had shown aggression toward David but he continued to avoid Saul's pursuits. Every time Saul heard of David's location, David would not be there when Saul arrived. First Samuel 23:25–26 describes Saul's pursuit. After this account,

Jonathan vanished from scripture until his death. We read only that he died fighting by his father's side (1 Samuel 31:1–2).

David later laments his friend in a poem called the "Psalm of the Bow" (2 Samuel 1:25–27). Let's examine these verses together. David referred to Jonathan as mighty. We can better understand this to be courage, reputation and success. We could say that he was a mighty spiritual warrior who loved God and feared him. Jonathan's death occurred at a high place. Mt. Gilboa is approximately a half mile high above the plain of Jezreel; a very vast, open plain which is most likely the future spot of the battle of Armageddon. David expressed his distress at Jonathan's death. His friend most likely died at a young age—in his twenties, which was David's age at this time. The word *distressed* is translated "to cramp or bind up." David was physically affected by Jonathan's death. So much so that it most likely caused him to have tightness in his stomach and chest. Then, David described what Jonathan meant to him. He said, "You have been pleasant to me." This expression describes Jonathan as agreeable and kind. Jonathan loved David. His love was selfless and bore quite a price. David said, "Your love was greater than the love I receive from the women in my life." David may have not felt the same kindred love from his wives as he had from Jonathan.

Jonathan proved his love to David in four ways.

- He gave his word to David that he would not betray him (verse 9).
- He asked David to affirm his love for him. Jonathan could see that David was questioning his love, so he reassured him, saying, "One day you will have the kingdom, so swear to me now, when that day comes, you will protect me." In other words, he was showing David that he really believed in his great destiny (verse 17).
- Jonathan proved his love by his deeds. In private and unknown to David, Jonathan temporarily deflected Saul's wrath from David to himself (verses 27–28).
- Jonathan proved his love because he kept his word. This was evident when he arranged to give David a signal to let him know whether it was safe for him to stay at court (verses 19–22).

David knew that he had a true friend—the kind of friend who sticks closer than a brother (Proverbs 18:24). This verse refers to the friend that we can have in the Lord. Jonathan proved that his friendship involved an unconditional, lasting love. Some years later, when David became king, he recalled a promise he had made. We know that Jonathan had a son named Mephibosheth (2 Samuel 4:4). This is a very short account of his descendant. Jonathan had died. But remember the promise he and David had made to each other? They formed an agreement that David was to protect Jonathan's family (1 Samuel 20:42). In this account of David and Mephibosheth (2 Samuel 9:1–13), David decided to inquire whether there was anyone in Jonathan's family to whom he could show kindness. Yes, he was told about Jonathan's son, Mephibosheth, who was lame from birth. David immediately sent for him, and treated him as royalty. Consider what David did for Mephibosheth:

- He restored Saul's personal estate to him.
- He supported him on a royal pension.
- He instructed Ziba, his fifteen sons and twenty servants to farm Mephibosheth's land and to treat him as if he were David's own son.
- He let him eat at his own table.

What kind of man would do this for another? A man with a magnanimous heart. Verse 7 says, "I will surely show you kindness for your father's sake." The word *kindness* means "loyal love". David's actions were rooted in his loyalty to Jonathan. And Mephibosheth's reaction was one of humility. He referred to himself as a dead dog; that is, worthless. He repeatedly bowed down to David, and at one point, fell prostrate on the floor. This was a man who had probably suffered his whole life from embarrassment, ridicule, and problems associated with immobility. And so, the love of two friends came full circle.

The love between two men can sometimes be misconstrued for homosexuality. David's culture, as in our culture, struggled with homosexual behavior. There is some unorthodox and unsubstantiated thought that David and Jonathan may have been homosexual lovers. However, there is no evidence of this postulation in scripture. As indicated in our study, both David and Jonathan expressed that their first love was for God. Their relationship with God served as a protection against the breaking of God's laws (Romans 1:26–28).

Personal Application

1. What exactly is a covenant and does it exist today? The word *covenant* in the Latin means a *coming together*. Covenants are referred to many times in scripture and are the source of great theological principles and blessings. In the case of Jonathan and David, their covenant was a binding or a bond with each other. A covenant is important for believers because it is both a promise and a protection. Jesus's sacrificial death and resurrection, sealed with his blood, instituted the New Covenant which spans the gulf between sinful man and eternal life with God (Matthew 26:26–28).

2. Is there a friend whom you love as much as Jonathan and David's love for each other? A friend whom you love as much as yourself? A friend whom you would sacrifice for or serve?

3. How should we view homosexuality? The Old Testament law explicitly states that homosexuality is an aberrancy to God's plan. God's law teaches that only male and female were created, that their creation was good in His eyes, and that they were created for each other's pleasure (Genesis 2:22–24). The lifestyle of homosexuality is described as an abomination, or a detestable action (Leviticus 18:22). Homosexuality is also depicted as a despicable act worthy of death (Leveticus 20:13). God clearly states in Romans 1:26–27 that homosexuals are morally fallen; the result of denying and disobeying him. There is hope for homosexuals, in that while they are sinners, as we all are, Christ loves them and died for their sins (Ephesians 2:4).

David: Friends for Life
Chapter 5
References

1 Samuel 18:1–15

1 Samuel 23:16–18 "And Jonathan, Saul's son, arose and went to David at Horesh, and encouraged him in God. Thus he said to him, 'Do not be afraid, because the hand of Saul my father will not find you, and you will be king over Israel and I will be next to you; and Saul my father knows that also.' So the two of them made a covenant before the LORD; and David stayed at Horesh while Jonathan went to his house."

1 Samuel 20:42 "Jonathan said to David, 'Go in safety, inasmuch as we have sworn to each other in the name of the LORD, saying, The LORD will be between me and you, and between my descendants and your descendants forever.' Then he rose and departed, while Jonathan went into the city."

1 Samuel 18:4 "Jonathan stripped himself of the robe that was on him and gave it to David, with his armor, including his sword and his bow and his belt."

1 Samuel 19:3 "I will go out and stand beside my father in the field where you are, and I will speak with my father about you; if I find out anything, then I will tell you."

1 Samuel 20:1–42

Numbers 10:10 "Also in the day of your gladness and in your appointed feasts, and on the first days of your months, you shall blow the trumpets over your burnt offerings, and over the sacrifices of your peace offerings; and they shall be as a reminder of you before your God. I am the LORD your God."

Psalm 81:3 "Blow the trumpet at the new moon, at the full moon, on our feast day."

Numbers 28:11–15 "Then at the beginning of each of your months you shall present a burnt offering to the LORD: two bulls and one ram, seven male lambs one year old without defect; and three-tenths of an ephah of fine flour mixed with oil for a grain offering, for each bull. And one male goat for a sin offering to the LORD; it shall be offered with its drink offering in addition to the continual burnt offering."

Leviticus 5:1–4 "Now if a person sins after he hears a public adjuration to testify when he is a witness, whether he has seen or otherwise known, if he does not tell it, then he will bear his guilt. Or if a person touches any unclean thing, whether a carcass of an unclean beast or the carcass of unclean cattle or a carcass of unclean swarming things, though it is hidden from him and he is unclean, then he will be guilty. Or if he touches human uncleanness, of whatever sort his uncleanness may be with which he becomes unclean, and it is hidden from him, and then he comes to know it, he will be guilty. Or if a person swears thoughtlessly with his lips to do evil or to do good, in whatever matter a man may speak thoughtlessly with an oath, and it is hidden from him, and then he comes to know it, he will be guilty in one of these."

1 Samuel 13:14 "But now your kingdom shall not endure. The LORD has sought out for Himself a man after His own heart, and the LORD has appointed him as ruler over His people, because you have not kept what the LORD commanded you."

1 Samuel 20:33 "Then Saul hurled his spear at him to strike him down; so Jonathan knew that his father had decided to put David to death."

1 Samuel 18:11 "Saul hurled the spear for he thought, 'I will pin David to the wall.' But David escaped from his presence twice."

1 Samuel 19:10 "Saul tried to pin David to the wall with the spear, but he slipped away out of Saul's presence, so that he stuck the spear into the wall. And David fled and escaped that night."

1 Samuel 23:14–18 "David stayed in the wilderness in the strongholds, and remained in the hill country in the wilderness of Ziph. And Saul sought him every day, but God did not deliver him into his hand. Now David became aware that Saul had come out to seek his life while David was in the wilderness of Ziph at Horesh. And Jonathan, Saul's son, arose and went to David at Horesh, and encouraged him in God. Thus he said to him, 'Do not be afraid, because the hand of Saul my father will not find you, and you will be king over Israel and I will be next to you; and Saul my father knows that also.' So the two of them made a covenant before the LORD; and David stayed at Horesh while Jonathan went to his house."

1 Samuel 30:6 "Moreover David was greatly distressed because the people spoke of stoning him, for all the people were embittered, each one because of his sons and his daughters. But David strengthened himself in the LORD his God."

Matthew 18:20 "For where two or three have gathered together in My name, I am there in their midst."

Psalm 27:1–3 "The LORD is the strength of my life; whom shall I fear? The LORD is the defense of my life; whom shall I dread? When evildoers came upon me to devour my flesh, my adversaries and my enemies, they stumbled and fell. Though a host encamp against me, my heart will not fear; though war arise against me, in spite of this I shall be confident."

1 Samuel 23:25–26 "When Saul and his men went to seek him, they told David, and he came down to the rock and stayed in the wilderness of Maon. And when Saul heard it, he pursued David in the wilderness of Maon. Saul went on one side of the mountain, and David and his men on the other side of the mountain; and David was hurrying to get away from Saul, for Saul and his men were surrounding David and his men to seize them."

1 Samuel 31:1–2 "Now the Philistines were fighting against Israel, and the men of Israel fled from before the Philistines and fell slain on Mount Gilboa. The

Philistines overtook Saul and his sons; and the Philistines killed Jonathan and Abinadab and Malchi-shua the sons of Saul."

2 Samuel 1:25–27 "How have the mighty fallen in the midst of the battle! Jonathan is slain on your high places. I am distressed for you, my brother Jonathan, you have been very pleasant to me. Your love to me was more wonderful than the love of women. How have the mighty fallen, and the weapons of war perished!"

1 Samuel 20:9 "Jonathan said, 'Far be it from you! For if I should indeed learn that evil has been decided by my father to come upon you, then would I not tell you about it?'"

1 Samuel 20:17 "Jonathan made David vow again because of his love for him, because he loved him as he loved his own life."

1 Samuel 20:27–30 "It came about the next day, the second day of the new moon, that David's place was empty; so Saul said to Jonathan his son, 'Why has the son of Jesse not come to the meal, either yesterday or today?' Jonathan then answered Saul, David earnestly asked leave of me to go to Bethlehem, for he said, 'Please let me go, since our family has a sacrifice in the city, and my brother has commanded me to attend. And now, if I have found favor in your sight, please let me get away that I may see my brothers.' For this reason, he has not come to the king's table. Then Saul's anger burned against Jonathan and he said to him, 'You son of a perverse, rebellious woman! Do I not know that you are choosing the son of Jesse to your own shame and to the shame of your mother's nakedness?'"

1 Samuel 20:19–22 "When you have stayed for three days, you shall go down quickly and come to the place where you hid yourself on that eventful day, and you shall remain by the stone Ezel. I will shoot three arrows to the side, as though I shot at a target. And behold, I will send the lad, saying, 'Go, find the arrows.' If I specifically say to the lad, 'Behold, the arrows are on this side of you, get them,' then come; for there is safety for you and no harm, as the LORD lives. But if I say to the youth, 'Behold, the arrows are beyond you,' go, for the LORD has sent you away"

Prov. 18:24 "A man of too many friends comes to ruin, but there is a friend who sticks closer than a brother."

2 Samuel 4:4 "Now Jonathan, Saul's son, had a son crippled in his feet. He was five years old when the report of Saul and Jonathan came from Jezreel, and his nurse took him up and fled. And it happened that in her hurry to flee, he fell and became lame. And his name was Mephibosheth."

1 Samuel 20:42 "Jonathan said to David, 'Go in safety, inasmuch as we have sworn to each other in the name of the LORD, saying, 'The LORD will be between me and you, and between my descendants and your descendants forever.' Then he rose and departed, while Jonathan went into the city"

2 Samuel 9:1–13

Matthew 26:26–28

Genesis 2:22–24 "The LORD God fashioned into a woman the rib which He had taken from the man, and brought her to the man. The man said, 'This is now bone of my bones, and flesh of my flesh; she shall be called Woman, because she was taken out of Man.' For this reason, a man shall leave his father and his mother, and be joined to his wife; and they shall become one flesh."

Leviticus 18:22 "You shall not lie with a male as one lies with a female; it is an abomination."

Leviticus 20:13 "If there is a man who lies with a male as those who lie with a woman, both of them have committed a detestable act; they shall surely be put to death. Their blood-guiltiness is upon them."

Romans 1:26–27 "For this reason God gave them over to degrading passions; for their women exchanged the natural function for that which is unnatural, and in the same way also the men abandoned the natural function of the woman and burned in their desire toward one another, men with men committing indecent acts and receiving in their own persons the due penalty of their error."

Ephesians 2:4–5, "But God, being rich in mercy, because of His great love with which He loved us, even when we were dead in our transgressions, made us alive together with Christ (by grace you have been saved)."

Romans 1:28 "And just as they did not see fit to acknowledge God any longer, God gave them over to a depraved mind, to do those things which are not proper."

6

David: Man on the Run

"My times are in Your hand; deliver me from the hand of my enemies and from those who persecute me."

—Psalm 31:15

At the age of twenty, David was forced to leave Saul's palace and the place he knew as home. This was because of Saul's relentless determination to kill him. He went into the wilderness of Judah and lived out a "Robin Hood" type of existence for almost ten years. What is recorded of David's activities during this time is only a fraction of what really happened. For this study, we will examine his life while he is on the run. David developed a strategy that involved provision, strength and protection while dealing with encounters with Saul.

Sanctuary at Nob (1 Samuel 21:1–9)

Where does one seek help when one is all alone? Perhaps the church, the synagogue or the parish. David fled to the city of Nob, which also was called "the city of priests." It was a religious center. He sought sanctuary and protection with Ahimelech, the high priest at Nob. As a result of their travels, David and his men were hungry and asked Ahimelech for some bread. The only bread the priest had was holy bread, and this had already been consecrated to God. Both the Old and New Testament refer to holy bread (Leviticus 24:5–9). Jesus spoke of it in Matthew 12:1–8. As Jesus and his disciples were walking through the fields of grain on the Sabbath, the disciples began to pick the buds of wheat and eat them. The Pharisees immediately jumped on this violation of the law and accused them of working on the Sabbath. Jesus, however, disputed their claim by using the illustration of David eating consecrated bread that was reserved for priests alone. The Pharisees were so law-focused that they failed to compassionately understand the basic needs of their people. Jesus reminded them that inner spiritual purity is more important than outward law keeping.

David admitted to Ahimelech that he left Saul's palace in such haste that he brought no weapons with him. So, he asked for a spear or a sword. Amazingly, Ahimelech offered him Goliath's sword, which he had been preserving. David took it, exclaiming that it was one of a kind. And truly, it was just as large and heavy as David remembered when he had fought Goliath. But David was now older and a man, no longer a boy. So, probably he was able to handle the size of the sword at this time.

David's Refuge (1 Samuel 21:10–15)

In the next account, David chose a very unlikely place of escape. It was to king Ackish in the Philistine city of Gath. Yes, the pagan city of Gath where Goliath had lived. Why would David go there? Well, this is also the reaction of king Ackish's servants. One theory is that David became tired of running. And he thought that if he could remain hidden in an enemy population, he could rest for a while. But no, King Ackish's servants recognized him and David became afraid for his life. Feigning mental illness, he fled from the city.

After David left Gath, we read that he sought refuge in a cave called Adullum (1 Samuel 22:1–5). The word *Adullum* means "refuge". It may be that David's family also feared for their lives, as we read that his brothers and his father's household joined with him in that cave, as well as four hundred men. Verse 2 says this group was distressed, in debt, or unhappy with Saul's leadership. We might compare this to the Robin Hood story. David formed a band of brothers and became their Robin Hood. They were not there for long, however, before they were warned that they needed to leave for their safety's sake. We have David's diary, so to speak, in the book of Psalms. David wrote at least two psalms while he was in the cave of Adullum—Psalm 57:1–11 and Psalm 142:1–7. These passages reveal the desperate situation David was in. One has a sense that his life was in danger. We read of despair and alarm. In times like this, who did David go to? The Lord!

Next, David discovers that he must provide protection for his followers and his country (1 Samuel 23:1–13). By now, David's army had grown to six hundred men. He found it hard to ignore the plight of his fellow Judeans, as they were being attacked by the Philistines. Keilah was located only three miles away but was near the Philistine territory line. The important theme in this account is the communication David had with God. Notice that in verse 1, David's army told him of the Philistine attack. Immediately in verse 2, David went to God for direction on what to do. And the conversation continued. David asked, listened and waited for the Lord's response. Was it a verbal response? Likely not, but we really do not know because in those days God communicated differently. We definitely have his message and words written in the Bible and that is his communication to us today. How comforting to know that the Lord was there and ready to respond. He is always available...to David, to you, to me. Now, David was torn between what his men wanted and what God wanted. Verse 3 says that his men were in a panic of fear at the thought of fighting the Philistines. But David united his men behind him, and at the risk of leaving their safe haven in the cave, they destroyed the Philistines and took their livestock. In that battle, the son of the high priest, Ahimelech, was God's representative. As he went into battle, he held an ephod, the linen garment that priests wore which represented divine inquiry. In simple terms, it was a symbol of their request to God for his protection. Verse 11 tells us that the men of Kielah betrayed David and relayed word to Saul of his location. Saul immediately sent out a search party for him. We know that Saul's rule was great. He had advantages over David, such as power, men, and resources. But we also know that God is greater and that God was on David's side! (Psalm 103:11).

Saul continued his pursuit of David (1 Samuel 23:14–15, 19–29). Again we see that the local people reported back to Saul. And Saul blessed them for doing this however, he then commanded them to find David. There are two psalms which reference this occasion—Psalm 31:22 and 17:9. These verses describe David as he feels alarm, fear, and isolation in the presence of his enemies. Saul received notice that the Philistines had invaded Judea, just at the moment when his men were closing in on David. There was no other explanation except that this was providential. God's orchestration at its best! And let's give Saul some credit. He distinguished himself by sacrificing his personal interests for the sake of his country's national security. Saul suddenly began to use religious language, saying, "Look what God has done for me by showing me where David was hiding." He saw this as a blessing from God, however, this was short-lived.

The Cave Experience (1 Samuel 24:1–22)

We continue to move on to David's next hide out. He went to the wilderness of En Gedi. En Gedi is a large spring on the steep western shore of the Dead Sea. Today, it is a beautiful, lush wooded acreage with a waterfall and natural springs. David took refuge here because of the high rock ledges and caves. But, Saul was immediately informed as to where David was hiding. Let's examine the text. David immediately became conscience stricken, for he knew that he had come close to competing with something that is God's prerogative alone (Hebrews 10:30). David learned an important lesson in this account. A leader must rise above his zealous followers. You will recall when David's supporters discovered that King Saul was in the cave where they were hiding, they encouraged David to kill him. Let's compare two interesting verses—1 Samuel 23:7; 24:4a. Here we see that both David and Saul claimed that God was on their side. So, who was right? At this point, God had not delivered David into Saul's hands. In fact, he had protected him. And, God had not really delivered Saul into David's hand—at least for now. God would deal with King Saul in his own time. And we see that David actually rebuked his men, saying, "The Lord forbids that I do anything to my master (or ruler), for he is the Lord's anointed." You see, David recognized and safeguarded the sanctity of the man that God placed in power, just as we should do.

Let us examine David and Saul's conversation. David began by asking Saul why was it that he wanted to kill him. This was the root problem and he exposed it for what it was. David went on to say, "I've been advised to kill you, King Saul. But I took pity on you (had my eye on you) and chose not to do that." In self-defense, David stated that he was innocent and that Saul had no reason to kill him. He then brought God into the picture. God will be the judge and will vindicate. Here we see David use the phrases "dead dog and flea". Expressions like this were common at that time. This was David's effort to describe himself as lowly and even an object to be loathed. He expressed his humility at the same moment that he challenged Saul. As we know, fleas are difficult to catch. And so was David. Then David alluded to the fact that God will indeed arbitrate his case, judge his case, and acquit him! So, Saul listened to what he had to say. He acknowledged David and then started to weep. He said, "You are right. And you are a better man than I." Saul now experienced a rare moment of remorse. He recognized David's righteousness and his right to rule. He even said that the Lord should repay David for his goodness. You see, Saul, recognizing his vulnerability, then asked for more. He was thinking ahead of his family's name and safety. And David promised Saul in an oath that he would honor his requests. Then the two men parted ways. We might consider some other facts about this account.

1. God was grooming and educating David during this time to become king. How much better would it have been if David had said nothing to Saul? He really gained nothing by exposing himself. It did not change the king's attitude toward him because Saul already knew David had no ill motives. We know that Saul's words were just a pre-text. He had no intention of letting David become king, nor did he ask for forgiveness from David or from God. The only thing that resulted was that Saul got an oath from David.

2. The second thing is that God gave Saul another chance to get right with him. Stubborn Saul refused to acknowledge his need of God. We will further examine Saul's life in another lesson.

3. This account teaches us that we ought to recognize a good thing when we see it. Saul had opportunity to really see David's heart. This was a moment when he could have made a decision to let go of his hatred of David. After

all, David had spared Saul's life. In turn, God has spared our lives from eternal death. And, he has given us many opportunities to turn to him (2 Corinthians 6:2).

A Sleeping Giant (1 Samuel 26:1–26)

In conclusion, we learn of Saul's final pursuit of David. Once again, Saul heard about David's place of hiding. So, the king and three thousand chosen men went to the hill of Hekilah in search of David. And again, the Lord miraculously delivered David, his chosen one. It involved a secret mission that would take David into the heart of his enemy's camp. This was a formidable task which required great courage. Why was the expedition necessary? It is thought that David felt he had to put to rest Saul's aggression. He needed to prove once and for all that he and King Saul were totally different in character. David asked for a volunteer to accompany him, and Abishai did not hesitate. He said, "I will go with you." What kind of man would volunteer for a suicide mission? The kind of man who had seen God's hand of provision, strength and protection in David's life. Picture this huge encampment of three thousand men, all asleep. Saul is in the middle, in more of an enclosed area—a trench or a ditch. His trusted commander was by his side and his spear close by. As David and Abishai crept around the men, not one awoke nor even stirred. There is a reason for this. The text says that God caused a deep sleep to come upon them. We know of two other previous times where God caused a deep sleep to come upon someone—Genesis 2:21 and Genesis 15:12. Abishai leaned over and whispered to David, "Let me thrust my spear into Saul." He also acknowledged the miracle at hand that God had given the victory to David. He could see that it truly was a miracle that no one had woken up. So, Abishai respected David's decision to not kill Saul. At that moment, David said, "The Lord will take care of him. I just know that his life will not end at my hand." Think of the temptation it must have been for David to not end it once and for all.

From a distance, David woke up the camp by calling to Abner, who was Saul's commander, and he pointed out his dereliction of duty; for Abner should not have been asleep. Notice how pretentious Saul was in his response. He again called David his son. He also urged David to return to the camp. Well, that would have ended in disaster! David would have most certainly been killed by Saul and his men. David stood his ground and proceeded to do the following:

- He embarrassed Abner in front of all his men by showing that he had not done his job in protecting Saul.
- He proved that he was at Saul's side and had the ability to kill him, as he held up Saul's spear and water jug.

- He inquired the reason why Saul persisted in his effort to pursue him, but all the while showing great respect for his position.
- He stated that Saul was keeping him from his true inheritance of becoming king.

Think of the army of men who were listening and had never heard reasons or defense for either side. There may have actually been men who defected from Saul's army to join David after they formed their own opinions at this time. In verse 23, David brings attention to the Lord; and in summary, David says the following things about the Lord.

- God rewards each man for his integrity and loyalty.

    o   Do we have evidence that Saul is this kind of man?
    o   Do we have evidence that David is this kind of man?

- God had anointed Saul as king, for the time being.
- God was at work in this situation, helping David.
- God would be faithful to him and spare his life once again from dangerous King Saul. The evidence of God's faithfulness is undeniable and marvelous!

Saul concluded by giving David a blessing. This is the reward that is mentioned at the end of the chapter. He also said that David would be successful. David had been a man on the run during much of his early life. But he persisted in not letting fear and discouragement overwhelm him.

Personal Applications

1. David's actions required great bravery. We know that his courage came from God. How does this apply in our lives? Are there times when you do not address wrongful decisions or behavior because of a lack of courage? Psalm 94:17 says that God will give us the incentive to speak out and the words to say.
2. Saul seemed to reach a place of spiritual complacency. His ears had become spiritually deaf. His heart had become spiritually cold. Have you ever ignored God's voice and eventually become dull of hearing? (Hebrews 5:11 and 4:7) God's patience is persistent and enduring ...to a point (Genesis 6:3).
3. We know that David must have tired of Saul's constant pursuit of him. Are we sometimes tempted to "just give up" with some person or situation in

our lives? (Psalm 31:15). It should give us comfort to know that God can and will deal with a person or a situation that causes us such grief. God is always present and desires the best outcome for us (Psalm 67:1). We see that David influenced his men to know these things about God and they loved and respected him for it.

4. How patient should we be with one who seeks to abuse or even harm us? (1 Samuel 26:23). David refused to repay Saul for his unthinkable actions against him. The famous option of turning the other cheek is not utilized much today. But, Jesus taught this choice of actions and associated it with loving our enemies (Matthew 5:39, 43–46). Jesus calls upon us to take a higher road. This means that in the face of hate:

- We should not resist an evil person.
- We should seek to better understand our brother and even our enemy.
- We should be charitable to our enemy.
- We should love those who hate us.

David: Man on the Run
Chapter 6
References

1 Samuel 21:1–9

Leviticus 24:5–9 "Then you shall take fine flour and bake twelve cakes with it; two-tenths of an ephah shall be in each cake. You shall set them in two rows, six to a row, on the pure gold table before the LORD. You shall put pure frankincense on each row that it may be a memorial portion for the bread, even an offering by fire to the LORD. Every Sabbath day he shall set it in order before the LORD continually; it is an everlasting covenant for the sons of Israel. It shall be for Aaron and his sons, and they shall eat it in a holy place; for it is most holy to him from the LORD's offerings by fire, his portion forever."

Matthew 12:1–8

1 Samuel 21:10–15

1 Samuel 22:1–5

Psalm 57:1–11

Psalm 142:1–7

1 Samuel 23:1–13

Psalm 103:11 "For as high as the heavens are above the earth, so great is His loving-kindness toward those who fear Him."

1 Samuel 23:14–15 "David stayed in the wilderness in the strongholds, and remained in the hill country in the wilderness of Ziph. And Saul sought him every day, but God did not deliver him into his hand. Now David became aware that Saul had come out to seek his life while David was in the wilderness of Ziph at Horesh."

1 Samuel 23:19–29

Psalm 31:22 "As for me, I said in my alarm, I am cut off from before Your eyes; nevertheless, You heard the voice of my supplications when I cried to You."

Psalm 17:9 "From the wicked who despoil me, my deadly enemies who surround me"

1 Samuel 24:1–22

Hebrews 10:30 "For we know Him who said, 'Vengeance is mine, I will repay' and again, 'The Lord, He will judge His people.'"

1 Samuel 23:7 "When it was told Saul that David had come to Keilah, Saul said, "God has delivered him into my hand, for he shut himself in by entering a city with double gates and bars"

1 Samuel 24:4a "The men of David said to him, 'Behold, this is the day of which the LORD said to you, 'Behold; I am about to give your enemy into your hand, and you shall do to him as it seems good to you.'"

2 Corinthians 6:2 "He says, 'At the acceptable time I listened to you, and on the day of salvation I helped you. Behold, now is the accepted time, behold, now is the day of salvation'"

1 Samuel 26:1–26

Genesis 2:21 "So the LORD God caused a deep sleep to fall upon the man, and he slept; then He took one of his ribs and closed up the flesh at that place."

Genesis 15:12 "Now when the sun was going down, a deep sleep fell upon Abram; and behold, terror and great darkness fell upon him."

Psalm 94:17 "If the LORD had not been my help, my soul would soon have dwelt in the abode of silence."

Hebrews 5:11, 4:7 "Concerning him we have much to say, and it is hard to explain, since you have become dull of hearing. He again fixes a certain day, 'Today,' saying through David after so long a time just as has been said before, 'Today if you hear His voice, do not harden your hearts.'"

Genesis 6:3 "Then the LORD said, 'My Spirit shall not strive with man forever.'"

Psalm 32:15 "My times are in Your hand; deliver me from the hand of my enemies and from those who persecute me."

Psalm 67:1 "God be gracious to us and bless us, and cause His face to shine upon us."

1 Samuel 26:23 "The Lord will repay each man for his righteousness and his faithfulness; for the Lord delivered you into my hand today, but I refused to stretch out my hand against the Lord's anointed."

Matthew 5:39, 43–46 "But I say to you, do not resist an evil person; but whoever slaps you on your right cheek, turn the other to him also. You have heard that it was said, 'You shall love your neighbor and hate your enemy.' But I say to you, love your enemies and pray for those who persecute you, so that you may be sons of your Father who is in heaven…For if you love those who love you, what reward do you have?"

David: A Virtuous Woman?

"Then David said to Abigail, 'Blessed is the Lord God of Israel, who sent you this day to meet me!'"

—1 Samuel 25:32

In this study, we will examine the different women in the life of David. The account of Bathsheba will be examined in a succeeding chapter. As trust and confidence in David's leadership ability actualized, we find evidence of his increasing popularity as a military leader and a potential ruler for the nation of Israel. As a single man, he was also to gain the attention of a royal princess.

An Honorable Reputation (1 Samuel 18:5–16)

The Israelite people, and specifically, the women respected and loved David. He may have been a charming figure for some, but for many, David was admired for his courage and the stand he took in dealing with King Saul. David behaved wisely in all situations. So, King Saul gradually increased his responsibility as commander of the troops for a couple reasons. He knew David could defeat the enemy, but also, there was a high likelihood that David might be killed in battle. Don't forget that David was a threat to King Saul's position. Notice also that even Saul's servants respected David. He was defeating the Philistines in every battle, and on one occasion, as he and King Saul returned home, the women came out to greet them. They were very joyous, singing and dancing and playing musical instruments. This was probably not an unusual response, for we read in Exodus 15:20–21, of an earlier time, when the Israelite women used this same expression of joy; only it was for their heavenly king! The Exodus account, of course, describes the escape of the Israelites from Egypt and the drowning of the Egyptians in the Red Sea. Now, in this account of David and Saul, we must give attention to what the women sang; "Saul has slain his thousands and David his ten thousands." It is not certain that the women meant to praise David more than Saul. It was common in Hebrew poetry for intensity to build within the verse, as we observe in verse seven. Regardless, Saul did take offense, and we see that he became jealous, suspicious, and angry with David from that day forward. In fact, in verse 15, we read that Saul actually became afraid of David. As we know, there were times when Saul tried to spear David, but David always managed to escape, with God's delivering help; and this gave David even more popularity. When Saul saw that he could not destroy David personally, he determined to let the Philistines kill him. Before we move into the account of Saul's daughters, we should again observe David's behavior. Verse 13 says he went in and out before the people. Transparency and visibility is many times the secret to acceptance. The people grew to love him because they saw what he did. Verse 14 says that he again behaved wisely. And why? Because the Lord was with him.

Michal (1 Samuel 18:17–30)

King Saul's two daughters, Merab and Michal, were of an acceptable age to marry. Initially Saul proposed that David marry his oldest daughter, Merab. However, it is not evident that Saul kept his promise to reward David for killing Goliath with riches or tax exemption. Now, for reasons that are not clear, the marriage between David and Mareb did not take place, and Saul, instead, gave Mareb in marriage to another man. However, the king learned that his daughter, Michal, was in love with David. David may very well have reciprocated this love in verse 26. The Bible shares Saul's thinking with us in verse 21. Saul arranged for his daughter to participate in a dangerous plot. The more we read about David and Saul, the more contrast we see in their personalities. One was a good man, the other was not. Saul seemed to care for his daughter's feelings but ruthlessly planned for her to ensnare the man she loved. David, on the other hand, responded in a humble way regarding both women. In verses 18 and 23, we read that King Saul decided he would require David to work for his daughter, Michal. What did he require? One hundred Philistine foreskins. This refers to the unbelieving Philistines not being circumcised. God required his people to be circumcised, as a defining feature that they were different and set apart unto God. With that background, why would Saul have required a hundred foreskins?

- First, he may have thought this assignment to be an impossibility for David. He thought that David would be killed.
- Circumcision would have been the greatest humility the Philistines could imagine.
- Foreskins would be a lightweight load to carry back from the battlefield, versus heads, for example.

- This was the best way to verify the number of deaths. To bring back proof.

We read that David accomplished the task and more. He did what Saul had thought an impossibility. He brought back two hundred foreskins. Finally, in verse 27, we read that Michal became David's wife. At first, we know that this was a good marriage, because Michal really loved him. And as time went on, the Lord's blessing was increasingly on David. Verse 28 says the Lord was with David, and verse 30 indicates that he was successful and had a highly esteemed name. David and Michal's good relationship seemed to be short-lived, however. Michel's true character is revealed in our next account.

David's Escape (1 Samuel 19:11–18)

Saul sent messengers to David's house to kill him. And Michal helped him escape by setting up a smoke screen for the messengers. She put an image, or a household idol, a statue of a god in their bed. Then she disguised it to be a likeness of David. You may ask, "Why would David, who loved God so much, have this statue in his house?" It is more probable that the statue did not belong to David, but to Michal. The messengers took back the notice that David was sick and Saul said, "Bring him in his bed and I will kill him." So, as the messengers searched the house, they found the disguise. When Saul heard of the foil, he became furious and accused Michal of deceiving him. Michal's response tells us her heart. Verse 17 Michal lied when she said that David would have killed her if she had not helped him escape. Michal may have responded in this way out of fear or retaliation. Even so, her reaction appears to have been an inclination of pretentiousness and dishonesty.

Some time had passed and we again read of Michal in 2 Samuel 3:13–16. The background of this account is that Abner, Saul's commander, was trying to keep his position in the kingdom. He cunningly asked for David's cooperation and we read of David's response. David and Michal had been involuntarily separated. In the meantime, Saul had given Michal as wife to another man! (1 Samuel 25:44). So we learn from this that David wanted her back and this would have been a condition of his agreement to become king.

Ark of the Covenant (2 Samuel 6:12–23)

There is one more account of Michal, and this occurred after David had become king. In fact, this passage refers to Jerusalem as the city of David...an uncommon title today, since Jerusalem is a multiethnic and multifaith city. It had been many years since the ark of the covenant had been separated from its owners, the Israelites.

David had retrieved the ark, which bore the name of God, himself, and represented God's presence.

First, we know that David offered a sacrifice of thanksgiving to God. Next, he blessed the people in the name of the Lord. Then, he generously fed the people with bread, meat, and fruit. The account says that David danced before the Lord with all his might. That means with great enthusiasm. He and others entered the city with exuberant shouting and trumpet playing. His attire was a linen Ephod, which is a sheath-like garment worn by the high priest. It would have been worn only in a religious ceremony. So, based on the circumstances, David's actions were appropriate, in that he viewed the return of the ark as a spiritual event. Religious dances on occasions of great national blessing were usually performed by women only. David danced with a readiness to please and honor God. When all was said and done, David returned home to Michal and to bless his household. Household servants were not normally allowed to take part in religious ceremonies but here we see that David valued all people equally at a time when this was not the norm. He also returned home to an angry and cold wife. She said with contempt, "You uncovered yourself today." This means that he took off his royal robe to put on the linen ephod. It does not mean that he exposed himself. She also did not like the fact that he was dancing and leaping. Michal saw David as lowering himself to the level of his subjects, the inferior class. She was embarrassed. She was ashamed. The public view of David reflected on Michal as well. Her reputation was tied to his. How did God view this? God saw David's heart and how it was honoring to him, and it was a humble heart. He was a person who had no trouble acknowledging God's goodness, and he honored him with every activity. Note David's response to Michal (2 Samuel 21).

1. He defended his position by saying that the Lord chose him over her father, to rule the people. This was a personal and sensitive reminder.
2. He did not accept Michal's accusation that his motive was to embarrass her, and he said that his motive was to please the Lord.
3. He showed no remorse for his actions and instead, told her that he would continue to be abased before the Lord so that God may receive the honor due him.
4. David rejected any notion that his reputation was ruined. He said, "The maidservants will view me in even higher esteem."

David and Michal's marriage produced no children.

Abigail (1 Samuel 25:2–23)

The second woman in David's life entered during that period of time when David was separated from Michal. David and his men had traveled into the Desert of Maon. The Bible tells us a descendant of Caleb lived there. The text states that Nabal was of the house of Caleb. Caleb was the man who accompanied Joshua into the land flowing with milk and honey to scout it out as perspective territory for the Israelites. He is described as having a different spirit, and he followed Joshua and God wholeheartedly when others did not. God blessed Caleb with an inheritance in the promised land, which included property and a large family. However, we read that Nabal did not resemble his ancestor, Caleb, and had a very adverse character. He is described as a harsh and evil man. In fact, his name actually means fool. But clearly, Nabal was blessed with material possessions, since he was wealthy and had considerable influence in the community. The day came when David found himself in a most compromising position. He and his men were in a wilderness area of Israel without any food to eat. So, David remembered Nabal. He was a farmer who raised one thousand goats and three thousand sheep. But, David decided to appeal to Nabal for another reason. Nabal "owed him one". David previously had an experience with Nabal's shepherds and had afforded them protection when they needed it. However, Nabal's response was churlish (rude in a mean-spirited way). He denied that he knew who David was, and he refused to comply with David's request. This caused David to view Nabal as an enemy. He and his men prepared to harm and even kill Nabal, his servants, and possibly Abigail, Nabal's wife. Now, Abigail is described as a woman of good understanding and a woman of beauty. To possess good understanding meant that she was intelligent and had good insight. But let us focus on her beautiful character. When she heard of Nabal's response to David, she immediately made preparations to help David. The text says she made haste. She wasted no time in preparing food for the troops.

The account says that Abigail secretly rode her donkey on a hidden road to find where David was hiding. We have already seen that she was industrious. She didn't just wave off the problem, but she took action. It is clear that she had the gift of generosity. She packed up what she thought David needed. We also know that Abigail was a respectful person. She immediately jumped off the donkey, threw herself to the ground and bowed low before David. David later wrote about this same humility (Psalm 95:6–7). Abigail's address was quite impressive, especially in context that women in that day held their tongue, and even more so with a stranger. It is evident that God gave her the words to say.

A Godly Woman (1 Samuel 25:24–31)

Verse 24, Abigail was willing to take her husband's deserved punishment. She offered herself as a sacrifice to satisfy the payment for wrongs done. In Psalm 54:6, David spoke of a time when he generously offered an animal for his sin. Abigail took this one step further. She was willing to sacrifice her life for her husband's sin. This took exceptional courage and was an extraordinarily noble act. We might remember, however, that there was one other who bore the ultimate sacrifice, when he offered himself upon the cross of calvary. This was Jesus Christ, who paid for all the world's sin (Hebrew 9:28).

Verse 25, Abigail detached herself from her husband, describing him as a man of folly. She explained that she was not present when Nabal had met with David's men. We too, sometimes need to separate ourselves from the evil conditions, situations, and even people that we are subject to. David wrote about his dissociation with the ungodly in Psalm 4:3.

Verse 26, Abigail was a peacemaker. She not only prevented a destructive attack on her husband and servants, but her words indicate that she wished only peace and protection for David. She said, "Let your enemies and those who seek harm for you be as Nabal." What did she really mean here? She said that it was not worthy of David to take vengeance on so despicable a person as Nabal. So, she recognized David's integrity and reputation. David inscribed God's words in Psalm 34:14 that instruct us to do what is good and pursue peace. It is clear that Abigail was led by God. She was a peace driven person (Psalm 119:165).

Verse 27, Abigail made the wrong right. She offered her gift of food, saying it specifically was for David and his men. But notice her use of the word, "maidservant" and throughout the text she refers to David as Lord. She was submissive to David, and effortlessly showed her respect for him. Many years later, David recognized how God had delivered him from contentious people, and placed him in his position as king. He had experienced that God would humble his enemies (Psalm 18:43–44). Again, we see God working in David's life.

Verse 28, Abigail had a relationship with God! She referenced him twice in this verse, and it is really her first mention of him. Here, Abigail tried to separate David's military role from the personal vendetta he now pursued. In an earlier account, David acknowledged this truth (1 Samuel 24:12). In the end, David would thank Abigail for her advice. And, as Abigail referenced, David's house would be enduring.

Verse 29, Abigail's expressions indicate she was cultured. This verse shows poetic repetition. She described David as being "bound in the bundle of the living." Bundle in the Hebrew means treasure pouch. David's life was highly treasured by God. Abigail also described David's enemies as being "slung out from a sling-shot." His enemies would be thrown away from his life. What promises of blessing Abigail shared with David! And they were words of encouragement to him (Psalm 135:4).

Verses 30–31, Abigail's language appears to be prophetic. David is not king at this time, but Abigail referred to his future role as appointed ruler over Israel. David would embark on his journey to become king with a clear conscience. She concluded with a reminder for him to remember her when he became king. Because she and David had kindred minds; both intelligent and both faithful to God, she wanted to continue to encourage him.

According to Psalm 59:10, David had learned to let God fight his battles. The translation means that God will cause him to look upon his enemies. Note that David was not to take action in bringing about vengeance.

Abigail's inspiration brought an immediate and positive response from David. David recognized God's hand in Abigail's visit. He thanked the Lord and thanked Abigail for her advice. He knew that this woman had literally kept him from bringing unnecessary harm to many people. He observed her peace and heeded her words, and in his heart, he respected her person. Now, as Abigail returned home, she found her husband hosting a party. And in the morning, she honestly told him what she had done. Nabal most likely became upset, leading to a disabling stroke. "He became like a stone" is evidence that Nabal had become paralyzed. Ten days later Nabal died. "Vengence is mine, says the Lord" and David proclaimed great relief when he heard the news (Psalm 54:5). Soon a message arrived from David, asking Abigail to become his wife. Once again, this virtuous woman expressed humility and bowed to the earth, offering to wash the feet of the servants who delivered the message. Abigail became David's wife, along with another woman, Akinoam, the Jezreelitis. We only know that she was from Jezreel, a town in the mountains of Judah. They each had a son by David (2 Samuel 3:2–5). David also had four other wives as listed in these verses.

Personal Applications

1. Why were the women in David's life significant? How could they be examples to us? David had good reason to respect women, as evidenced by Abigail's godly testimony. He wrote about the closeness of a mother-child relationship in Psalm 35:14. We know that David remained married to his wives, Abigail, Akinoam, and Bathsheba, for most of his life. He recognized a woman's importance in child bearing and rearing (Psalm 127:5). However, David's writings do not speak much of women. We can establish from the biblical accounts that David responded favorably towards women because of his interactions with them in this study.

    *   He earned Michel's hand in marriage, by meeting Saul's requirements (1 Samuel 18:25–26).

- He enjoyed the admiration given him by the maidservants and women of Jerusalem, but did not unwisely take advantage of their attention (1 Samuel 18:6).
- He called Abigail "blessed" and "respected her person", thus, demonstrating appreciation for her godliness (1 Samuel 25:33, 35).

2. The old cliché "Behind every great man is a great woman" may be true in David's case!

3. Today, we live in a culture where marriage seems to have less value than God would want. His desire is that marriage, as ordained in Genesis 2:24, be our standard. Marriage is a covenant between a man and a woman, just as Christ joins with believers (his church) in a covenant relationship. Men and women each have distinct roles within their union. The man is to give special attention to loving his wife. And the wife is to give priority to respect her husband (Ephesians 5:22–33).

4. What should our attitude be regarding the unfaithful and/or disloyal spouse? We have read of Michal, who disregarded David's purity of heart in his worship of the Lord. We have learned how Nabal was demeaning and evil, most likely also to Abigail. We are to love each other, even as Christ loves the church (Ephesians 5:28–29).

David: A Virtuous Woman?
Chapter 7
References

1 Samuel 25:32

1 Samuel 18:5–16

Exodus 15:20–21 "Miriam the prophetess, Aaron's sister, took the timbrel in her hand, and all the women went out after her with timbrels and with dancing. Miriam answered them, 'Sing to the LORD, for He is highly exalted; the horse and his rider He has hurled into the sea.'"

1 Samuel 18:17–30

1 Samuel 18:26 "When his servants told David these words, it pleased David to become the king's son-in-law."

1 Samuel 18:21 "Saul thought, 'I will give her to him that she may become a snare to him, and that the hand of the Philistines may be against him.' Therefore, Saul said to David, 'For a second time you may be my son-in-law today.'"

1 Samuel 18:18, 23 "But David said to Saul, 'Who am I, and what is my life or my father's family in Israel, that I should be the king's son-in-law?' So, Saul's servants spoke these words to David. But David said, 'Is it trivial in your sight to become the king's son-in-law, since I am a poor man and lightly esteemed?'"

1 Samuel 19:11–18

1 Samuel 19:17 "So Saul said to Michal, 'Why have you deceived me like this and let my enemy go, so that he has escaped?' And Michal said to Saul, 'He said to me, 'Let me go! Why should I put you to death?'"

2 Samuel 3:13–16 "David said, 'I will make a covenant with you, but I demand one thing of you, namely, you shall not see my face unless you first bring Michal, Saul's daughter, when you come to see me.' So David sent messengers to Ish-bosheth, Saul's son, saying, 'Give me my wife Michal, to whom I was betrothed for a hundred foreskins of the Philistines.' Ish-bosheth sent and took her from her husband, from Paltiel, the son of Laish. But her husband went with her, weeping as he went, and followed her as far as Bahurim."

1 Samuel 25:44 "Now Saul had given Michal his daughter, David's wife, to Palti the son of Laish, who was from Gallim"

2 Samuel 6:12–23

2 Samuel 6:21 "So David said to Michal, 'It was before the LORD, who chose me above your father and above all his house, to appoint me ruler over the people of the LORD, over Israel; therefore, I will celebrate before the LORD'."

1 Samuel 25:3

Psalm 95:6–7 "Come, let us worship and bow down, let us kneel before the LORD our Maker. For He is our God, and we are the people of His pasture and the sheep of His hand."

Psalm 54:6 "Willingly I will sacrifice to You; I will give thanks to Your name, O LORD, for it is good." ().

Hebrews 9:28 "So Christ also, having been offered once to bear the sins of many, will appear a second time to those who eagerly await Him."

Psalm 4:3 "But know that the LORD has set apart the godly man for Himself."

Psalm 34:14 "Depart from evil and do good; seek peace and pursue it."

Psalm 119:165 "Those who love Your law have great peace, and nothing causes them to stumble."

Psalm 18:43–44 "You have delivered me from the contentions of the people; You have placed me as head of the nations; a people whom I have not known serve me. As soon as they hear, they obey me; foreigners submit to me."

1 Samuel 24:12 "May the LORD judge between you and me, and may the LORD avenge me on you; but my hand shall not be against you."

Psalm 135:4 "For the LORD has chosen Jacob for Himself, Israel for His own possession."

Psalm 59:10 "My God in His lovingkindness will meet me; God will let me look triumphantly upon my foes."

Psalm 54:5 "He will recompense the evil to my foes; destroy them in Your faithfulness."

2 Samuel 3:2–5 "Sons were born to David at Hebron: his firstborn was Amnon, by Ahinoam the Jezreelitess; and his second, Chileab, by Abigail the widow of

Nabal the Carmelite; and the third, Absalom the son of Maacah, the daughter of Talmai, king of Geshur; and the fourth, Adonijah the son of Haggith; and the fifth, Shephatiah the son of Abital; and the sixth, Ithream, by David's wife Eglah. These were born to David at Hebron."

Psalm 35:14 "I went about as though it were my friend or brother; I bowed down mourning, as one who sorrows for a mother."

Psalm 127:5 "How blessed is the man whose quiver is full of them; they will not be ashamed when they speak with their enemies in the gate."

1 Samuel 18:25–26 "Saul then said, 'Thus you shall say to David, The king does not desire any dowry except a hundred foreskins of the Philistines, to take vengeance on the king's enemies.' Now Saul planned to make David fall by the hand of the Philistines. When his servants told David these words, it pleased David to become the king's son-in-law."

1 Samuel 18:6 "It happened as they were coming, when David returned from killing the Philistine, that the women came out of all the cities of Israel, singing and dancing, to meet King Saul, with tambourines, with joy and with musical instruments."

1 Samuel 25:33, 35 "And blessed be your discernment, and blessed be you, who have kept me this day from bloodshed and from avenging myself by my own hand. Nevertheless, as the LORD God of Israel lives, who has restrained me from harming you, unless you had come quickly to meet me, surely there would not have been left to Nabal until the morning light as much as one male. So, David received from her hand what she had brought him and said to her, 'Go up to your house in peace. See, I have listened to you and granted your request.'"

Genesis 2:24 "For this reason a man shall leave his father and his mother, and be joined to his wife; and they shall become one flesh."

Ephesians 5:22–33

Ephesis 5:28–29 "So husbands ought also to love their own wives as their own bodies. He who loves his own wife loves himself; for no one ever hated his own flesh, but nourishes and cherishes it, just as Christ also does the church."

8

Saul: Success to Failure

"Samuel said to Saul, "You have acted foolishly; you have not kept the commandment of the LORD your God, which He commanded you.""
—1 Samuel 13:13

For just one study, we return to the life of King Saul to examine his character and the series of wrong choices that took him down a difficult road and far from God. But let us begin with a question, "What did God require of Saul?" "What does God require of us?" There are basic requirements for everything—from the need for nourishment to protection from danger. But there are also requirements necessary for human and spiritual interaction. Such as required obedience from your children for their own good. In this study we will consider God's requirements for Saul.

Saul's Beginning (1 Samuel 9:1–6)

The Lord had agreed to Samuel the prophet, or seer, that he would allow Israel to have a king. Saul was a tall, striking Benjamite, from the tribe of Benjamin, who appeared quite naive and "un-kingly" in many ways. Though his father was a man of some influence, Saul had little to commend him to the high position of king except his impressive physic. God had to convince both Saul and the people that he was the right man for the job. One day, Saul was on a mission to find his father's lost donkeys, and his journey took him straight to Samuel (1 Samuel 9:14–21). The Lord had revealed to Samuel his choice for king. This does not mean that Saul satisfied God's ultimate requirements, but only that he was graciously letting the people have their own way. When Samuel told Saul that he was God's choice for king, Saul could only respond that he was unworthy of such a role. This is important, because as we will see later, Saul's humility would eventually turn to pride.

Saul's Anointment and Appointment (1 Samuel 10:1, 17–27)

Sometime later, Samuel gathered the leaders of Israel together. He reminded them of their foolish insistence on having a king, despite the fact that it was not God's will. Samuel then set up what could be called a somewhat amateur selective service process. It would have been accomplished by drawing lots; rather like drawing the short straw. Through this selective process, the tribe of Benjamin was separated out. Then the clan of Matri was pulled from that group; then the family of Kish, and finally, Saul was chosen. The casting of lots has been documented seventy times in the Old Testament and in most instances, God controlled the outcome, as he did in this account. How interesting that Saul was not even present for his selection. David, of course, was also not present when he was chosen as king; but rather, was tending sheep in the field. Indicative of Saul's humility was his attempt to avoid the glare of publicity. Alas, he was found hiding in an area that held the military equipment. He was brought out in public, standing tall over all the other men. Samuel pointed him out, and the people shouted, "Long live the king!" This exclamatory phrase that England still uses today, originated with King Saul, in the Bible! And since Saul was Israel's first king, Samuel found it necessary to develop some guidelines and principles on how he should rule. Thus, the interpretation for the statement "behavior of royalty". Samuel anointed Saul with oil, which was symbolic of setting a person apart for divine service—that is, service to God. So, we see here in the very beginning of Saul's life, that his first and most important obligation and assignment would be to serve God. As Saul departed to his home, valiant men of God went with him. And we read that God touched their hearts, probably to offer their service as his cabinet and advisors.

Saul's Reign

Saul's career had begun but the role God played in his life would be limited. Saul was just a novice king when his people were attacked by the Ammonites. It so happened that the king of the Ammonites attempted to make a treaty with the town that had been attacked. If the town surrendered, he would pluck out every right eye of the citizens. If they resisted, the Ammonites would kill them. The citizens made a wise decision and asked for seven days of grace during which Saul came to their rescue. In 1 Samuel 11:6, we are told that the Spirit of God came upon Saul. This was an empowering presence of God but not indication of a personal relationship with him, as David had. We read in following verses that he defeated the Ammonites. Saul's response can be found in 1 Samuel 11:13–15. Saul gave God all the glory and Samuel then conducted a covenant renewal ceremony, probably on the occasion of Saul's one year anniversary as king.

In the second year of Saul's reign, he selected an army of three thousand men to fight the Philistines. Here, Saul took things into his own hands by giving burnt offerings to God, which he should not have done. He did this on his own authority, instead of waiting patiently for direction from Samuel, who would have conveyed God's message to Saul (1 Samuel 10:8). You see, Saul did not know the proper procedure of offering a sacrifice; he needed instructions. There were to be seven days of waiting, which was intended to teach Saul patience and dependence on God. By not waiting the full seven days, he showed a number of weaknesses that made him unfit for king, including impatience and self-reliance. By taking things into his own hands, it showed that he did not trust either God or Samuel for these and future decisions. When Samuel found out, he said, "Saul, what have you done? You have acted foolishly and not kept God's commands." This was only two years into Saul's kingship! (1 Samuel 13:13–14). Since Saul reigned for forty years, God minimally tolerated him for thirty-eight of those forty years. God was more than patient and how tragic that Saul's relationship with him was not better. Now, did David offer burnt offerings to God without waiting for direction? Yes, and let's examine that (2 Samuel 24:25). In this case, however, David acted in obedience to God (I Samuel 13:18–19).

What can be learned from this? First, our obedience to God is very important and not to be taken lightly. In fact, God requires it! Second, a lot of patience is necessary to fully follow God's ways. Third, there are consequences for disobedience and choosing our way over God's ways.

The Hunger Test (1 Samuel 14:24–46)

In the next account, we find a situation where Saul with his son, Jonathan and his armor-bearer decide to attack a group of Philistines. God gave them the victory and then the rest of Saul's army joined in the fight. But prior to Saul sending his men into battle, he instructed them to not eat anything. Perhaps he thought that fasting would please God and give them a military advantage. But this is not validated because there is no evidence that Saul requested it of God. Or possibly he wanted to instill obedience in his men. It was not a good decision, because his men's best performance depended on adequate nourishment. Jonathan failed to receive the message that he was not to eat. He was not physically there with Saul and the rest of the men. So, at the end of the fighting, he came upon a honeycomb dripping with honey. He reached out and took the honey and eagerly ate it. When Jonathan later heard of his father's command, he stated that his father had acted unwisely (1 Samuel 14:29–30). Jonathan said, "The honey made me feel better!" And he further said, "The men would have fought with more energy and would have killed more Philistines, had they eaten." Now, what happened next, occurred after Saul's men had defeated their enemy. Saul's men were so hungry that they killed the animals in the field; not even taking the time to prepare and cook the meat. You may recall an Old Testament law regarding restraint from eating blood. This account occurred when God gave instructions to Noah (Genesis 9:4). It happened again later to the Israelites and the law of Moses in Leviticus 3:17. When Saul heard what his men had done, he recognized that consumption of blood was a sin against God and he then made provisions for them to cook the meat properly. We read in 1 Samuel 14:35 that he set up an altar to God. He offered a propitiation sacrifice to the Lord, which indicated an act of repentance for this sin. Saul then planned to fight against the Philistines a second time. The priest suggested praying about it, so Saul did seek God's counsel. But God did not answer him immediately. Saul interpreted this as an indication that there was still sin in the camp (regarding the food incident). So, who had done something wrong? He decided to draw lots, or straws. As we discussed before, this method was used to distinguish one person or group from another. Through a process of elimination, Jonathan was found to be the culprit, because as we know, he had eaten the honey, even though he acted blamelessly. This account was clearly a test for Saul (1 Samuel 14:43). To Jonathan, it was important to be willing to submit to God's punishment if need be. And Saul brought on the verdict. Jonathan must indeed die. It seemed that Saul let his pride and concern for his own authority take over common sense and the stark reality of his own son dying. He even took an oath to kill his son (1 Samuel 14:44). However, the people would not let this happen. They said, "There is no reason to do this" (1 Sam. 14:45). They exonerated Jonathan and apparently, Saul accepted this. Because in the next verse, Saul saw that his people were not with him and he returned home (1 Samuel 14:46).

We know that Saul was a man of war and was quick to go to battle. According to ancient custom, war was a primary way for a new king to establish his sovereignty. Saul, who ruled for forty years, expanded Israel's territory (1 Samuel 14:47–48). The Amalekites were an indigenous race of wicked people who threatened Saul's governance. They were members of the original Canaanites who had occupied Palestine before Israel. There is historical record that they were the first of many pagan armies to attack the Israelites after they left Egypt. God, at that time, promised to wipe them off the face of the earth. Because, this set a precedence for all other opposition groups in that region for many years to come (Exodus 17:14–16). The description of a banner is the same as the phrase "under the ban", used elsewhere in scripture. It meant to utterly destroy, according to God's directive (1 Samuel 15:1–35). We can take one major point from this account. Did Saul do as God required and commanded? No, he should have utterly destroyed the Amalekites, including all animals and the king; hence, Saul received a punishing rebuke from Samuel. Again, we have yet another example of Saul's disassociation with God and his intended will. Saul had a pattern of troubling behavior.

Verse 13 indicates that Saul lied to Samuel.

Verse 15 shows that Saul heeded his own preference, his *own* way of doing things over what God wanted.

Verse 17 states that Saul had a problem with pride and disobedience.

Verse 19 says that Saul did evil in the sight of the Lord.

Verse 20 is an example of his refusing to believe he had done anything wrong.

Verse 21 Saul blamed his own people for his mistakes.

Now, as Samuel pointed out to Saul, God's delight is in complete obedience, as compared to rebellion, stubbornness and rejection of God's word. Saul had not met God's requirement. Verse 24 shows us Saul's true heart. In one breath, he admitted wrong, and in the next, he placed blame on others. Samuel said, "This doesn't cut it, Saul," and he personally took care of destroying King Agag.

A Tormented King (1 Samuel 28:3–25)

Things continued to worsen for King Saul. Once God rejected him as king, he also removed his empowering spirit from him. And he replaced it with what is called a distressing spirit. If your Bible translation refers to this spirit as evil, the translation of the word evil refers to the effect it had upon Saul. It caused him to be troubled and tormented (1 Samuel 16:14–15). One horrific action that Saul took after this happened was to murder God's designated priests (1 Samuel 22:11–18). This account reveals the great disrespect Saul had for the religious leaders of that time and for God. We have noted a number of negative character traits in Saul that include jealousy of David's success and popularity, paranoia, a non-understanding nor acceptance of the truth, uncontrollable anger, and now a disregard for life. Saul did not even provide a fair trial for the priests. He simply executed the eighty-five men.

To further explain Saul's psychological and spiritual instability, we observe that his belief in an all-sufficient God was lacking. Saul expelled mediums and spiritists from the land, as he should, according to Mosaic law (Leviticus 19:31). Notice that God reminds his people to seek after *him*, for *he* is their God. God had stern words for his people concerning any involvement with the spirit world (Deuteronomy 18:9–12). God took this very seriously and the penalty for practicing witchcraft was death (Leviticus 20:27). The word sorcery is translated pharmakia, from which we get our word pharmacy. Witchcraft and spiritism involve mind altering practices, including drug enhancement. At the heart of witchcraft is the desire to know and to manipulate events that are not ours to control. Only God has that power. Remember Satan's first temptation to Eve, "You *can* become like God?" (Genesis 3:4–5). Since the garden of Eden, Satan's major focus has been to divert human hearts away from worship of God. He entices us with suggestions of self-power, self-realization, and spiritual enlightenment apart from submission to God. So, to become involved in witchcraft in any way is to enter Satan's realm. Why should we seek any power apart from the source of all power, God? (Isaiah 8:19–20). According to this descriptive literary reference, the dawn brings light! People who are engaged in witchcraft are in spiritual darkness. Now, a fear entered Saul, as he looked at the great Philistine army. He inquired of the Lord, but the Lord, again, did not respond. So, Saul went to "the other" source of power, contrary to his original conviction. He consulted a witch. His desire was to bring up Samuel, who had previously died. Well, the woman was greatly surprised, since this realm of power was not something she usually had—to bring up someone's spirit from the dead. But Samuel did come up from the dead to talk to Saul. Samuel's message was one of even more dread and fear than Saul could have imagined. Samuel told him that Israel would be defeated by the Philistines and that the next day, he and his sons would also die. Saul's response was a hunger strike. Shouldn't his response have been to turn back to God and plead to him for his life? But there is no record that he ever did this.

Saul's Death (1 Samuel 31:1–13)

The last account of Saul is that of his death. We find that Saul responded as so many hopeless people do; with taking their lives into their own hands. He committed suicide, once he realized that his armor-bearer would not kill him. There is an interesting twist regarding the end of Saul's life (2 Samuel 1:1–16). It is certain that the Amalekite did not actually kill Saul, for Saul had fallen on his own sword. But the Amalekite just happened upon Saul's body and took advantage of the situation. He then made it his story, that he had killed him. We realize that David sorrowfully responded to this. Remember all the times when David had opportunity to kill King Saul but did not do it? Saul was God's anointed king for a certain time. Now, David brought it to the Amalekite's attention that he had no right to kill Saul. It is ironic that Saul lost his kingdom because he failed to annihilate the Amalekites. Now the one who said he was an Amalekite did so because he claimed to have destroyed Saul.

Personal Applications

1. There are three lessons we can learn from Saul's life.

    a. Obey the Lord and seek to do his will. From the very start of his reign, Saul had the perfect opportunity. All he had to do was seek the Lord with his whole heart. However, like so many others, Saul chose a different path. And he made a feeble attempt at pleasing God. Notice that he did go to God for things, but he did not wait and listen for God to direct him.

b. We should not misuse the power given to us. There is no question of Saul's abuse of God's power. The overriding reason for this is pride that so easily creeps into our hearts when we become knowledgeable, influential, or successful in some way. Pride can destroy relationships with family and friends; but most important, with God.

c. Lead the way God wants you to lead; 1 Peter 5:2–4 gives the ultimate guidance on how to do this. It was written as a tool for pastors but can be applied to our individual situations. How much different Saul's life would have been if he had only followed the principles of 1 Peter! Consider that God's requirement for Saul, as well as for us, is to:

- Willingly be a spiritual leader
- Make certain that all actions are the product of unselfish motives
- Do not abuse the trust ascribed to you
- Be an example to others by caring, loving and serving

2. How does this play out in your life? The thing that God requires of us is obedience. Can we truly say that all of our thoughts, words and deeds are pleasing to God? Do we include him into every thought we have, everything we say, and everything we do?

3. Interest in witchcraft and Satanism has dramatically increased in the past several decades. God's first commandment still holds true after thousands of years (Exodus 20:3). God had stern words for and punishment for the violator who would turn to any practice associated with the occult. We do not need to fear Satan if we belong to the Lord Jesus (1 John 4:4).

Saul: Success to Failure
Chapter 8
References

1 Samuel 9:1–6

1 Samuel 9:14–21

1 Samuel 10:1, 17–27

1 Samuel 11:6 "Then the Spirit of God came upon Saul mightily when he heard these words, and he became very angry."

1 Samuel 11:13–15 "The next morning Saul put the people in three companies; and they came into the midst of the camp at the morning watch and struck down the Ammonites until the heat of the day. Those who survived were scattered, so that no two of them were left together. Then they offered sacrifices of peace offerings before the Lord; and there Saul and all the men of Israel rejoiced greatly."

1 Samuel 10:8 "And you shall go down before me to Gilgal; and behold, I will come down to you to offer burnt offerings and sacrifice peace offerings. You shall wait seven days until I come to you and show you what you should do."

1 Samuel 13:13–14 "Samuel said to Saul, "You have acted foolishly; you have not kept the commandment of the Lord your God, which He commanded you, for now the Lord would have established your kingdom over Israel forever. But now your kingdom shall not endure. The Lord has sought out for Himself a man after His own heart, and the Lord has appointed him as ruler over His people, because you have not kept what the Lord commanded you."

2 Samuel 24:25 "David built there an altar to the Lord and offered burnt offerings and peace offerings. Thus, the Lord was moved by prayer for the land, and the plague was held back from Israel."

1 Samuel 13:18–19 "So God came to David that day and said to him, "Go up, erect an altar to the Lord on the threshing floor of Araunah the Jebusite. David went up according to the word of God, just as the Lord had commanded"

1 Samuel 14:29–30 "Then Jonathan said, 'My father has troubled the land. See now, how my eyes have brightened because I tasted a little of this honey. How much more, if only the people had eaten freely today of the spoil of their enemies which they found! For now, the slaughter among the Philistines has not been great.'"

Genesis 9:4 "Only you shall not eat flesh with its life, that is, its blood."

Leviticus 3:17 "It is a perpetual statute throughout your generations in all your dwellings: you shall not eat any fat or any blood."

1 Samuel 14:35 "And Saul built an altar to the Lord; it was the first altar that he built to the Lord."

1 Samuel 14:43 "Then Saul said to Jonathan, 'Tell me what you have done.' So Jonathan told him and said, 'I indeed tasted a little honey with the end of the staff that was in my hand. Here I am, I must die!'"

1 Samuel 14:44 "Saul said, 'May God do this to me and more also, for you shall surely die, Jonathan.'"

1 Samuel 14:45 "But the people said to Saul, 'Must Jonathan die, who has brought about this great deliverance in Israel? Far from it! As the LORD lives, not one hair of his head shall fall to the ground, for he has worked with God this day.' So the people rescued Jonathan and he did not die."

1 Samuel 14:46 "Then Saul went up from pursuing the Philistines, and the Philistines went to their own place."

1 Samuel 14:47–48 "Now when Saul had taken the kingdom over Israel, he fought against all his enemies on every side, against Moab, the sons of Ammon, Edom, the kings of Zobah, and the Philistines; and wherever he turned, he inflicted punishment. He acted valiantly and defeated the Amalekites, and delivered Israel from the hands of those who plundered them."

Exodus 17:14–16 "Then the LORD said to Moses, 'Write this in a book as a memorial and recite it to Joshua, that I will utterly blot out the memory of Amalek from under heaven. Moses built an altar and named it The LORD is My Banner'; and he said, 'The LORD has sworn; the LORD will have war against Amalek from generation to generation.'"

1 Samuel 15:1–35

1 Samuel 15:9 "But Saul and the people spared Agag and the best of the sheep, the oxen, the fatlings, the lambs, and all that was good, and were not willing to destroy them utterly; but everything despised and worthless, that they utterly destroyed"

1 Samuel 15:24 "Then Saul said to Samuel, "I have sinned; I have indeed transgressed the command of the LORD and your words, because I feared the people and listened to their voice."

1 Samuel 15:13 "Samuel came to Saul, and Saul said to him, "Blessed are you of the LORD! I have carried out the command of the LORD.""

1 Samuel 15:15 "Saul said, "They have brought them from the Amalekites, for the people spared the best of the sheep and oxen, to sacrifice to the LORD your God; but the rest we have utterly destroyed.""

1 Samuel 15:17 "Samuel said, 'Is it not true, though you were little in your own eyes, you were made the head of the tribes of Israel? And the LORD anointed you king over Israel.'"

1 Samuel 15:19 "Why then did you not obey the voice of the LORD, but rushed upon the spoil and did what was evil in the sight of the LORD?"

1 Samuel 15:20 "Then Saul said to Samuel, "I did obey the voice of the LORD, and went on the mission on which the LORD sent me, and have brought back Agag the king of Amalek, and have utterly destroyed the Amalekites.""

1 Samuel 15:21 "But the people took some of the spoil, sheep and oxen, the choicest of the things devoted to destruction, to sacrifice to the LORD your God at Gilgal"

1 Samuel 15:24 "Then Saul said to Samuel, "I have sinned; I have indeed transgressed the command of the LORD and your words, because I feared the people and listened to their voice.""

1 Samuel 16:14–15 "Now the Spirit of the LORD departed from Saul, and an evil spirit from the LORD terrorized him. Saul's servants then said to him, 'Behold now, an evil spirit from God is terrorizing you.'"

1 Samuel 22:11–18

1 Samuel 28:3–25

Leviticus 19:31 "Do not turn to mediums or spiritists; do not seek them out to be defiled by them. I am the LORD your God."

Leviticus 20:27 "Now a man or a woman who is a medium or a spiritist shall surely be put to death. They shall be stoned with stones, their bloodguiltiness is upon them"

Genesis 3:4–5 "The serpent said to the woman, 'You surely will not die! For God knows that in the day you eat from it your eyes will be opened, and you will be like God, knowing good and evil.'"

Isaiah 8:19–20 "When they say to you, 'Consult the mediums and the spiritists who whisper and mutter,' should not a people consult their God? Should they consult the dead on behalf of the living? To the law and to the testimony! If they do not speak according to this word, it is because they have no dawn."

1 Samuel 31:1–13

2 Samuel 1:1–16

1 Peter 5:2–4 "Shepherd the flock of God among you, exercising oversight not under compulsion, but voluntarily, according to the will of God; and not for sordid gain, but with eagerness; nor yet as lording it over those allotted to your charge, but proving to be examples to the flock. And when the Chief Shepherd appears, you will receive the unfading crown of glory."

Exodus 20:3 "You shall have no other gods before Me."

Deuteronomy 18:9–12 "When you enter the land which the LORD your God gives you, you shall not learn to imitate the detestable things of those nations. There shall not be found among you anyone who makes his son or his daughter pass through the fire, one who uses divination, one who practices witchcraft, or one who interprets omens, or a sorcerer, or one who casts a spell, or a medium, or a spiritist, or one who calls up the dead. For whoever does these things is detestable to the LORD; and because of these detestable things the LORD your God will drive them out before you"

1 John 4:4 "You are from God, little children, and have overcome them; because greater is He who is in you than he who is in the world."

David: Accession to the Throne

"And David realized that the LORD had established him as king over Israel, and that He had exalted his kingdom for the sake of His people Israel."

—2 Samuel 5:12

Now that Saul was dead, the way was open for David to take the throne without lifting his hand against the Lord's "anointed". This chapter begins with David, once again, going before God for direction (2 Samuel 2:1–3). Even though David knew he was to be appointed king, he still went to the Lord before every activity, to confirm that he was doing his will. Hebron was located nineteen miles southwest of Jerusalem. The city was strategically well suited for the inauguration of David's rule over Judah, as it was located at the highest elevation of any town in Israel (2 Samuel 2:4–7). Unique as it may sound, David became king in stages. First, he reigned over Judah and later over all of Israel. Initially, it was the men of Judah who came to anoint him. Recall that David had previously been anointed by the prophet Samuel. One might ask, "Why did he need to be anointed again?" That first anointing was at God's direction. It was God who gave his approval. The second anointing was the decision of the people of Judah. Note that Judah is only one tribe of twelve tribes, but it was a start for David as he became king, and he ruled over Judah for six years. The Jebusites came to David's attention because they were a group that wanted to pay tribute to the now deceased King Saul, and they made sure that his body was buried. This pleased David greatly, which again shows his respect and honor for his predecessor.

Those first few years as king were troubling for David because Saul's forty-year-old son, Ishbosheth, took the reign over Israel. Ishbosheth was the man whom Saul had given to Michel, David's wife. Right by Ishbosheth's side was Abner, Saul's military commander. And what we will find is that Isbosheth was but a pawn in the hand of Abner. Needless to say, there were a few conflicts that involved David, Isbosheth and Abner.

Abdication and Murder (1 Samuel 3:6–39)

Abner planned a wrestling match, similar to the contest between Saul's army and the Philistines. (2 Samuel 2:12–17). Twelve men of Benjamin (Saul's tribe) were to fight twelve men of Judah (David's men). It was hand to hand combat. David's men killed their opponents, and then, war broke out; which resulted in a victory for David. It is probable that the men used daggers, since the location of this battle is called Helkath Hazzurim, or field of sharp swords. The supporters of Saul's family were still determined to resist David's rule but 2 Samuel 3:1 gives us more insight. David only became stronger and the house of Saul became weaker.

The next dispute is a personal one and it concerns Abner, the former commander of Saul's army. He was not only a man to be feared, but he was a man who knew how to twist the truth in order to get what he wanted (2 Samuel 3:6–11). The account tells us that Abner appropriated Saul's concubine. A concubine is a prostitute. It was not uncommon for kings, during this period of time, to have concubines; in fact, King Solomon, David's son, had three hundred women! (1 Kings 11:3). The phrase "Turned his heart away" indicates that an excessive number of women in Solomon's life distracted him from the attention he would have given to God. Abner's effort to take Saul's concubine meant that this was an attempt to claim the throne. It was common procedure that the concubines naturally followed whomever succeeded to power and the throne. When Ishbosheth accused Abner of wrongdoing, Abner used the accusation to his advantage by shifting his allegiance to David (2 Samuel 3:12). However, he asserted that the land was his own; as one who controls it, including the people. David was perceptive to Abner's insidious protest and realized the solution would be to collaborate, and not to disagree. He may also have realized that he needed Abner as a resource. However, David used this situation for his own advantage and wanted something in return. He desired that his wife, Michal, come back to him! (2 Samuel 3:13–21). And Abner arranged for this to materialize. As Michal left Ishbosheth, he followed her, weeping. It was now more apparent than ever, that Abner clearly had the authority over Ishbosheth's personal life and government. Abner not only scolded Ishbosheth, telling him to go home; but he then proceeded to arrange for David's kingship over the rest of Israel. Abner then said he would be willing to step aside but he knew Ishbosheth could not govern long without him. David expressed his appreciation to Abner by preparing a feast, and this caused Abner to become more than generous. He offered to bring all of Israel together to consummate David's right to the throne.

The account continues and a new character is introduced. His name is Joab. He was David's nephew and a commander in his army. Joab had a history with Abner. Joab had always suspected that Abner was untrustworthy. And on a previous occasion, Joab and his two brothers had followed Abner, when consequently, one of the brothers was killed by Abner. So, now, Joab was interested in taking revenge. Joab tried to convince David that Abner was not a man of peace, as David thought he was. But David was unwilling to take any action, and Joab proceeded to take matters into his own hands and he killed Abner (2 Samuel 3:22–30). David took no initiative to punish Joab but he did place a curse on Joab's descendants. He said, "Let this guilt rest on Joab's descendants." In other words, the reputation of the family would be ruined and whatever happened, was meant to be. David left it in God's hands. In memory of Abner, David declared a memorial day, complete with hired mourners. He informed the people that his hands were clean and that he had nothing to do with Abner's death, just in case there was some suspicion. David, himself, personally grieved for Abner. In fact, he demonstrated his grief by fasting (2 Samuel 3:31–39). Even Ishbosheth lamented Abner's death, despite the rift that had now separated them. There were two men, Rekab and Baanak, both Benjamites, who thought that Ishbosheth was responsible for the death; so they took it upon themselves to punish him. They made a forced entry into his home, giving the appearance that it was a robbery, and they killed Ishbosheth. Then they cut off his head and took it to David as a trophy, hoping for a reward, since Ishbosheth had been David's rival for the throne (2 Samuel 4:9–11). David's response was identical to his reaction when he learned of King Saul's death (2 Samuel 1:11–12, 16). He mourned for Ishbosheth. David then ordered the two murderers to first have their hands and feet amputated and then to be executed (2 Samuel 4:12). Why the cutting off of the hands and feet? These body parts were the instruments of the bad deed. Their feet took them there and their hands committed the murder. David regarded their act as an unjustified assault on a defenseless man, and royalty at that. His retribution also reflected his genuine concern and dedication to Saul and his family. Eventually, this gruesome series of events paved the way for David's transition from leading the tribe of Judah to becoming king over all of Israel. Consider that David did not give in to the violence around him and he remained innocent of the blood of his rivals. David may very well have recalled these events when he wrote Psalm 1:1–2. In this text, we observe that David's success in rising above the people he was around was due to his sensitivity to God. He listened to God and meditated on what God said. He delighted in what God wanted and he anticipated the ways that God would lead. May this be a lesson for us!

The Long-Awaited Throne (2 Samuel 5:1–5)

After those troublesome years, David remained in Hebron until the elders of Israel came to him and made a covenant to establish him as king of all Israel. The elders recognized that David and the people of Judah truly were their brothers, by heritage and by faith. They also acknowledged that even when Saul was king, David was the true leader. The third thing the elders recognized was that David was the one with whom the Lord communicated and the one whom He had anointed. What an honor, after all this time, for David to finally hear these words! And even more important, it was God's time (2 Samuel 5:2). It was time for God's promise to be fulfilled. David wrote Psalm 89 in honor of God's covenant with him (Psalm 89:1–4; 19–21). So, at the age of thirty, David was crowned king over all of Israel. The role of shepherd is again introduced. David, who began as a shepherd boy, would act by divine appointment as the shepherd of all Israel. His rule would be over all tribes (Psalm 80:1–2). We may want to insert David's name into these verses, because they certainly seem to describe him. But they actually are a description of God. God is Israel's shepherd (Psalm 23:1). God would lead and direct David during his reign as king. And God would be David's shepherd.

Jerusalem Conquered (2 Samuel 5:6–12)

At this point in time, David brought his men into Jerusalem, making it the capitol city of Israel and the City of David. Jerusalem is an ancient city that dates from at least 1,700 BC. We first read about it in Genesis 14:18. The name Salem was later lengthened to Jerusalem. We know that God had promised to give Jerusalem to his people (Zechariah 1:14). However, the city was inhabited by Jebusites, who had remained there after Joshua led the Israelites into the land of Canaan. David was well aware of Jerusalem because it was only eight miles from Bethlehem, where he grew up. He probably often thought "Jerusalem is in the heart of the land that belongs to us, by God's promise." He most likely dreamed of capturing the city for God. Many years earlier, God made a promise that his people should inherit and inhabit the land of Canaan. It started with Abraham, who at one time had lived in Hebron (Genesis 13:18; Genesis 15:18–21). It was God's plan all along that his people should take over their land, and this included the city of Jerusalem. David ensured that God's plan would come to fruition (2 Samuel 5:6–8). Jerusalem seemed impregnable because previous attempts to invade it had failed. The Jebusites now threatened that even the lame and the blind would be strong enough to resist David. But David responded that because of the Jebusite's hate for God's people, even the lame and the blind would end in defeat. And how would David do it? Verse 8 says that he climbed up a water shaft. The city's water source came from a large underground pool which was connected to the surface by a vertical forty-foot shaft in which the people could lower their buckets to draw up the cold, clear water. It was in this way that David and his men captured the city of Jerusalem. There is significance regarding the names, the city of David and city of Zion. Names are important to us, but they are even more important to God. In fact, we know that he calls his children by name (Isaiah 43:1). God's message was that Jerusalem would be tied to his name (Psalm 132:13–14).

David's first achievement as king was to rebuild Jerusalem and make improvements. He wanted to fortify and strengthen it and make it habitable for his people. He also removed the idols of the Jebusites at the same time. We are told that David contacted Hiram, King of Tyre, for help with his project (2 Samuel 5:9–12). Tyre was a Phoenician port city about thirty-five miles north on the Mediterranean Sea. Hiram's generosity to David may have been driven by a desire to generate business for his city. Tyre needed trade routes that were now controlled by David. It is evident that David and Hiram's friendly arrangement continued well into Solomon's reign. Hiram provided both of them with lumber to build their palaces and the temple.

We see God's plan and work in David's accession to the throne of Israel (2 Samuel 5:12).

- God had finally established David as king of Israel.
- David's kingdom was brought to power for the sake of his people, Israel... not necessarily for David's sake.
- David *knew* that God was instrumental in his becoming king.

Personal Applications

1. Do *you* know, without a doubt, that God is fulfilling his plan in your life? (1 John 5:13). This verse says that we can *know*; not wonder, not assume, not doubt, but *know* if we will have eternal life with God. But notice how important the Son of God's name is. He wants us to believe in the name of the Son of God, whom he has identified as Jesus Christ. Eternal life with Jesus Christ will be far greater than David's experiences as king.

2. Our custom and laws declare prostitution a crime. How can we justify a king of Israel owning concubines? Concubines held positions as slaves. They were owned and mostly used for the bearing of children. It is true that David's many wives and concubines caused problems in his life. This custom was allowed to continue, even though it was clearly not God's first choice for David.

3. Since God knows our names, it is certain that he cares very deeply for each of us. Do you know the significance of your name?
4. David, as we are learning, was a great leader. Describe a true spiritual leader in your life.

David: Accession to the Throne
Chapter 9
References

2 Samuel 2:1-3 "Then it came about afterwards that David inquired of the LORD, saying, 'Shall I go up to one of the cities of Judah?' And the LORD said to him, 'Go up.' So David said, 'Where shall I go up?' And He said, 'To Hebron.' So David went up there, and his two wives also, Ahinoam the Jezreelitess and Abigail the widow of Nabal the Carmelite. And David brought up his men who were with him, each with his household; and they lived in the cities of Hebron."

2 Samuel 2:4–7 "Then the men of Judah came and there anointed David king over the house of Judah. And they told David, saying, 'It was the men of Jabesh-gilead who buried Saul.' David sent messengers to the men of Jabesh-gilead, and said to them, 'May you be blessed of the LORD because you have shown this kindness to Saul your lord, and have buried him. Now may the LORD show lovingkindness and truth to you; and I also will show this goodness to you, because you have done this thing. Now therefore, let your hands be strong and be valiant; for Saul your lord is dead, and also the house of Judah has anointed me king over them.'"

2 Samuel 2:12–17

2 Samuel 3:1 "Now there was a long war between the house of Saul and the house of David; and David grew steadily stronger, but the house of Saul grew weaker continually."

2 Samuel 3:6–11

1 Kings 11:3 "He had seven hundred wives, princesses, and three hundred concubines, and his wives turned his heart away"

2 Samuel 3:12 "Then Abner sent messengers to David in his place, saying, 'Whose is the land? Make your covenant with me, and behold, my hand shall be with you to bring all Israel over to you.'"

2 Samuel 3:13–21

2 Samuel 3:22–30

2 Samuel 3:31–39

2 Samuel 4:9–11 "David answered Rechab and Baanah his brother, sons of Rimmon the Beerothite, and said to them, 'As the LORD lives, who has redeemed my life from all distress, when one told me, saying, 'Behold, Saul is dead,' and thought he was bringing good news, I seized him and killed him in Ziklag, which was the reward I gave him for his news. How much more, when wicked men have killed a righteous man in his own house on his bed, shall I not now require his blood from your hand and destroy you from the earth?'"

2 Samuel 1:11–12, 16 "Then David took hold of his clothes and tore them, and so also did all the men who were with him. They mourned and wept and fasted until evening for Saul and his son Jonathan and for the people of the LORD and the house of Israel, because they had fallen by the sword. David said to him, 'Your blood is on your head, for your mouth has testified against you, saying, 'I have killed the LORD's anointed.'"

2 Samuel 4:12 "Then David commanded the young men, and they killed them and cut off their hands and feet and hung them up beside the pool in Hebron. But they took the head of Ish-bosheth and buried it in the grave of Abner in Hebron."

Psalm 1:1–2 "How blessed is the man who does not walk in the counsel of the wicked, nor stand in the path of sinners, nor sit in the seat of scoffers! But his delight is in the law of the LORD, and in His law he meditates day and night."

2 Samuel 5:1–5

Psalm 89:1–4, 19–21

Psalm 80:1–2 "Oh, give ear, Shepherd of Israel, You who lead Joseph like a flock; You who are enthroned above the cherubim, shine forth! Before Ephraim and Benjamin and Manasseh, stir up Your power and come to save us!"

Psalm 23:1 "The Lord is my shepherd; I shall not want."

Genesis 14:18 "And Melchizedek king of Salem."

Zechariah 1:14 "So the angel who was speaking with me said to me, 'Proclaim, saying, 'Thus says the LORD of hosts, I am exceedingly jealous for Jerusalem and Zion.'"

Genesis 13:18 "Then Abram moved his tent and came and dwelt by the oaks of Mamre, which are in Hebron."

Genesis 15:18–21 "In that day the LORD made a covenant with Abram, saying, 'To your descendants I have given this land, from the river of Egypt as far as the great river, the river Euphrates: the Kenite and the Kenizzite and the Kadmonite and the Hittite and the Perizzite and the Rephaim and the Amorite and the Canaanite and the Girgashite and the Jebusite.'"

2 Samuel 5:6–8 "Now the king and his men went to Jerusalem against the Jebusites, the inhabitants of the land, and they said to David, 'You shall not come in here, but the blind and lame will turn you away'; thinking, 'David cannot enter here.' Nevertheless, David captured the stronghold of Zion, that is the city of David. David said on that day, 'Whoever would strike the Jebusites, let him reach the lame and the blind, who are hated by David's soul, through the water tunnel.' Therefore they say, 'The blind or the lame shall not come into the house.'"

"But now, thus says the LORD, your Creator, O Jacob, and He who formed you, O Israel, do not fear, for I have redeemed you; I have called you by name; you are Mine!" (Isaiah 43:1).

Psalm 132:13–14 "For the LORD has chosen Zion; He has desired it for His habitation. This is My resting place forever; here I will dwell, for I have desired it."
2 Samuel 5:9–12
2 Samuel 5:12 "And David realized that the LORD had established him as king over Israel, and that He had exalted his kingdom for the sake of His people Israel."
1 John 5:13 "These things I have written to you who believe in the name of the Son of God, so that you may know that you have eternal life."

David Puts God First

On the day I called, You answered me; You made me bold with strength in my soul.

—Psalm 138:3

The New King

In this study, we will focus on David's first actions as king. He went into office with certain goals in mind, just as our elected officials do. He had plans to keep his people safe, to return the ark of the covenant to Jerusalem, and above all, to honor God in all his ways. But, as we know, there are usually obstacles that interfere with our goals. In this first case, it was the constant threat of enemy forces against Israel. The Philistines were one such force. David's stint in the wilderness during his political asylum with the Philistine King Ackish did not afford him additional protection now. The aggression was all about the land, as it pervades in today's Palestinian conflict. The Philistines were an aggressive, warlike people whose goal was to conquer territory. David had learned to never make a major decision without first asking God. So, as the Philistines were preparing to attack, he turned to the Lord. How did David put God first in this account? His immediate response was to take shelter in a stronghold. The Hebrew translation states that this was a fort; a secure place of shelter that David had apparently made ready for himself and others in case of attack. But here, he found peace and quiet. He needed to pray, to seek God alone, where he could concentrate and listen. This was his spiritual stronghold.

The Godly King (2 Samuel 5:17–25)

David received assurance from the Lord that he would give him the victory. In fact, God would *hand* him the victory, it says. This informs us that there were to be few and possibly no casualties. The author of 2 Samuel writes to the outcome of the battle as a breakthrough of waters. The account is described as David's army plowing right through the middle lines—down the center. And the Philistines dropped all around them. The remaining Philistines left their idols on the battlefield, which they had brought for protection. David, at once, burned the idols as they left them. He wanted to eliminate this insult to the God that he knew was living and involved. The Philistines scattered and regrouped to make a second attack. Again, David was given specific strategy and position by God. Notice that David inquired again of the Lord. Each time there was a new development, he went to Him.

Is this our first reaction with life situations? Consider the following personal application of this account.

- Let's say we receive news of a life changing situation for ourselves or for a family member.

  - o Would our first reaction be to immediately pray about the situation?
  - o Or would our first response be to react...emotionally or physically?

- As time goes on, the circumstances become more complex and we think about the situation frequently and perhaps worry or grieve.

  - o Would subsequent responses include praying at every turn; Returning to the Lord repeatedly and making this return habitual?
  - o Or would we weaken and give in to the immediate pressures?

- There are updates with the situation that seem to change every day, resulting in very complicated issues.

  - o Depending on the update, do we return to God in prayer as soon as we hear the news? For example, if good news, do we thank him? If the news is not so good, do we frame our prayers to plead for his help? Do our prayers increase in intensity and in frequency? Do we let God know of our serious intention to get his help by sacrificing... fasting, serving, studying his word, or spending more time with him? See, these are signs to God that we are seriously in need of his help (Philippians 4:6–7).

In truth, David took advantage of his relationship with God that afforded him protection. He sought God's mind with every development, and he gave him the credit; as verse 20 says, "The Lord has broken through my enemies." Now, with the second battle, God told David to circle around the enemy and attack from all sides. And this time, God sent a great sound of troops marching, coming from above the trees. The sound literally drove the Philistines in fear as far as twenty miles away, with David in hot pursuit, because God told him to advance quickly. What was the result of David putting God first in military challenges? God's hand of intervention. God became involved in a big way and the same could happen to us today! The more often we go to him, the more he will feel welcome to intervene in our lives.

The Human King (1 Samuel 6:1–12)

In review of our study of David, we have read how he first established himself as a political leader when he united Israel and declared Jerusalem the capitol. Then, we read how David established himself as a military leader, when he defeated enemy peoples. In this next account, David will attempt to show himself as a spiritual leader. The ark of the covenant had a notable role in Israel's history because it symbolized the presence of God with his people. But by the time David became king, probably very few Israelites even knew what the ark was or where it was. The ark was actually located at the house of Abinadab. There is no evidence that Saul had ever recognized the ark for its importance. And in the previous generation, the people of Beth-Shemesh treated the ark as a curiosity item (1 Samuel 6:19–7:1). The Old Testament law taught that no one should touch the ark; and in this story, seventy men died because they disrespected it. The ark had now lain dormant for fifty years, except that its mere presence at Abinadab's house had benefited him personally. David decided that he wanted to restore the honor of God's name to his people who had been devoid of spiritual leadership from Saul's reign. David had good intentions and had even invited thirty thousand Israelites to come together in Jerusalem for the joyous occasion of the ark's return. This was no small gathering, and the Chronicler—that is, 1 Chronicles 13:2–3 records David's speech to the assembly's multitude. However, even David forgot God's rules on how to transport the ark (Exodus 25:14; Numbers 4:15). The ark was so holy that it was only to be carried with long poles on the shoulders of priests. And it was not to be touched. How did David arrange to have the ark transported? On a cart pulled by cows. Now, we know this to be a Philistine practice (1 Samuel 6:1–2, 7–8). The Philistines did not regard God's laws, so they did not respect their treatment of the ark; and in some ways, these practices just continued, even though the ark was no longer in Philistine possession. It may seem like such a small, moot point to us, but not to God! First, we know that David disobeyed God. Next, Uzzah fell over dead because he had acted irreverently and reached out to support the ark. He had ignored God's clear instructions, which were to never touch the ark. Remember that God's glory means a great deal to him and his glory was revealed in this object; this gold covered box called the ark. Initially, David was distraught and angry. There are three possible reasons for this.

1.   He may have realized that he had overlooked or forgotten about God's specific commands concerning the ark and was angry at himself for being so careless.
2.   It is more likely that he misunderstood, even though he had good intentions and wanted to please the Lord.
3.   It is very probable that he had been publicly humiliated. This national celebration was in front of thirty thousand onlookers. It was apparent to the crowd that God did not approve of David's actions. In the people's eyes, David's relationship with God may have been in question. His reputation as a spiritual leader had been diminished.

But what was God saying through this? He was saying that his word and his rules do not change! (1 Chronicles 15:13). God was saying that he is no respecter of persons. He would not bend the rules, even for his king. And God does not change his requirements to suit cultural or societal mores!

Finally, David learned that God is not only interested in who honors him, but *how* he is honored. After this incident, David's anger soon gave way to fear (2 Samuel 6:9–13). It was now that David realized he had disobeyed God in the way he had transported the ark. He also possibly saw Uzzah's death as a result of his failure to correctly oversee the transport of the ark. David's reaction to this is interesting. He suddenly just wanted to get the ark off his hands. His joy and anticipation had turned to fear and regret. So, he found a local Levite priest named Obed-Edom with whom to place the ark. The priest took it into his home for three months. During that time, God greatly blessed Obed-Edom and his entire household. The word "blessed" in this case means the opposite of what you might think. It means to bless God. So, the blessing Obed-Edom received was more of a personal relationship with God that included worship and brought him and his family happiness. When David learned that Obed-Edom was being blessed with the "dangerous ark" at his home, he realized that the ark itself was not the problem, and he wanted the same blessing for himself and his city. So, he made plans to move the ark again, and this time, the procedure was different (1 Chronicles 15:14–15). "The priests and the Levites sanctified themselves", meaning, they consecrated themselves to the Lord. They dedicated their actions in a prayerful way to God. And this time the ark entered into Jerusalem as God had determined it should, so many years before. This time David put God first!

The Ambitious King (2 Samuel 7:1–17)

In this study, we have noted that David put God first immediately with the conquest of the Philistines. We also learned that David eventually put God first according to the ceremonial action of returning the ark to God's people. Last, we will read that because David put God first, God made a very important covenant between David and himself. It is regarding David's desire to provide only the best worship conditions and a place of holiness worthy of God. This account begins with a discussion between David and Nathan. Nathan was a prophet of God to the nation of Israel. Remember that a prophet is God's designee to use as a vehicle for his communication to people. So, Nathan, who was in the Virgin Mary's ancestral line, communicated God's message to David. David realized that he had not given God his best. He compared his newly built cedar palace to God's house, which was still a modest tent or tabernacle. And Nathan's response shows that he had great respect for his king, because God was with him. In verse 3, David's plan seemed reasonable enough to Nathan at first; but he was quick to change his mind when ordered by the Lord. Nathan delivered God's message that he did not want David to build a temple for him. You see, God is very particular about the manner in which we worship him (Psalm 24:3–5). And God did not need David's help to accomplish his plan. What we read here is that David decided that God needed *his* help! David had reached a comfortable and secure place in his term as king and was looking for one more project! He had almost started to think that he could do things to impress God. But God refused to accept David's generosity. We also realize that David's perspective concerned only the present. He could envision a temple—another building project, that when complete, would elevate the status of worship. David must have been deeply disappointed to learn that God would never allow him to build the temple. There is great theological significance in God's promise to David in verse 12. Solomon, his son (seed), would be God's designated person to build his holy temple. Why him and not David? (1 Chronicles 28:3). It was because David was a man of war and was involved in the shedding of blood. But then, God's message was that he would establish a covenant with David. In verse 16, David's linage, his people, and his throne would be established forever. All the promises that God gave to Abraham and his seed were now brought to rest on David. And, looking forward, it prepared for the Messianic hope that would inspire Israel's faith. David, himself, acknowledged his linage as being associated with the coming Messiah, also known as "The Anointed" (Psalm 132:17). In this psalm the horn of the ox signifies strength. The lamp is a metaphor for the Davidic dynasty. The two metaphors signify strength through the Messiah. We are informed that the hope of the Messiah culminates in the coming of the Lord Jesus Christ, who came from David's linage. There was a later, similar promise given to the prophet Isaiah in Isaiah 9:7. This verse speaks of the Messiah, who will be seated on David's throne and will bring eternal peace and justice. And then, regarding Jesus Christ's birth, a message to Mary in Luke 1:31–33.

David, at the time, did not know the Messiah would be Jesus Christ, but God had revealed to him the promise of this Messianic kingdom. And how precious, that this comes at a time when David experienced deep disappointment. This was the message from God that Nathan the prophet delivered to David. What was David's reaction? (2 Samuel 7:18–29). David went before God because he realized that he had been out of line. Sometimes, God does not want us to do anything. He wants us to just wait for him to speak to us (Psalm 46:10). As David waited and prayed, he knew who God was, and he revered Him. We know this because of the frequency David used the phrase, "O Lord God". It occurs nine times in eleven verses. David's first intent in his prayer was to acknowledge God's lordship. Given the fact that God was his leader, his ruler, the one whom he must submit to, David did this very willingly. We also see that in his prayer, David accepted God's decision with dignity and welcomed his future plan. He knew that God was trustworthy, for he had seen evidence of it over and over in his life.

Personal Applications

1. As David prepared to face the Philistines, he first went to God. Do we do what David did? It is absolutely necessary for us, when we pray in earnest over something, to get alone with God in a quiet place, away from people, TV, and all interruptions. And God will honor this.

2. You might say, "But we are living in different times than David. God's rules for David are outdated and not applicable to our lives today." How can we understand this better? We must recognize that God has the ability and interest to change our thinking to accept His ways, no matter the era of time. If we invite him to influence our minds, our thinking with coincide with his (Isaiah 2:3).

3. Since worship is so important to God, how can we best do this? *Webster's* definition of worship is:

   a. Excessive admiration for someone
   b. The act of showing respect and love for God by praying

   While this definition is limited and insufficient, it is possible to gain an understanding that we must first know who God is. Then we are able to admire him, then love him, and finally worship him. Worship is telling or showing God that we love him. John 4:23–24 says that we must worship in spirit and in truth. This is not possible without the aid of the Holy Spirit, who communicates our attitude, prayers, and thoughts to God.

David Puts God First
Chapter 10
References

2 Samuel 5:17–25

Philippians 4:6–7 "Be anxious for nothing, but in everything by prayer and supplication with thanksgiving let your requests be made known to God. And the peace of God, which surpasses all comprehension, will guard your hearts and your minds in Christ Jesus."

2 Samuel 6:1–8

1 Samuel 6:19, 7:1

1 Chronicles 13:2–3 "David said to all the assembly of Israel, 'If it seems good to you, and if it is from the LORD our God, let us send everywhere to our kinsmen who remain in all the land of Israel, also to the priests and Levites who are with them in their cities with pasture lands, that they may meet with us; and let us bring back the ark of our God to us, for we did not seek it in the days of Saul.'"

Exodus 25:14 "You shall put the poles into the rings on the sides of the ark, to carry the ark with them."

Numbers 4:15 "When Aaron and his sons have finished covering the holy objects and all the furnishings of the sanctuary, when the camp is to set out, after that the sons of Kohath shall come to carry them, so that they will not touch the holy objects and die."

1 Samuel 6:1–2, 7–8 "Now the ark of the LORD had been in the country of the Philistines seven months. And the Philistines called for the priests and the diviners, saying, 'What shall we do with the ark of the LORD? Tell us how we shall send it to its place.' Now therefore, take and prepare a new cart and two milk cows on which there has never been a yoke; and hitch the cows to the cart and take their calves home, away from them. Take the ark of the LORD and place it on the cart; and put the articles of gold which you return to Him as a guilt offering in a box by its side. Then send it away that it may go.'"

1 Chronicles 15:13 "Because you did not carry it at the first, the LORD our God made an outburst on us, for we did not seek Him according to the ordinance."

2 Samuel 6:9–13

1 Chronicles 15:14–15 "So the priests and the Levites consecrated themselves to bring up the ark of the LORD God of Israel. The sons of the Levites carried the ark of God on their shoulders with the poles thereon, as Moses had commanded according to the word of the LORD"

2 Samuel 7:1–17

2 Samuel 7:3 "Nathan said to the king, "Go, do all that is in your mind, for the LORD is with you.""

Psalm 24:3–5 "Who may ascend into the hill of the LORD? And who may stand in His holy place? He who has clean hands and a pure heart, who has not lifted up his soul to falsehood, and has not sworn deceitfully. He shall receive a blessing from the LORD and righteousness from the God of his salvation" ().

2 Samuel 7:12 "When your days are complete and you lie down with your fathers, I will raise up your descendant after you, who will come forth from you, and I will establish his kingdom."

1 Chronicles 28:3 "But God said to me, 'You shall not build a house for My name because you are a man of war and have shed blood.'"

2 Samuel 7:16 "Your house and your kingdom shall endure before Me forever; your throne shall be established forever."

Psalm 132:17 "There I will cause the horn of David to spring forth; I have prepared a lamp for Mine anointed."

Isaiah 9:7 "There will be no end to the increase of His government or of peace, on the throne of David and over his kingdom, to establish it and to uphold it with justice and righteousness, from then on and forevermore. The zeal of the LORD of hosts will accomplish this."

Luke 1:31–33 "And behold, you will conceive in your womb and bear a son, and you shall name Him Jesus. He will be great and will be called the Son of the Most High; and the Lord God will give Him the throne of His father David; and He will reign over the house of Jacob forever, and His kingdom will have no end."

2 Samuel 7:18–29

Psalm 46:10 "Cease striving and know that I am God; I will be exalted among the nations, I will be exalted in the earth."

Isaiah 2:3 "That He may teach us concerning His ways, and that we may walk in His paths."

John 4:23–24 "But an hour is coming, and now is, when the true worshipers will worship the Father in spirit and truth; for such people the Father seeks to be His worshipers."

David and Bathsheba

Against You, You only, I have sinned and done what is evil in Your sight.

—Psalm 51:4

It happened one evening. The spring air was refreshing, the moon lit up the world. The king awoke from a light sleep and, restless, he began to walk about, eventually going out onto the palace porches. And there, at a short distance from his palace, the lighted sky exposed a beautiful woman, bathing on her rooftop. Are you intrigued? This might describe an evening at the royal palace. Let's read the account.

The Tempted: David (2 Samuel 11:1–5)

By now, David had eighteen wives and concubines. Did he need that many? And was God pleased with this? We know that many wives would result in turning David's heart away from God. And we know this because of God's previous warnings to his people and many examples prior to David. What was God's rule on this? (Deuteronomy 17:15–17). These commands were designed by God to prevent the king from trusting completely in military might (horses), from worshipping foreign gods, which many wives would bring from their cultures, and from relying on wealth instead of God. At the time of this account, David was in his midforties and was a very successful king (2 Samuel 8:15). Warring with other nations had become the norm, but David had always experienced victories God had given him. And 2 Samuel 8:14 says that the Lord preserved David wherever he went. In our text, we read that David had remained behind in Jerusalem while his armies went out to fight the battles. The Ammonites had been soundly defeated the previous fall, so this spring conflict was a mop-up campaign. David probably had some downtime. It may be that he was also experiencing some restlessness. He most surely had all of his needs met by his many wives; but on this occasion, as he looked upon Bathsheba, it was a matter of temptation and giving in to that temptation. What was the temptation?

The Temptation: Lust

We read that Bathsheba was very beautiful to behold. To be tempted is not a sin because that is out of our control. It happens to everyone. David may have been surprised to see Bathsheba because it is likely that her location was at least partially hidden from his view. This is because her home is thought to have been in a garden. The longer a man nurtures this kind of temptation, the more difficult to leave it alone. Second Timothy 2:22 gives this advice. The strength to leave a temptation is to immediately run from it and run to God in prayer. It is possible that David did not do this. He may not have even thought of God at that moment, as he had done so many other times, while in questionable situations. Could this be because David was not walking close with God because of his distraction with his wives? We have no evidence of this, but it could very well be. There is another aspect to the situation that cannot be ignored. Bathsheba was married. This meant David's responsibility to avoid her was at a higher level. Jesus taught about adultery in Matthew 5:27–28. Adultery is also addressed in the Ten Commandments, "Thou shall not commit adultery" and this is what Jesus referred to. Notice that temptation becomes sin when the temptation is allowed to become an action, even in our minds. James 1:14–15 speaks to how this happens. A man's desires are many times sexual in nature. There is an inner craving that draws a person out, like a fish being drawn out from its hiding place. This craving is enticed, as a fish is enticed with bait. In this case, David both built and baited his own trap. First John 2:16–17 speaks more to the concept of lust and bodily appetites. The lust of the eyes refers to man's covetous and selfish nature. The world, as described here, is the vast number of people and systems that are hostile to the God of the Bible. The world competes with God and one cannot love both it and the Father at the same time. There are many temptations that come from the world and one such temptation is intimate relationships outside of marriage, even back in David's time.

The Temptress: Bathsheba

Our first impression of Bathsheba is that because she was bathing in public, even at nightfall, she is indiscreet. Proverbs 11:22 describes an immodest woman. A beautiful woman who lacks good judgment is like a jewel in a pig's snout. One might take this as a warning! Women's apparel in the Old Testament consisted of a very modest and loose robe. It covered everything; probably similar to what Muslim women wear today. And the New Testament addresses proper dress for women (1 Timothy 2:9–10). These verses set the standard for women's dress from the first century up until now. A woman's appearance should be one of modesty. And then the verses go on to apply greater importance to a woman's behavior, such as good works. It may not have been unusual for a woman to bathe in public at that time for the following reasons. Verse 4 says she was cleansing from her impurity. This means she had just finished her menstrual cycle and was meeting a ritual requirement of cleanliness. She would have been indisposed during this time of impurity and probably sought relief to be outside and enjoy the surroundings away from the interior home. David sent his men to fetch her and she may have been taken against her will. Now, the unthinkable happened and Bathsheba soon sent word to David that she was pregnant. This would have caused a real crisis in that culture, for adultery could have been punishable by death, according to Leviticus 20:10. Bathsheba's pregnancy would have revealed that adultery was a possible factor, since Uriah was not home during this time. It would have brought great embarrassment to the family. Here she was, the granddaughter of one of David's advisors and the wife of one of his most valiant men. Now that we have reflected on Bathsheba as a temptress, this brings us to the very real possibility of a tempter. This would be someone with incredibly evil motives and power.

The Tempter: Satan

Satan is known as the great deceiver and a destroyer. He is determined to dethrone God by tempting us to sin against him. Consider the following verses:

- He is the father of sin and human conditions. He is the source and expert in lying and murder (John 8:44).
- Satan, the god of this world, has blinded the eyes of many to the truth of their sin (2 Corinthians 4:4).
- Satan appears beautiful and pleasing to the eye. He can even cause a beautiful and pleasing experience (2 Corinthians 11:14). In this way he deceives us into thinking our experience is of God or that he is God.
- Satan's realm is the universe, thus the term "heavenly places." He plans and schemes, and is a powerful force to be reckoned with. However, if we take advantage of the armor that God has provided us, we have no need to fear him (Ephesians 6:11–12).
- Satan paces the earth, looking for opportunities to harm or even kill Christians (1 Peter 5:8). He is an adversary. But even more common is his role as a tempter. The word devour means to drown. His goal is to tempt us into deep situations where there seems to be no way out.

How does this information apply to the account of David and Bathsheba? It is completely applicable! Knowing that Satan is the great deceiver, we can identify some ways that David was deceived and tempted.

- David thought he could sin and get away with it (Psalm 10:11). He was deceived into thinking there would be no consequences; that he could play with fire and not get burned. But Satan's deception goes even further.

- Satan deceived David into thinking about the positive results or the pleasures of that sin. The pleasure lasted only for a moment, in the grand scheme of things (Hebrews 11:25). The context of this verse in Hebrews is of Moses; who gave up the pleasures of palace life and all of the sensual delights which would have distracted him from rescuing his enslaved people.

- David was deceived into thinking that his sin was not really that bad. So, is there such a thing as very serious sin verses less serious sin? One might categorize less serious sin as things like impatience, selfishness, an uncontrolled gossiping tongue, complaining, overeating, fear, or worry. These are sins that are more common; thus we might think of them as less serious. If we could only see every sin as the big deal that it is, we would soon realize that we are rebellious. Romans 6:23 certainly does not distinguish degrees of sin. The Puritans described sin in the following way.

> *"Unmask to me sin's deformity, that I may hate it, abhor it, flee from it. Let me never forget that the heinousness of sin lies not so much in the nature of the sin committed, as in the greatness of the person sinned against."*

- David may have been deceived at the time into thinking that he was not fully responsible for his actions and responses. It is human nature to want to blame someone else for what we are compelled to do! We do know, based on Psalm 51 that David eventually would take full responsibility for his actions.

- Satan probably tried to deceive David into thinking that just going astray this once would not hurt anything. After all, he had been so obedient to God, and he was the king! He was the man whose heart was after God's own heart! Romans 7:21-24 describes what temptation is like to the believer. The desire to give into temptation conflicts with what God wants for us. Even if we want to do good, evil is right there with us! Our body, our emotions, our will all tell us to do one thing; to get instant gratification. An example of this gratification might be the sense of satisfaction one has when gossiping about another person. But God's law, his rules, which we say we should delight in and value, conflict with gratification. It's like a war within us. Every time we choose to give in to what our mind and body want, we give opportunity for sin to gain mastery over us. Unfortunately, tragedy followed David. And many more people would be negatively affected by David's one sin.

The Tragedy (2 Samuel 11:6–17)

What we know of Uriah's heritage is that he was a Hittite. The Hittites were one of the seven Canaanite nations. Many of the Hittites, going back generations during the time of Joshua, had intermarried with the Israelites. The contrast between them and Israel was similar to differences between people in diverse communities. Uriah and his family continued to be identified as Hittites. But Uriah seemed to have been totally immersed in the Jewish culture. He was an admirable man who was 100 percent dedicated to David and his army. We can compare him to the dedicated men and women of today's armed forces, because he exhibited all the qualities of a hero.

- In verse 8, we read that he forfeited his own pleasures, sacrificing for his king. David sent him home to clean up, hoping he would spend some intimate time with Bathsheba. But we know that did not happen, because of his great loyalty to David.
- In verse 9, we read further that Uriah was so loyal to David that he slept at his door, willing to serve and protect him as needed.
- In verse 11, we find that Uriah felt guilty enjoying the finer things in life, when others did not.
- Uriah seemed to greatly respect the ark of the covenant; indicating his support for Judaism.

David made several attempts to correct or hide the wrong that had been done. His first idea to send Uriah home was not successful. Then he came up with another plan. He thought if he got Uriah intoxicated, that Uriah would then want to go home to his wife. That did not work either. David's third plan was much more ambitious. He assigned Uriah to the front lines of battle. He orchestrated the plan through Joab, his trusted military commander. And just as predicted, David's army suffered casualties, including Uriah, who died at the front line. You might say, "How could David have planned such an awful thing?" David was in a perilous situation. And a desperate situation requires a desperate plan. But, more important, David had temporarily left God out of his life. Nowhere in the account are we told that David goes to the Lord. The cover-up continued (2 Samuel 11:18–27). Joab thought that

David might be angry at the news that he lost men, including Uriah. But the opposite was true. David devalued Uriah's tragic death. He said, "It could have happened to any of us! What happened today is history. Move on and plan for tomorrow." Unfortunately, there seemed to be no remorse, at least for the present time. He may have been unaware of God's anger, even though he had broken at least four of the ten commandments. His covetousness, adultery, murder, and lying were viewed by God as being evil. Did God let go of David and wait for him to eventually find his way back to him? No, for we read in the next chapter that God wanted David back and he used his prophet, Nathan, to bring this about.

The Totality (2 Samuel 12:1–15)

It was two years later that God confronted David with his sin. Nathan was a true and courageous man of God, to be willing to go to King David with such a message. His message exposed David's heart and his sin. David was like the rich man who robbed the poor man of his only and most cherished possession. God reminded David of his goodness to him. He had anointed him king. He had delivered him from Saul. He had given him land and victory over his enemies. But God's wrath would bring great sorrow to David. God promised to do the following.

- God promised to plague the house of David with violence. David's family members would die needlessly and tragically.
- God promised to raise up adversity within his family. David's son, Absalom, would eventually divide and conquer the royal family.
- God promised to reassign David's wives, a valuable commodity, and give them to others, in a public fashion, thereby causing humility to fall upon David.
- God promised to cause utter contempt for David by his enemies.
- God promised to allow David's young son to die.

Nathan brings God's assessment of David. According to David's own judgment regarding the rich man and the poor man, he, himself, deserved to die for this sin. Instead, David's own son would die, according to God's judgment. And the reason God could not ignore David's behavior is that he is very serious about sin. But as we know, God is also merciful (Romans 9:15). How did God show mercy to David? (Ephesians 2:4). David writes later about God's reaction (Psalm 51).

- God is always loving, kind and merciful, no matter what we do (verse 1).
- God is able to remove or forgive our sin and our guilt (verse 2).
- God judges sin (verse 4).

- God desires truth and wants us to admit to the truth about our sin (verse 6).
- God's presence will never leave us (verse 11).
- God requires a broken spirit and a contrite heart regarding our sin (verse 17).
- God is pleased with righteousness (verse 19).

God had to show David his sin. Once David recognized the brevity of it, he became remorseful. And it was because of God's grace that he promised David would not lose his life (II Samuel 12:13).

Personal Application

1. Have you ever been confronted by God with your sin? And then experienced his wrath? And, finally his grace, or unmerited favor? I have! It gets your attention very quickly! I felt God's wrath because it hit me personally and financially, and it was immediate. I had no idea my sin was so great, but God, in his mercy and grace, showed me and brought me to repentance. Knowing that I displeased God that much was more devastating to me than anything else! If you are not aware of your sin, ask God to show it to you, and he will! Then, encounter how wonderful his grace can be and you will eventually thank him for that experience.

2. In addition to being tempted sexually, in what other ways can we be tempted? Remember that Jesus, in his humanity, was tempted (Mark 1:13). The sinless son of God experienced the same kind of temptations from Satan (Hebrews 4:15). Jesus, who is our role model, told the tempter to leave, and we have the power to do that as well (Matthew16:23).

3. Is it possible to never be tempted to sin? (1 Corinthians 10:12–13). These verses say that:

   a. If we think we are not tempted to sin, we had better take a closer look, because it is then that we have already fallen to the temptation of unbelief that Satan puts before us.
   b. We can expect to be fooled and even overtaken by temptation
   c. God, who is faithful to us, also knows what our limitations are
   d. God, who is aware of and sensitive to our weaknesses, will then either provide the strength we need to endure that temptation or provide a way out of it. Isn't God good?

4. How do we know when a temptation is from Satan or from ourselves? Because man's nature has been inherently corrupt since the fall, as explained in Genesis 3:22, man is susceptible to the temptations put before him by

Satan and other sinful men. But sin originates within us as well. David wrote about the rebelliousness that Israel expressed towards God. Psalm 78:36-39 Their defiance emerged from deceitful mouths (hearts). God's incomprehensible love for Israel overcame his anger towards them, as he acknowledged their inherently sinful ways (flesh). We are, in effect, carbon copies of Israel, as we devise our own temptation and then succumb to it. Praise God that his compassion remembers our human (sinful) tendencies and forgives us.

David and Bathsheba
Chapter 11
References

2 Samuel 11:1–5

Deuteronomy 17:15–17 "You shall surely set a king over you whom the LORD your God chooses, one from among your countrymen you shall set as king over yourselves; you may not put a foreigner over yourselves who is not your countryman. Moreover, he shall not multiply horses for himself, nor shall he cause the people to return to Egypt to multiply horses, since the LORD has said to you, 'You shall never again return that way.' He shall not multiply wives for himself, or else his heart will turn away; nor shall he greatly increase silver and gold for himself."

2 Samuel 8:15 "So David reigned over all Israel; and David administered justice and righteousness for all his people."

2 Timothy 2:22 "Now flee from youthful lusts and pursue righteousness, faith, love and peace, with those who call on the Lord from a pure heart."

Matthew 5:27–28 "You have heard that it was said, 'You shall not commit adultery' but I say to you that everyone who looks at a woman with lust for her has already committed adultery with her in his heart."

James 1:14–15 "But each one is tempted when he is carried away and enticed by his own lust. Then when lust has conceived, it gives birth to sin; and when sin is accomplished, it brings forth death."

1 John 2:16–17 "For all that is in the world, the lust of the flesh and the lust of the eyes and the boastful pride of life, is not from the Father, but is from the world. The world is passing away, and also its lusts; but the one who does the will of God lives forever."

Proverbs 11:22 "As a ring of gold in a swine's snout, so is a beautiful woman who lacks discretion"

1 Timothy 2:9–10 "Likewise, I want women to adorn themselves with proper clothing, modestly and discreetly…but rather by means of good works, as is proper for women making a claim to godliness."

Leviticus 20:10 "If there is a man who commits adultery with another man's wife, one who commits adultery with his friend's wife, the adulterer and the adulteress shall surely be put to death."

John 8:44 "The devil was a murderer from the beginning, and does not stand in the truth because there is no truth in him. Whenever he speaks a lie, he speaks from his own nature, for he is a liar and the father of lies."

2 Corinthians 4:4 "The god of this world has blinded the minds of the unbelieving so that they might not see the light of the gospel of the glory of Christ, who is the image of God."

1 John 1:8 "If we say that we have no sin, we are deceiving ourselves and the truth is not in us."

2 Corinthians 11:14 "Even Satan disguises himself as an angel of light. Therefore, it is not surprising if his servants also disguise themselves as servants of righteousness, whose end will be according to their deeds."

Ephesians 6:11–12 "Put on the full armor of God, so that you will be able to stand firm against the schemes of the devil. For our struggle is not against flesh and blood, but against the rulers, against the powers, against the world forces of this darkness, against the spiritual forces of wickedness in the heavenly places."

1 Peter 5:8 "Be of sober spirit, be on the alert. Your adversary, the devil, prowls around like a roaring lion, seeking someone to devour."

Psalm 10:11 "He says to himself, "God has forgotten; He has hidden His face; He will never see it."

Hebrews 11:25 "Choose rather, to endure ill-treatment with the people of God than to enjoy the passing pleasures of sin."

Romans 6:23 "For the wages of sin is death, but the free gift of God is eternal life in Christ Jesus our Lord."

Romans 7:21–24 "I find then the principle that evil is present in me, the one who wants to do good. For I joyfully concur with the law of God in the inner man, but I see a different law in the members of my body, waging war against the law of my mind and making me a prisoner of the law of sin which is in my members. Wretched man that I am! Who will set me free from the body of this death?"

2 Samuel 11:6–17

2 Samuel 11:18–27

2 Samuel 12:1–15

Romans 9:15 "For He says to Moses, 'I will have mercy on whom I have mercy and I will have compassion on whom I have compassion'"

Ephesians 2:4 "But God, being rich in mercy, because of His great love with which He loved us."

Psalm 51

2 Samuel 12:13 "Then David said to Nathan, 'I have sinned against the LORD.' And Nathan said to David, 'The LORD also has taken away your sin; you shall not die.'"

Mark 1:13 "And He was in the wilderness forty days being tempted by Satan; and He was with the wild beasts, and the angels were ministering to Him."

Hebrews 4:15 "For we do not have a high priest, who cannot sympathize with our weaknesses, but we have One high priest (Jesus Christ) who has been tempted in all things as we are, yet without sin."

Matthew 16:23 "But He turned and said to Peter, 'Get behind Me, Satan! You are a stumbling block to Me; for you are not setting your mind on God's interests, but man's.'"

1 Corinthians 10:12–13 "Therefore let him who thinks he stands take heed that he does not fall. No temptation has overtaken you but such as is common to man; and God is faithful, who will not allow you to be tempted beyond what you are able, but with the temptation will provide the way of escape also, so that you will be able to endure it."

Genesis 3:22 "Then the LORD God said, 'Behold, the man has become like one of Us, knowing good and evil.'"

Psalm 78:36-39 "But they deceived Him with their mouth and lied to Him with their tongue. For their heart was not steadfast toward Him or were they faithful in His covenant. But He, being compassionate, forgave their iniquity and did not destroy them; and often He restrained His anger and did not arouse all His wrath. Thus He remembered that they were but flesh."

12

Consequences of David's Sin

"I acknowledged my sin to You, and my iniquity I did not hide."
—Psalm 32:5

There is a familiar verse that reads, "Train up a child in the way he should go, and when he is older, he will not depart from it" (Proverbs 22:6). Consequences of poor parenting or even a parent's sin often reflect upon the children (Numbers 32:23). In this lesson, we will study the consequences of David's sin with Bathsheba and Uriah, and how those mistakes led to so much sorrow for him and others. Sin took David to a place he may never have intended to go, and cost him more than he ever thought he would pay.

The Wrath of God (2 Samuel 12:15b–23)

As a result of David and Bathsheba's sin, the Lord struck David's child and he became ill. This was the first in a series of painful events that David would experience as a result of his sin. Your question might be, "But I thought God was good!" Yes, but in David's own words, Psalm 7:11 says that God displays his wrath every day. God's wrath is towards the sin, not the sinner (Romans 1:18). And it is God's right to deal with sin as he wants (Genesis 18:25). We must be careful not to equate God's anger with our own anger. What makes a perfect and holy God angry is when his character has been violated or if anything harms his relationship with his people. David had violated God, thus, compromising their relationship; and God took action by striking down his son. How do we know the child's death was a direct consequence of David's sin? (2 Samuel 12:13–14; James 1:15). The death that James speaks of is spiritual death, or separation from God. God does not let sin go unnoticed, and in our text, we see its seriousness. But it is possible to have the same victory over sin that Christ experienced with his death on the cross. For Christ did not sin, as we know. But he took on the guilt, shame and punishment of our sin. Romans 6 is a perfect description of how sin can take over our lives. A few choice verses will help us to realize this truth (Romans 6:10–14). How can we better understand this passage? For it will help us to recognize the brevity of our sin.

- It is possible to resist the control that sin tries to claim in our lives
- The secret is giving our whole person to God, that is, every member or part of our being, for him to control.
- This happens through our expression to God that we want this identity with him and control by him.
- The result is that sin has less dominance in us; and godliness, or resistance to sin, becomes more dominant.
- The new reign of God's grace (his favor expressed by forgiveness) sets free what has been a reign or dominance of sin, transforming us into the likeness of Christ. His grace transforms us.

The Peace of God

Another important point in this account is the remarkable peace that David had after the death of his first child (Psalm 29:11). How could he have immediately praised and worshipped God at a time like this? The text shows that David grieved, pleaded with God, and fasted when he heard of his child's illness. He was so distraught that his household servants were concerned for his health. But as soon as the child died, he arose, bathed, changed his clothes, ate, and went to worship God. The servants were shocked to see the change in him, for they expected him to experience a greater appearance of loss. David had accepted the fact of his child's death and was able to recognize the reasons for its occurrence. But it was God's peace that enabled him to do this. Why did David have peace? The answer is found in verse 13. David said, "I have sinned against the Lord." David recognized his sin and repented of it. In fact, Nathan told David that he had been forgiven. We know that the Lord did not treat David according to the law, since Leviticus 20:10 required death as a punishment for adultery. Instead, David received God's forgiveness, thus retaining his life. God chastens us, not to get even with us for our offense, but to restore us. And David wrote about God's goodness to him in Psalm 32:1-11, to encourage others to seek God. We know that this psalm is probably a companion to Psalm 51, which describes David's sin with Bathsheba. In Psalm 32, David acknowledges some important things about sin and forgiveness.

- The word "blessed" is descriptive of the joy one has with forgiveness (verse 1).

- David's sin was covered, meaning he was forgiven fully (Romans 4:7).
- God did not hold anything against David (He does not "impute iniquity") (verse 2) (2 Corinthians 5:19).
- David realized the consequences of sin ("my bones grow old") as taking a toll on his body (verse 3).
- God's heavy hand is expressed as guilt and it immobilized David (verse 4).
- David's strength was sapped and he lost his vitality (verse 4).
- Once David confessed his sin to God, restoration occurred (verse 5) (1 John 1:9).
- Finally, David asked God to instill in him a willing spirit. He wanted to continue to serve him (verse 8).

David's responsiveness to God is evidence of his worship. 2 Samuel 12:20 says that he went into the house of the Lord and worshipped. Do you wonder what that worship must have been like? True worship is not confined to singing, praising, reading scripture, or listening to an exposition of a spiritual leader's interpretation or message. True worship is acknowledgment of God's person, power, and preferences. So, the highest form of worship is to be obedient to him by what he has told us in his word. Jesus said that real worship includes the Holy Spirit (John 4:24). For David, the Holy Spirit opened his path of communication to God. For us, the Holy Spirit opens our path of communication to Jesus Christ and then to God.

There was no sign that David blamed God as so many people do, with the loss of a child. Verse 16 says that instead, he pleaded with God but he did not try to bargain with God. In verse 23, David said to his servants, "He shall not return to me." David had accepted the consequences. So, as he went to worship the Lord, he would have thanked God, remarkable in itself, for the loss, the punishment, and most of all, for the sovereignty God had shown through this heartbreaking experience. David clearly saw God's holiness and the expectations for his people, as the prophet Samuel had experienced while still a child (1 Samuel 3:18). Samuel recognized God at work in his life and gave God control. At this moment of God-centered worship, David humbly submitted to "whatever seemed good to God". Most often in our lives, as we accept and submit, peace will follow.

The Blessings from God (2 Samuel 12:24–25)

David resumed his life with Bathsheba. David, who had received solace from God, recognized Bathsheba's grief and now had the capacity to love her and comfort her. We also read that Bathsheba, for the first time, was called David's wife. God drew that line between adultery and marriage; which, in his eyes, is pure. Then God confirmed his love for them with the conception of another son who would be named Solomon. The product of the now consecrated and legitimate marriage in God's eyes, was a son that "God loved". Soon after Solomon's birth, God sent Nathan, the prophet, to tell David and Bathsheba that the baby should be named Jedidiah, which means beloved of the Lord. At that time, a name change was a really big deal! There are other instances in the Bible where God changed someone's name, with powerful results.

- Abram to Abraham (Genesis 17:5). This meant an identity change for Abraham. He went from being a father of one to a father of many nations.
- Sarai to Sarah (Genesis 17:15). Sarah's new name means princess over many, not just one child.
- Jacob to Israel (Genesis 35:10). God strengthened Israel's character which helped bring about God's plan for the twelve tribes of Israel.

What we know of the renaming of Solomon is that it probably was not embraced as God would have wanted. For the name "Solomon" continued to be used in biblical references. Finally, our study will close with an important confirmation that David's personal problems did not influence his effectiveness as king. This was evident in the military campaign of Rabbah.

God's Blessing of Wealth (2 Samuel 12:26–31)

Joab, David's commander, had one military expedition left in his conquest of the Ammonites. It was the Ammonite capitol of Rabbah. Joab reported to David that he had taken over the city's water supply. But Joab wanted David to gain credit for the city's fall. So, he urged David to lead the final assault himself. David soon found himself in a very advantageous position. After the city's capture, David took the wealth of the city that included a seventy-five-pound golden crown that had belonged to the Ammonite king. He also enslaved the Ammonite survivors, as was his practice with all captured Ammonites, and he returned in triumph to Jerusalem. It should be noted that David did not imprison these people, which he could have easily done. He saw it more efficient to use them as human resources for building projects, i.e., picks, axes and brickmaking are mentioned. And it may be that some of these captives later worked on the temple construction under King Solomon (1 Kings 9:15–22). Israel became stronger and wealthier under King Solomon than any other king. And one of the advantages he used to his favor was slave labor for his building projects. The descendants of conquered native or Canaanite tribes were assigned jobs that required the most physical labor.

The consequences of David's sin did not prove to be too great for him. His life during these years, tumultuous as it was, revealed unique skill to recover and be successful in the different roles in which he was involved.

- David recognized his vulnerability as a human being. David's loss of a child drained his physical, emotional, and spiritual strength (Ps. 32:4). He was able to identify his own sin and humble himself (Psalm 32:5).
- With the conquest of Rabbah, David led his kingdom with dignity, while appreciating man's need to be humbled (Psalm 9:20).
- Even as the city of Rabbah lost its main line to vitality, its source of water, David rallied because his water line was the Lord (Psalm 63:1).

Personal Applications

1. How resilient are you, when life's defeating problems or sins overtake you? Do you receive peace and God's blessings through his forgiveness?

2. Comparing David's sin with our sin, does this mean that every time we sin, we will go through each of the same phases of repentance and grief as he experienced? No, because the impact of our sin will be different and God's conviction upon us will be different. But, key to this is having a sensitive heart that responds to a call of repentance (Psalm 51:17).

3. Is physical death a consequence of sin? According to Genesis 3:19, physical death was a direct consequence of Adam and Eve's sin. It is the plight of all humans to die, because of our human condition of sinfulness (Romans 6:23). This death is both physical and spiritual.

4. Why do babies and children die? First of all, God is not pleased when we, including babies and children, suffer and/or die. Jesus welcomed the little children to come to him (Matthew 19:14). Children are not sinless before God, because their sinful nature is inherited (Psalm 51:5). We can gain comfort in knowing that all babies and children who have not reached an age where they recognize their sinfulness (age of accountability), go to heaven after death.

5. Does the Bible approve or condone slavery? There are many examples of slavery in the Bible, going back to Abraham's servant, Hagar in Genesis 16. The most poignant account of slavery is the plight of the Hebrew people in Egypt. Unfortunately, slavery continues today in greater numbers than ever before. Slavery in the Bible was different in those times than it is today. It was largely defined by social/economic class and not race. Many people sold themselves in order to live. The Bible does not condone slavery as it was in Bible times, but instead, gives guidelines that would prevent abuse

of slaves. Colossians 4:1 In Genesis 1:27 God stated that all men were created in his image. While this was God's perfect plan for mankind, sin distorted what was originally good. The Bible focus is on the freeing aspect that salvation offers from the enslaving tenets of sin. Ephesians 6:9.

Consequences of David's Sin
Chapter 12
References

Numbers 32:23 "Be sure your sin will find you out."

2 Samuel 12:15–23

Psalm 7:11 "God is a righteous judge, and a God who has indignation every day."

Romans 1:18 "For the wrath of God is revealed from heaven against all ungodliness and unrighteousness of men who suppress the truth in unrighteousness."

Genesis 18:25 "Far be it from You to do such a thing, to slay the righteous with the wicked, so that the righteous and the wicked are treated alike. Far be it from You! Shall not the Judge of all the earth deal justly?"

2 Samuel 12:13–14 "Then David said to Nathan, 'I have sinned against the LORD.' And Nathan said to David, 'The LORD also has taken away your sin; you shall not die. However, because by this deed you have given occasion of the LORD to blaspheme, the child also that is born to you shall surely die.'"

James 1:15 "Then when lust has conceived, it gives birth to sin; and when sin is accomplished, it brings forth death."

Romans 6:10–14 "For the death that He (Christ) died, He died to sin once for all; but the life that He lives, He lives to God. Even so consider yourselves to be dead to sin, but alive to God in Christ Jesus. Therefore do not let sin reign in your mortal body so that you obey its lusts, and do not go on presenting the members of your body to sin as instruments of unrighteousness; but present yourselves to God as those alive from the dead, and your members as instruments of righteousness to God. For sin shall not be master over you, for you are not under law but under grace."

2 Samuel 12:13 "Then David said to Nathan, 'I have sinned against the LORD.' And Nathan said to David, 'The LORD also has taken away your sin; you shall not die.'"

Leviticus 20:10 "If there is a man who commits adultery with another man's wife, one who commits adultery with his friend's wife, the adulterer and the adulteress shall surely be put to death."

Psalm 29:11 "The LORD will give strength to His people; the LORD will bless His people with peace."

Psalm 32:1–11

Romans 4:7 "Blessed are those whose lawless deeds have been forgiven, & whose sins have been covered."

1 John 1:9 "If we confess our sins, He is faithful and righteous to forgive us our sins and to cleanse us from all unrighteousness."

2 Corinthians 5:19 "God was in Christ reconciling the world to Himself, not counting their trespasses against them, and He has committed to us the word of reconciliation."

1 John 1:9 "If we confess our sins, He is faithful and righteous to forgive us our sins and to cleanse us from all unrighteousness."

John 4:24 "God is spirit, and those who worship Him must worship in spirit and truth."

1 Samuel 3:18 "So Samuel told Eli, the priest, everything and hid nothing from him. And Eli said, "It is the LORD; let Him do what seems good to Him."

2 Samuel 12:24–25 "Then David comforted his wife Bathsheba, and went in to her and lay with her; and she gave birth to a son, and he named him Solomon. Now the LORD loved him and sent word through Nathan the prophet, and he named him Jedidiah for the LORD's sake."

Genesis 17:5 "No longer shall your name be called Abram, but your name shall be Abraham; for I have made you the father of a multitude of nations."

Genesis 17:15 "Then God said to Abraham, "As for Sarai your wife, you shall not call her name Sarai, but Sarah shall be her name."

Genesis 35:10 "God said to him, 'Your name is Jacob; you shall no longer be called Jacob, but Israel shall be your name.' Thus, He called him Israel."

2 Samuel 12:26-31

1 Kings 9:15–22

Psalm 32:4 "For day and night Your hand was heavy upon me; my vitality was drained away as with the fever heat of summer."

Psalm 32:5 "I acknowledged my sin to You, and my iniquity I did not hide; I said, 'I will confess my transgressions to the LORD'; and You forgave the guilt of my sin"

Psalm 9:20 "Put them in fear, O LORD; let the nations know that they are but men."

Psalm 63:1 "O God, You are my God; I shall seek You earnestly; my soul thirsts for You, my flesh yearns for You, in a dry and weary land where there is no water."

Psalm 51:17 "The sacrifices of God are a broken spirit; a broken and a contrite heart, O God, You will not despise."

Genesis 3:19 "By the sweat of your face you will eat bread till you return to the ground, because from it you were taken; for you are dust, and to dust you shall return."

Romans 6:23 "For the wages of sin is death, but the free gift of God is eternal life in Christ Jesus our Lord."

Matthew 19:14 "But Jesus said, 'Let the children alone, and do not hinder them from coming to Me; for the kingdom of heaven belongs to such as these.'"

Psalm 51:5 "Behold, I was brought forth in iniquity, and in sin my mother conceived me."

2 Samuel 12:23 "David knew that when he died, he would once again see his son. He said, "I shall go to him.""

Colossians 4:1 "Masters, grant to your slaves justice and fairness, knowing that you too have a Master in heaven."

Genesis 1:27 "God created man in His own image, in the image of God He created him; male and female He created them."

Ephesians 6:9 "And masters, do the same things to them, and give up threatening, knowing that both their Master and yours is in heaven, and there is no partiality with Him."

13

David: The Tragedy of Fatal Attraction

"Now therefore, the sword shall never depart from your house, because you have despised Me."

—2 Samuel 12:10

The previous chapter spoke of the birth of Solomon. David went on to have more children in addition to Solomon. Two of David's sons, Absalom and Amnon, followed after their father's example of adultery and murder. Immediately we are reminded of Nathan's prophecy to David in 2 Samuel 12:10 and how it was beginning to be fulfilled. It meant that David's family would have avenging death as a consequence of his transgressions with Bathsheba and Uriah.

The Terrible Truth (2 Samuel 13:1–20)

This biblical account is a prototype of what you might see in a movie theatre today. It has all the elements of contemporary entertainment—love, lust, immorality, hate, plot, vengeance, and family disunity. The main characters are the interrelated children of David. They are half brothers and sister; having two different mothers (2 Samuel 3:2–3). Absalom and Tamar's mother was Maccah. Amnon, David's firstborn, was the child of Ahinoam, one of David's first wives, chosen around the same time as Abigail. We are told that Amnon loved Tamar, his half-sister. This love was initially an affectionate kind of love that quite possibly started out as a caring kind of affection between siblings. But later, it developed into a lustful kind of attraction. Amnon became infatuated with Tamar to the point of his becoming anorexic. We read that the cause of his illness was the fact that she was a virgin. It would have been an impossibility for Amnon to not be aware of the consequences for them both. He was torn between his passion and their future welfare. What were the consequences?

(Deuteronomy 22:13–21). Amnon most likely knew the laws that defined and punished the one who violated a virgin. Let's examine the truth and its consequences.

Consequences for Amnon	Consequences for Tamar
Gratification of Amnon's intimate desires	Loss of Tamar's virginity – since it was improper at that time, the future marriage would expose her condition, resulting in a public reprimanding in front of the elders at the city gate. This would bring shame on her and her family.
Unwise council from Jonadab – encouraged dishonesty to get what he wanted. *How does God view false friends who give us ungodly counsel? See verse 5. How should we deal with this?* (1 Corinthians 15:33).	Tamar's future husband and family would hate and reject her. He would be forced to marry her if she could prove that she was indeed a virgin. If she had been raped, the rapist would also hate her (Deuteronomy 22:28–29).
Jonadab encouraged Amnon to believe that he deserved what he wanted. Amnon, as eldest son and king elect, had every need and desire met. He had his father's love, a life of luxury and comfort, and a promising future.	Tamar would be condemned to a life of psychological pain, rejection, and loss.
There would be punishment and a fine for the offender if found guilty.	If found to be a nonvirgin, the woman would be stoned to death.

The account is described as follows.

- Amnon became love-sick for his half-sister, Tamar.
- He sexually desired her and eventually succumbed to those desires.
- He consulted with his good friend and uncle Jonadab, a man of questionable character.
- Jonadab noticed that Amnon had lost weight and proceeded to give Amnon some bad advice.
- The plan was for Amnon to pretend he was ill and to request of his father that Tamar bring him some food. The use of the word *cakes* means "heart". It could be there are two meanings here. Amnon asked for some food but wanted Tamar's heart.
- When Tamar brought the food, Amnon assertively suggested that she sleep with him.

- The plan backfired, as Tamar was repulsed by the idea.
- Her response is described in verses 12–13:

  o She felt forced to comply – "forced" is a word often associated with rape in the Old Testament.
  o She knew of the disgrace this would bring to them both—Amnon would be thought of as a fool and she would be shamed.
  o She thought of an alternative plan—that is, Amnon could honorably request her hand in marriage.

- Amnon rejected Tamar's reasoning and raped her.
- Immediately Amnon hated her. The word "then" in verse 15 shows an instant reaction to the previous verse 14.
- Amnon's hatred was very great; much greater than his love had been for her. Psychology describes this kind of hate for one's victim. Experts in this area characterize two types of rape motivations—anger and power. Anger is not planned. But power is planned, as in Amnon's case. The rapist fantasizes about the way his victim will enjoy the power or forcefulness he uses. Amnon's anger was the result of Tamar's rejection of his display of power. His low self-esteem was further diminished and he hated her for that. How different things would have been if Amnon would have made the best choice, like Job did in a similar situation (Job 31:1).
- Amnon wanted to be rid of this reminder of his sin and dismissed Tamar from his house and his life.
- Tamar stood her ground because she knew what lay ahead of her. She refused to leave. Exodus 22:16 gives us insight of what should happen next.
- Tamar responded that there was something worse than the rape itself and that would be, facing the cultural rejection from friends, family, and a future spouse.
- Amnon again became forceful, and had a servant throw Tamar out and lock the door. He referred to her as a "woman", which only further describes his resentment of her, when in verse eleven, he had called her his sister.
- Tamar was devastated and she responded as such.

  o She placed ashes on her head. Sprinkling dust or dirt on one's person symbolized grief or humility. David later wrote in Psalm 72:9 how his enemies would have contact with dust in response to their rebellion to God and their humility.
  o Tamar responded by tearing her multicolored robe. This robe was symbolic of royalty and virginity. She now could no longer wear the garment that identified her.

o   She placed her hands on her head, which was typically a posture assumed by captives of war.

o   She wept bitterly and was inconsolable.

- Tamar fled to her brother Absalom's home for refuge and her brother knew immediately what had happened and gave her instructions. She was not to tell anyone and she was to stay secluded in his house.
- And then, Absalom said the unthinkable to Tamar. "He is your brother; do not take this matter to heart." Absalom minimized the devastation Tamar was experiencing.
- Tamar's state of mind is described as a continuing condition of desolation. This means that she suffered from a complete loss of hope (verse 20).
- The record does not end here.

Accountability (2 Samuel 13:21–23)

David's anger was most likely contained and there was no indication that he took disciplinary action. The Dead Sea Scrolls add a translation that said David would not hurt Amnon because he was his eldest son and he loved him. However, we know that David began his administration with justice (2 Samuel 8:15). David's failure to administer judgment and justice to *all* people in Israel, including his sons, eventually contributed to the greatest political crisis of his life. Namely, this was Absalom's national rebellion. In fact, we read of a subsequent complaint from Absalom in 2 Samuel 15:4, referencing his dissatisfaction with his father's leadership style and instead, stating confidence in his own ability. There will be more to come on this future rebellion by Absalom.

Payback (2 Samuel 13:24–33)

Absalom's outward reaction to Amnon's violation was one of indifference. But his hatred for him was an inward, simmering hostility. This hatred grew and grew for two long years until one day, Absalom finalized a plan in his mind.

- The occasion was a massive sheep-shearing event and accompanying feast. We could compare it to a nineteenth century barn-raising. The community came together to complete a project, working as teams, and then rejoiced over their productivity.

- Absalom had other ideas and capitalized on this opportunity to bring his brothers together, in hopes of isolating Amnon and killing him as retribution for Tamar.

- He asked for his father, David's, assistance in bringing their family together. When David disapproved of the idea, Absalom requested that Amnon at least join him. This captured David's attention. But rather than heed what may have been an intuition to resist Absalom, he permitted Amnon to go. The stipulation was that the other brothers should join him and this probably was based on the thinking that there would be safety in numbers and especially amongst family.

- Absalom instructed his servants to wait until Amnon was intoxicated with wine and then to strike him. He encouraged his servants to be courageous and valiant. What servant would not want to be like the mighty man of valor (David)? (1 Samuel 16:18). What servant would not want to be like David's choice men known for their courage and honor? (2 Samuel 6:1). So, the servants proceeded with the plan.

- In one stroke the murder was committed. The king elect was now dead. Remember how important it was to David that he never harm the king elect? This was the position David took with both Saul and Ishbosheth (1 Samuel 26:23).

- When news returned that Amnon was dead, the king's sons arose from their feast table, got on their donkeys, and fled. The Hebrew meaning of the word "fled" is to escape. Whether they felt entrapped by Absalom or feared their father's wrath, it is not certain.

- David, on the other hand, had received fallacious news from an unknown source that *all* his sons were dead. The rumor states, "Absalom killed all of the king's sons, leaving not one of them alive."

- David went into inconsolable grief, mourning his sons. In fact, his servants also mourned, for they all tore their clothes, and in a most extreme gesture, David lay on the ground. We know from other Old Testament examples, that this posture was a position of prayer. It allowed David to express the desperate attitude of his heart—an attitude which is clearly one of emptying himself of his power, will, self-gain, and possessions. He laid it all at God's mercy. David wrote about death and sorrow in Psalm 18:4-6. David compared his grief to his own death. Could it be that he actually wished death upon himself? We do not know, but once again, David cried out to the Lord, and as always before, the Lord heard him. The overwhelming grief of his son's death had brought him to his God.

- David's brother, Jonadab, arrived on the scene and had some advice for him. It seems that he had knowledge of the real facts and that only Amnon had died. He tried to console David. He also betrayed the confidence of

Absalom, his friend, by providing his identity as Amnon's murderer. What could have been his motive? Was it that he was a busy body, stirring the pot, so to speak? Was it that he saw the evil deed in its purest sense, and truly wanted justice to prevail? Was it that he valued David's confidence and relationship more than any other? Or was it that there might be something for him in this situation? Perhaps a promotion or public recognition. We know that Jonadab is described as very wise, with a translation that says that he was shrewd or crafty. It is likely that whatever Jonadab was up to, it probably was not good.

- In other quarters, Absalom had fled to his mother's native country and found refuge with Talmai, his maternal grandfather. Here he stayed for three years (2 Samuel 13:34–39).
- During this time, David and his sons continued to mourn. But eventually David realized that God's comfort had been sufficient. Verse 39 uses the word "comforted" to describe David's state of mind. The Hebrew translation of this word is to breathe strongly. It implies a consolation that, while yet grief-stricken, David was now able to recover, to take a deep breath and move forward with his life.
- As for Tamar, she is not mentioned again in this account. However, in chapter 14, we read that her name was carried forward to the next generation, when Absalom named his only daughter Tamar.

Rape and murder are never acceptable in the eyes of the Lord. Sins committed against mankind or against God can be described as sins of the heart. For the heart first produces evil thoughts, then evil words, then evil actions (Matthew 15:18–19). Yes, it is possible to become fatally attracted to the desires of our heart, and follow through, even though it may seem that we are driven to the bad deed. A solution that the Bible offers is found in Luke 10:27. If our love for God is agape love, it will take on these identifying traits:

- Our obligation to God is both social and moral. In other words, agape love results in benevolence and goodwill. It is characterized by an unselfish and unconditional desire to please God and man.
- Our thoughts and feelings (our heart) are focused on God.
- Our reasoning and decision making (our soul) is consecrated to God's mastery.
- Our ability, influence, and determination (our strength) are used to bring God glory.
- Our understanding and imagination (our mind) allows God to communicate with us.

- The natural result of giving God complete control over our heart, soul, strength, and mind is that we will love others as much as we love ourselves (and that is a lot!).

Personal Applications

1. Did the Lord see and care about a victim like Tamar? (Proverbs 15:3). Of course! He certainly knew of her circumstances and cared about her (Lamentation 3:33). The Lord is not only aware of our situation, but he cares; he identifies with it and does not want us to suffer (Psalm 34:18).

2. What happens when a father does not discipline his children? (Proverbs 22:15, Proverbs 29:17). In another account from the Bible, God had some harsh words for the priest, Eli, regarding his misbehaved sons (1 Samuel 3:12–13). David, in his position as father and king, should have taken action to rebuke Amnon, as Eli the priest should also have taken action with his adult sons, years earlier.

3. When we observe that criminals go unpunished for their crimes, it results in a type of injustice. How should our legal system deal with the necessary punishment for criminals? And how can we personally deal with a "soft" system that hesitates to punish? We can be assured that God greatly favors justice. A strong and godly Hebrew king named Jehoshaphat once implemented reforms and a court system in his government. (2 Chronicles 19:7). Based on this verse, a ruler or government should:

   a. Respect God's ways regarding justice/injustice
   b. Take careful action to proceed with maintaining a just system of law-keeping
   c. Avoid partiality and taking of bribes (Psalm 89:14, Proverbs 21:3)

We need to invite God's perfect justice and His righteousness to be at work in our lives and in our courts of law. Only then will correct decisions be made with regards to accountability (Micah 6:8).

David: The Tragedy of Fatal Attraction
Chapter 13
References

2 Samuel 12:10 "Now therefore, the sword shall never depart from your house, because you have despised Me and have taken the wife of Uriah the Hittite to be your wife."

2 Samuel 13:1–20

2 Samuel 3:2–3 "Sons were born to David at Hebron: his firstborn was Amnon, by Ahinoam the Jezreelitess; and his second, Chileab, by Abigail the widow of Nabal the Carmelite; and the third, Absalom the son of Maacah, the daughter of Talmai, king of Geshur."

Deuteronomy 22:13–21

1 Corinthians 15:33 "Do not be deceived: 'Bad company corrupts good morals.'"

Deuteronomy 22:28–29 "If a man finds a girl who is a virgin, who is not engaged, and seizes her and lies with her and they are discovered, then the man who lay with her shall give to the girl's father fifty shekels of silver, and she shall become his wife because he has violated her; he cannot divorce her all his days."

2 Samuel 13:12–13 "But she answered him, 'No, my brother, do not violate me, for such a thing is not done in Israel; do not do this disgraceful thing! As for me, where could I get rid of my reproach? And as for you, you will be like one of the fools in Israel. Now therefore, please speak to the king, for he will not withhold me from you.'"

2 Samuel 13:15 "Then Amnon hated her with a very great hatred; for the hatred with which he hated her was greater than the love with which he had loved her. And Amnon said to her, "Get up, go away!""

2 Samuel 13:14 "However, he would not listen to her; since he was stronger than she, he violated her and lay with her."

Job 31:1 "I have made a covenant with my eyes; how then could I gaze at a virgin?"

Exodus 22:16 "If a man seduces a virgin who is not engaged, and lies with her, he must pay a dowry for her to be his wife."

Psalm 72:9 "Let the nomads of the desert bow before him, and his enemies lick the dust."

2 Samuel 13:20 "So Tamar remained and was desolate in her brother Absalom's house."

2 Samuel 13:21–23 "Now when King David heard of all these matters, he was very angry. But Absalom did not speak to Amnon either good or bad; for Absalom hated Amnon because he had violated his sister Tamar. Now it came about after two full years that Absalom had sheepshearers in Baal-hazor, which is near Ephraim, and Absalom invited all the king's sons."

2 Samuel 8:15 "So David reigned over all Israel; and David administered justice and righteousness for all his people."

2 Samuel 15:4 "Moreover, Absalom would say, "Oh that one would appoint me judge in the land, then every man who has any suit or cause could come to me and I would give him justice."

2 Samuel 13:24–33

1 Samuel 16:18 "Then, one of the young men said, "Behold, I have seen a son of Jesse the Bethlehemite who is a skillful musician, a mighty man of valor, a warrior."

2 Samuel 6:1 "Now David again gathered all the chosen men of Israel, thirty thousand."

1 Samuel 26:23 "The LORD will repay each man for his righteousness and his faithfulness; for the LORD delivered you into my hand today, but I refused to stretch out my hand against the LORD's anointed"

Psalm 18:4–6 "The cords of death encompassed me, and the torrents of ungodliness terrified me. The cords of Sheol surrounded me; the snares of death confronted me. In my distress I called upon the LORD, and cried to my God for help; He heard my voice out of His temple, and my cry for help before Him came into His ears."

2 Samuel 13:34–39

Matthew 15:18–19 "But the things that proceed out of the mouth come from the heart, and those defile the man. For out of the heart come evil thoughts, murders, adulteries, fornications, thefts, false witness, slanders."

Luke 10:27 "And Jesus answered, You shall love the Lord your God with all your heart, and with all your soul, and with all your strength, and with all your mind; and your neighbor as yourself."

Proverbs 15:3 "The eyes of the LORD are in every place, watching the evil and the good."

Lamentations 3:33 "For He does not afflict willingly, or grieve the sons of men."

Psalm 34:18 "The LORD is near to the brokenhearted, and saves those who are crushed in spirit."

Proverbs 22:15 "Foolishness is bound up in the heart of a child; the rod of discipline will remove it far from him."

Proverbs 29:17 "Correct your son, and he will give you comfort; he will also delight your soul."

1 Samuel 3:12–13 "In that day I (God) will carry out against Eli all that I have spoken concerning his house, from beginning to end. For I have told him that I am about to judge his house forever for the iniquity which he knew, because his sons brought a curse on themselves and he did not rebuke them."

2 Chronicles 19:7 "Now then let the fear of the L ORD be upon you; be very careful what you do, for the L ORD our God will have no part in unrighteousness or partiality or the taking of a bribe."

Psalm 89:14 "Righteousness and justice are the foundation of Your throne; lovingkindness and truth go before You."

Proverbs 21:3 "To do righteousness and justice is desired by the L ORD more than sacrifice."

Micah 6:8 "He has told you, O man, what is good; and what does the L ORD require of you but to do justice, to love kindness, and to walk humbly with your God?"

14

Absalom, the Wayward Son

"Just as a father has compassion on his children, so the LORD has compassion on those who fear Him"

—Psalm 103:13

Absalom, David's son and criminal on the run, had become estranged from his father. It was three long years since they had seen each other. Let's face it, parenting is not easy! Add that to the demanding job of being king over a nation of people. Much of the child rearing in David's family might easily have been delegated to the mothers and the palace personnel. Present day studies show that dads strongly influence their children's lives. David, himself, wrote at length about the blessings of children and gave parental advice. In Psalm 127:3–5, David described how sons defend the family, how many children add to the diversity and enjoyment of the family, and how, as peacemakers, they enhance relationships with other families.

As we read David's reaction to Absalom, we become painfully aware of how much he missed his son. David pitied Absalom, who had not been able to participate in family gatherings. He later wrote about this in Psalm 103:13. In the documented short stories about Absalom, we will study his life and David's concern and care for his son, which never subsided with time nor with rejection.

A Father's Forgiveness (2 Samuel 14:1–24)

- A good friend knows and cares when you are suffering. David thought he had a good friend in Joab.
- Joab sought intervention from a wise woman. The word *wise* means "intelligent, skillful, and possibly cunning". This woman had a silver tongue and probably had a reputation of being a professional communicator;

something that most women who knew their place in that society, did not possess.

- Joab laid out the message he wanted her to communicate to the king.
- During her visit to King David, the woman pretended she was mourning the death of her husband but that her two sons had argued and now one of them was dead.
- She worried that her family's name, reputation, and safety would be compromised, including that of her remaining murderous son.
- She then constructed a similar comparison to the king's situation with his son, Absalom.
- She acknowledged that discerning good and evil is not always easy, and this wisdom needs to come from God.
- The king then became aware that the woman was avoiding the real reason for her visit.
- He surmised that it was Joab who had been the instigator.
- The woman admitted that it had been Joab's plan.
- David brought in Joab, who humbly fell to the floor, thanking David for his favor and for granting Absalom's return.
- David had one important command. That Absalom return only to his own home and that he not see David.

Had David only temporarily forgiven Absalom? Or was he, in fact, placing a house arrest on Absalom? Absalom, according to law, really should have been put to death for killing his brother. Why should Absalom have been executed for killing his brother? (Genesis 9:5–6). Because God knew that man's sinful ways would lead to murder, He gave Noah and all people rules to follow.

A Flawed Character (2 Samuel 14:25–33)

Absalom is described very clearly in physical terms. We also are made aware of the true character of his person.

- Absalom was greatly admired because of his good looks.
- Absalom had a head of beautiful hair that weighed three to six pounds, which he, himself, admired and coiffed.
- Absalom had a family of four children.
- Absalom attempted to contact Joab to schedule an appointment to see his father.
- Joab ignored Absalom's inquires… for a time.

- Absalom then set Joab's field on fire in an attempt to retaliate and get his attention.
- This did capture Joab's awareness, and he went to see Absalom, asking the reason for the arson.
- Absalom expressed his distress at being ignored and asked again to see his father.
- This resulted in David's granting permission to see him, and once they met, the reunion was sweet.

What character flaws might we see in Absalom in this account?

- The text describes the admiration and praise of the people for Absalom because of his handsome appearance. This flattery no doubt helped to contribute to an arrogance yet to be observed.
- Absalom's vanity is described in how his hair was cut and weighed. The fact that his hair is emphasized in two verses adds to its significance. Unfortunately, Absalom's love for his hair foreshadowed the way in which he would eventually die.
- Absalom is seen as impatient and vengeful in his reaction to Joab's refusal to help him see the king. In fact, Absalom insisted on getting his own way and took drastic action when he did not get what he wanted.
- Absalom placed blame on Joab for his situation. (It was Joab's fault that he needlessly moved back to Jerusalem and it was Joab's fault that the king would not see him.)
- Absalom used his situation to test his father by speaking of his own execution for his brother's death. He really did not expect to be executed, since it had not happened to date. But he challenged his father to do it.
- Once Absalom was reunited with his father, it appeared that he was temporarily humble and sincere.

The Takeover (2 Samuel 15:1–6)

Now that Absalom was back in Jerusalem and enjoying restored favor with his father, he began to feel comfortable enough to position himself with the public.

- Absalom had a following of fifty men who served as his own personal army. This army assured Absalom's protection and the enforcement of his plans.
- Every day at the city gate, people from all over Israel would come for legal help or business transactions. Why the city gate? City gates were the grand

central station; the public hub of activity. Here it was that important officials would be available to make decisions and solve problems.

- Absalom was now recognized and admired not only as the king's son, but as an intuitive, resourceful and cunning administrator. He had now assumed the role of gate coordinator. This involved greeting the customer or visitor with a welcome that included a kiss on the hand. He also gave advice or direction to gain their favor.
- After many years of this procedure, Absalom had steadily developed friends and respect, and had a large fan club.
- It is hard to say what David's reaction was to this, but he allowed it to continue.
- It was in this manner that Absalom won the hearts of the people. The word *stole* means "to deceive". So, we know that Absalom was deceptive in his plan and approach to take the popular vote away from David. A comparative use of this deception is found in Romans 16:18. Absalom no doubt used smooth words and flattering speech to deceive the easily deceived.
- Absalom now devised a new plan to take over the throne (Verses 7–12).
- Under the guise of worship, Absalom received David's permission and probably his support to travel to "his mecca". Hebron was the capitol city where David had initially become king over Judah and he no doubt had a huge following there. Was this the reason Absalom picked Hebron? To start a rebellion against their beloved King David?
- Absalom continued to deceive in order to gain support for his cause. Two hundred well-meaning men from Jerusalem even joined Absalom, thinking they were doing the right thing.
- The battle lines were beginning to be drawn. While Absalom gained in popularity and in strength, David failed to retain his public following after being king for many years.
- The dreaded news arrived by messenger that David was being deposed as king by Absalom, his own son.
- David relied on his close friends and household for advice. But he was still a wise and a kind king who, most of all, relied on God. David's description of this time in his life is written in Psalm 3:1–4.
- David's generosity extended to many people at the time that he felt it necessary to leave the palace for his own protection.

David Extends Kindness (2 Samuel 15:13–23)

David's servants	David made sure they got out safely and he personally watched each one leave the city.
Ittai the Gittite	The newest member of the palace staff, he is encouraged by David to remain protected at the palace. But Ittai insisted on being loyal to David, and proceeded to join him.
Zadak and Abiathar the high priests	Levites who safeguarded the ark of the covenant and received instructions from David to return to Jerusalem for their and the ark's well-being (2 Samuel 15:24–29).
Hushai the Archite and David's friend	He begged David to let him continue to be his loyal servant. David suggested that he be his secret agent in Absalom's new administration. He was to pass on information to Zadok and Abithar (2 Samuel 15:32–37)
Ziba, the servant of Mephibosheth	He met David with food for his entourage and gave him an update on Absalom's activities in Jerusalem. David, in return, stated that all that had belonged to Mephibosheth now belonged to Ziba (2 Samuel 16:1–4).
Shimei, a Benjamite from Saul's family	He met David on the road and began cursing him aggressively. He also tried to stone him. David had unusual insight as to this man's behavior and compared Shimei's judgment of him with God's judgment of his son, Absalom (2 Samuel 16:5–14).

At this point in the account, both David and Absalom are described as going before the Lord to worship. Their worship experiences should be compared to show the clear contrast of their relationships with God.

David's Worship (2 Samuel 15:30)

Location: The Mount of Olives

- David ascended up the Mount of Olives, which overlooks Jerusalem.
- He wept as he walked; probably shedding tears of regret that he had made mistakes, that his son had turned on him, and that he had lost his crown.
- His grief was agonizing, expressive, and public.
- He showed reverence to God by covering his head and removing his sandals, much as we would do when entering one's home.
- He prayed, bringing his request to God that Absalom's advisor, Ahithophel, provide counsel which would appear foolish.
- How very similar it was, many years later, when Jesus walked up the Mount of Olives to weep and pray, as he was being betrayed and rejected by his own people of Israel (Luke 19:41).

Absalom's Worship (2 Samuel 15:7–8, 12)

Location: Hebron

- Absalom wanted to re-pay the vow he owed the Lord. He had promised God that he would serve him if he would allow him to return to Jerusalem. This was what he told his father.
- He offered sacrifices, which was typically only the role of the priest.
- There is no evidence of prayer or the humility of worship that David exhibited. There is no evidence that Absalom repaid his vow to God. And there is no evidence of his grief over broken relationships.

The Advisors (2 Samuel 17:1–14)

- Hushai, David's friend, worked alongside Absalom as a secret agent and an advisor.
- He acknowledged him as the king and stated that whomever happened to be king, that man he would serve. However, he did not defect to Absalom but remained loyal to David.
- Absalom asked first for Ahithophel's advice on how to handle the situation with David.
- Ahithophel advised that Absalom claim David's ten concubines as his own.

- Absalom took his advice in a public fashion on the roof of his home. This action fulfilled the prophet Nathan's prophecy found in 2 Samuel 12:11–12.
- Ahithophel was so widely regarded, that, when he gave advice, it was as if it came from God.
- Ahithophel also wanted to pursue David with twelve thousand men, kill him, and bring back his army as prisoners.
- Ahithophel's advice pleased Absalom and the elders of Israel.
- Absalom now asked for Hushai's advice.
- Hushai said that Ahithophel's advice was not good.
- He stated that David was long gone, meaning that he had fled the country.
- He said that David's anger would be great and would result in the slaughter of Absalom's men.
- He advised that their action not necessarily be quick, but that more importantly, it be overpowering in numbers.
- He recommended that Absalom lead his men in battle.
- He quoted, "David would be pulled out of hiding even if they had to drag the river to find him!"
- Hushai's brilliant plan was readily accepted, and, unbeknownst to Absalom and company, the plan would allow David time to escape across the Jordan River.

The Warning and the Escape (2 Samuel 17:15–29)

- David's network of spies alerted him to immediately cross the river.
- As was always the case, word got back to Absalom that there were spies in his administration.
- There immediately ensued a hide and seek chase between Absalom's men and the spies.
- In a daring escape, David and all his people reached safety before morning light and camped at a place called Mahanaim.
- Based on 2 Samuel 2:29 Mahanaim is quite a distance from the Jordan. So, David had secured a place of safety for now.
- The next day, Absalom quickly formed an army, called Israel, and appointed Amasa as his military captain.
- They crossed the river and camped at Gilead, the Transjordan plain that stretches east from the Jordan River.
- David's camp and Absalom's camp are described as both being in the large territory of Gilead.

- Thousands of David's sympathizers, came out in support, from all regions of Israel.
- The leaders and people of Gilead extended hospitality to David by bringing food and provisions for his men.

The Military Campaign (2 Samuel 18:1–4, 6–8)

As we proceed to study the conflict between David's and Absalom's infantry, we may recognize similarities of war like to that of American history.

- The positioning of the two armies was close enough for combat even though this may not necessarily have been planned (2 Samuel 17:24).
- Local residents expressed their support for the troops by offering shelter and/or sustenance. (2 Samuel 17:28–29).
- David appointed captains over large divisions of troops: Joab, Abishai, and Ittai the Gittite. This was a promotion for Ittai, who was initially hired as a servant in David's household! (2 Samuel 15:19–20).
- David's protection was afforded by his men, even though David's wish was to go to battle himself. The crucial decision was made for David to lead from behind and not actively participate in battle. This method has been utilized throughout history as a strategy of strength, thus preserving the life of the one who gives the orders (2 Samuel 18:3).
- Absalom, on the other hand, seemed to have strayed away from his army, leaving him alone and vulnerable to the enemy. Ground combat dictates strength in numbers, not in isolation. We know that Absalom was alone because of an eyewitness, and at his capture he was immediately surrounded by David's men (2 Samuel 18:10, 15).
- The conflict between the two armies claimed many lives; twenty thousand men died that day (2 Samuel 18:7).
- The land was to blame for most of those casualties. Rough and unfamiliar terrain, described as a wilderness, as well as the environmental elements, were unfriendly to experienced and unexperienced troops alike. They also encountered a loss of orientation (2 Samuel 18:8).
- The evidence of destruction and death was apparent on the face of the land (2 Samuel 18:8).

A Royal Death (2 Samuel 18:5, 9–18)

The final account compares striking similarities to Saul's end of life experiences.

- David publicly instructed his military captains, to not take the life of Absalom. *David had commanded that Saul's life not be taken* (1 Samuel 26:9, 23).

- When Absalom encountered David's men, he was riding alone on a mule under a great terebinth tree. Why was he riding a mule, instead of a black stallion? A mule was the animal reserved for all royalty. The biblical record tells us that Jesus, King of the Jews, rode a donkey into Jerusalem (Matthew 21:1–2, 5). The terebinth tree, a type of oak, grows in the mid-east and is a shrub-like low-branched tree. In this case, the tree was larger in size than usual. *Both Saul and Absalom were hung: Absalom from a tree and Saul after death, from the city wall* (1 Samuel 31:10).

- Absalom's head became caught. The translation for head is "shaking". And although hair is not mentioned in the text, the imagery is of head movement resulting in an upward progression of Absalom's long flowing hair. His first reaction might have been to reach for his hair; an automatic response, but that would have caused him to let go of the reigns as the donkey rode on. His hair became entangled in the tree, causing him to dangle from the tree. How coincidental that Absalom's hair, the vanity of his pride, contributed to his end. Compare to Saul in 1 Samuel 31:4. *Both died a prideful death. Absalom's head became caught; Saul's head was removed* (1 Samuel 31:9).

- While Absalom was still dangling, a man reported to Joab what he had just witnessed (I Samuel 31:9).

- Joab criticized the eye witness for not killing Absalom. It is certain that Joab did not honor David's express command to spare Absalom's life.

- The eye witness realized that Joab preferred another person kill Absalom rather than himself. That man would then be guilty of the crime. *Another person claimed to have taken Saul's life; the Amalekite falsely made the claim* (2 Samuel 1:1–15).

- No bribe, even 1,000 shekels of silver (equivalent to $1,000) and a soldier's chief ornament, his belt, could persuade the eye witness to kill Absalom. *No amount of persuasion could bring Saul's armorbearer to kill him* (1 Samuel 31:4).

- Joab realized he was wasting his time and took action himself. He went to the scene and threw three spears into Absalom's heart (probably the thoracic-abdominal part of his body referred to as his heart). He surely was near to death, but Joab's armorbearers finished the job by striking him and killing him. *Both Saul and Absalom died on the battlefield* (1 Samuel 31:2).

- It is important to know that the armorbearers were doing their job by killing Absalom, as this was their role. Joab bore the sole responsibility of the death since the armorbearers must obey his orders. *The Philistines caused Saul's mortal wound, not the armorbearer* (1 Samuel 31:4). *Saul's armorbearer did not kill him* (1 Samuel 31:8–10).

- Many years later, as David lay on his death bed, he gave instructions to his son, Solomon, regarding Joab (1 Kings 2:5–6).
- As was the custom, Joab blew the trumpet, in announcement of David's victory (1 Samuel 13:3).
- The people responded to the sound of the trumpet by rushing to Joab's side. Simultaneously, however, Israel (Absalom's men) fled in full retreat (1 Samuel 31:7).
- Joab held back the crowd while Absalom's body was taken down and thrown into a pit-like grave. It was covered with large stones. This type of burial meant the ultimate disgrace for a member of the royal family, who would have been expected to have a dignified burial.
- Ironically, Absalom had prematurely erected a monument in his own honor. The location of the monument pillar was in the King's Valley, otherwise known as the Kidron Valley in Jerusalem. A similar monument ascribed to Absalom stands there today. It reaches sixty-five feet high and dates back to the first century. It was once said that a man who deserves a monument does not need one and a man who needs a monument does not deserve one!
- Absalom stated that he had no son to carry forward his name as a memorial. However, we know that he did have three sons (2 Samuel 14:27). It is probable that the sons died prior to their father's death.

Personal Applications

1. Absalom was deserving of death, according to Old Testament law. Do Old Testament rules apply to today's culture? Has God changed his mind over time? Has man changed since the days of Noah? No, neither God nor man has changed (Malachi 3:6). God demands as compensation nothing less than the life of the murderer. Human life holds ultimate value in God's eyes because we are made in his image. David acknowledged in his writings that God does not let wickedness go unpunished (Psalm 9:12, Nahum 1:3).

2. Certainly, we see evidence that Absalom had an affinity with his appearance. Is vanity wrong? The Hebrew meaning of the word vanity means that which is unsubstantial, futile, or useless. Solomon speaks of vanity as an evil affliction in this short life that we live on earth (Ecclesiastes 6:12). He compares it to a different kind of life focus; that of joyfulness (Ecclesiastes 5:20).

3. Where should the line be drawn when it comes to being confident as compared to being proud, as we saw with Absalom? (Psalm 101:5b). God does not tolerate a high look, which is described as haughty (Proverbs 3:26). We can find all the confidence we need in the Lord.

4. What kind of legacy will you leave? Can you say, as Mary said in Luke 1:48, that future generations will call you blessed? Absalom left a legacy of delusory, deceit, and disloyalty.

5. Was God's sovereignty at work in this account? Yes, God protected the crown reserved for David. His covenant with David would stand for the entirety of David's life. How is God's sovereignty at work in your life?

Absalom, the Wayward Son
Chapter 14
References

Psalm 127:3–5 "Behold, children are a gift of the Lord, the fruit of the womb is a reward. Like arrows in the hand of a warrior, so are the children of one's youth. How blessed is the man whose quiver is full of them; they will not be ashamed when they speak with their enemies in the gate" ().

Psalm 103:13 "Just as a father has compassion on his children, so the Lord has compassion on those who fear Him."

2 Samuel 14:1–24

Genesis 9:5–6 "Surely I will require your lifeblood; from every beast I will require it. And from every man, from every man's brother I will require the life of man. Whoever sheds man's blood, by man his blood shall be shed, for in the image of God he made man."

Psalm 9:12 "For He who requires blood remembers them; He does not forget the cry of the afflicted."

Nahum 1:3 "The Lord is slow to anger and great in power, and the Lord will by no means leave the guilty unpunished."

1 Samuel 15:1–6

Romans 16:18 "For such men are slaves, not of our Lord Christ but of their own appetites; and by their smooth and flattering speech they deceive the hearts of the unsuspecting."

Psalm 3:1–4 "Lord, how my adversaries have increased! Many are rising up against me. Many are saying of my soul, 'There is no deliverance for him in God.' But You, O Lord, are a shield about me, my glory, and the One who lifts my head. I was crying to the Lord with my voice, and He answered me from His holy mountain."

I Samuel 15:13–23

I Samuel 15:24–29

I Samuel 15:32–37

2 Samuel 15:30 "And David went up the ascent of the Mount of Olives, and wept as he went, and his head was covered and he walked barefoot. Then all the people who were with him each covered his head and went up weeping as they went."

Luke 19:41 "When He approached Jerusalem, He saw the city and wept over it."

2 Samuel 15:7–8, 12 "Now it came about at the end of forty years that Absalom said to the king, 'Please let me go and pay my vow which I have vowed to the Lord, in Hebron. For your servant vowed a vow while I was living at Geshur in Aram, saying, 'If the Lord shall indeed bring me back to Jerusalem, then I will serve the Lord.' And Absalom sent for Ahithophel the Gilonite, David's counselor, from his city Giloh, while he was offering the sacrifices.'"

2 Samuel 17:1–14

2 Samuel 12:11–12 "Thus says the Lord, 'Behold, I will raise up evil against you from your own household; I will even take your wives before your eyes and give them to your companion, and he will lie with your wives in broad daylight. Indeed, you did it secretly, but I will do this thing before all Israel, and under the sun.'"

2 Samuel 17:15–29

2 Samuel 2:29 "Abner and his men then went through the Arabah all that night; so they crossed the Jordan, walked all morning, and came to Mahanaim."

2 Samuel 18:1–4, 6–8

2 Samuel 17:24 "Then David came to Mahanaim. And Absalom crossed the Jordan, he and all the men of Israel with him."

2 Samuel 17:28–29 "They brought beds, basins, pottery, wheat, barley, flour, parched grain, beans, lentils, parched seeds, honey, curds, sheep, and cheese of the herd, for David and for the people who were with him, to eat; for they said, 'The people are hungry and weary and thirsty in the wilderness.'"

2 Samuel 15:19–20 "Then the king said to Ittai the Gittite, 'Why will you also go with us? Return and remain with the king, for you are a foreigner and also an exile; return to your own place. You came only yesterday, and shall I today make you wander with us, while I go where I will?'"

2 Samuel 18:3 "But the people said, 'You should not go out; for if we indeed flee, they will not care about us; even if half of us die, they will not care about us. But you are worth ten thousand of us; therefore, now it is better that you be ready to help us from the city.'"

2 Samuel 18:10, 15 "When a certain man saw it, he told Joab and said, 'Behold, I saw Absalom hanging in an oak. And ten young men who carried Joab's armor gathered around Absalom.'"

2 Samuel 18:7 "The people of Israel were defeated there before the servants of David, and the slaughter there that day was great, 20,000 men."

2 Samuel 18:8 "For the battle there was spread over the whole countryside, and the forest devoured more people that day than the sword devoured."

2 Samuel 18:5, 9–18

1 Samuel 26:9, 23 "But David said to Abishai, 'Do not destroy him, for who can stretch out his hand against the LORD's anointed and be without guilt? The LORD will repay each man for his righteousness and his faithfulness; for the LORD delivered you into my hand today, but I refused to stretch out my hand against the LORD's anointed.'"

Matthew 21:1–2, 5 "When they had approached Jerusalem and had come to Bethphage, at the Mount of Olives, then Jesus sent two disciples, saying to them, 'Go into the village opposite you, and immediately you will find a donkey tied there and a colt with her; untie them and bring them to Me. Say to the daughters of Zion, 'Behold your King is coming to you, gentle & mounted on a donkey.'"

1 Samuel 31:10 "They put his weapons in the temple of Ashtaroth, and they fastened his body to the wall of Beth-shan."

1 Samuel 31:4 "Then Saul said to his armor bearer, 'Draw your sword and pierce me through with it, otherwise these uncircumcised will come and pierce me through and make sport of me.'"

1 Samuel 31:9 "They cut off Saul's head and stripped off his weapons, and sent them throughout the land of the Philistines, to carry the good news to the house of their idols and to the people."

2 Samuel 1:1–15

1 Samuel 31:4 "But Saul's armor bearer would not kill him, for he was greatly afraid. So Saul took his sword and fell on it."

1 Samuel 31:2 "The Philistines overtook Saul and his sons; and the Philistines killed Jonathan and Abinadab and Malchi-shua the sons of Saul."

1 Samuel 31:8–10 "It came about on the next day when the Philistines came to strip the slain, that they found Saul and his three sons fallen on Mount Gilboa. They cut off his head and stripped off his weapons, and sent them throughout the land of the Philistines, to carry the good news to the house of their idols and to the people. They put his weapons in the temple of Ashtaroth, and they fastened his body to the wall of Beth-shan."

1 Kings 2:5–6 "Now you also know what Joab the son of Zeruiah did to me, what he did to the two commanders of the armies of Israel, to Abner the son of Ner, and to Amasa the son of Jether, whom he killed; he also shed the blood of war in peace. And he put the blood of war on his belt about his waist, and on his sandals on his feet. So act according to your wisdom, and do not let his gray hair go down to Sheol in peace."

1 Samuel 13:3 "Jonathan smote the garrison of the Philistines that was in Geba, and the Philistines heard of it. Then Saul blew the trumpet throughout the land, saying, 'Let the Hebrews hear.'"

1 Samuel 31:7 "When the men of Israel who were on the other side of the valley, with those who were beyond the Jordan, saw that the men of Israel had fled and that Saul and his sons were dead, they abandoned the cities and fled."

2 Samuel 14:27 "To Absalom there were born three sons, and one daughter whose name was Tamar."

Malachi 3:6 "For I, the Lord, do not change."

Ecclesiastes 6:12, For who knows what is good for a man during his lifetime, during the few years of his futile life? He will spend them like a shadow. For who can tell a man what will be after him under the sun?

Ecclesiastes 5:20 "For he will not often consider the years of his life, because God keeps him occupied with the gladness of his heart."

Psalm 101:5b "No one who has a haughty look and an arrogant heart will I endure."

Proverbs 3:26 "For the Lord will be your confidence and will keep your foot from being caught."

Luke 1:48 "For, behold, from this time on all generations will count me blessed."

15

A Time for Mourning and a Time of Healing

There is an appointed time for everything.
And there is a time for every event under heaven.

—Ecclesiastes 3:1

The book of Ecclesiastes provides remarkable instruction from the pen of King Solomon. While he had not yet written ecclesiastical wisdom literature, the instruction, in retrospect, bears applicability to 2 Samuel 18–21. "The times"—that is, all human activity, including David's lifetime—is in God's hand. References from Ecclesiastes correlate with a time of mourning and a time of healing in this study of David.

A Time of Mourning (2 Samuel 18:1–33)

Absalom was dead. No father ever wants to hear the horrible news of their child's death. Yet we know that death is a consequence of life, as Ecclesiastes 1:4 says. Who would deliver the news of Absalom's death? Two men stepped forward, eager to serve in this way. They are identified as a Cushite (Ethiopian) and a courier, Ahimaaz, the son of Zadok, the priest, who shared a warm relationship with David. Both were swift runners and both were known to David. We might view this as unusual, that not only one, but two men volunteered for such a grievous duty. Joab initially denied Ahimaaz the responsibility; most likely because he may have wanted to protect Ahimaaz in case the news was not well received. Instead, Joab dispatched the Cushite, thinking that he was perhaps more knowledgeable about the situation or was even more expendable. However, Ahimaaz was not to be denied, and finally convinced Joab to let him go. David saw both runners from a distance and could have assumed that since Ahimaaz was closer, that the news was good. Ahimaaz's message was that Absalom's army had, indeed, been defeated. "But," said David, "How about my son?" Ahimaaz told him that he did not know. Ahimaaz, it seems, could not bear to tell David the honest truth. David then gave his attention to the Cushite, who had now arrived. The Cushite repeated the same good news to David that his army had been victorious. The king persisted in asking further about his son. And the Cushite revealed the grave account of Absalom's death. How did this news impact David? Visualize him sitting between the two gates after hearing the battlefield report. All merchant and legal business would have adjourned as the news circulated, causing shock, apprehension, and uncertainty. In deep despair, David retreated to the closest and most private spot—a room above the city gate of Mahanaim. There, he wept in anguish and cried out with regret that he had not died in Absalom's place. We are reminded that most parents would willingly die for their child. David would have done anything to have his son back, regardless of Absalom's hatred for him. We read that David did not weep alone. The city declared it a day of mourning and his people, who shared his grief, also wept. As the mourning continued, a silent strength took over the city and David's people temporarily rallied behind him. Meanwhile, in private quarters, Joab paid David a visit.

A Time of Regret (2 Samuel 19:5–8)

Joab brought a scolding message of rebuke to David for his insensitivity toward his people and even his own military officers. The message revealed that what had been strong had broken down (Ecclesiastes 3:3b). Joab's accusations unfolded some stark realities and unrealistic blame.

- That David had brought embarrassment to everyone he personally knew
- That he favored his enemies over his friends
- That he didn't care about his leaders or servants
- That he valued Absalom's life over the life of any other

Joab also brought a two-fold message of warning and advice to David.

- That the people now were threatening to abandon him
- That a disaster of the worse kind was immanent and would be unlike anything that David had experienced
- That he should pull himself together and face the people
- That he should offer encouragement to them

The plain truth became obvious to David. For he responded immediately to Joab's message and went to the city gate. This was just what his followers needed and expected. His presence was healing. The people could see that he cared for them and that he remained strong for them. There were others, however, who did not agree, and these were the men of Israel.

A Time of Reconciliation (2 Samuel 19:9–14)

Although the leader of Israel, Absalom, was dead and David remained alive, the people in the land continued to be unsettled and divided. Their loyalties to Absalom had been strong and were not quickly abandoned. Steadily there were murmurings of uniting behind David. However, David noticed that his own tribe of Judah had not voiced their loyalty to him. So, he sent his priests, Zadok and Abiathar, a request to publicly extend their support of him. The phrase, "my bone and my flesh" is repeatedly used in this passage. It signifies something as being part of oneself or of the same bloodline. These were David's feelings for Judah. As a son of Jesse, David was intimately related to this tribe. It was time for reconciliation of grievances and forgiveness (Ecclesiastes 3:5). Of note is that Amasa, David's nephew who assumed Joab's position as commander of the army, had previously betrayed David by pledging his allegiance to Absalom. Now, David reinstated Amasa's services as commander of his army. This would later cause its own set of problems. Soon to follow, with a providential change of heart, Judah surprised David by rallying its support to reappoint him as king; and word was soon sent for him to return to Jerusalem.

A Time of Relocation (2 Samuel 19:15–18)

The message from Judah was, "Return"! This must have been music to David's ears. It had been a year since he had vacated his position as king. He could now go home to Jerusalem—home to the palace and the life he had enjoyed before everything went so wrong with Absalom. The invitation from Judah was welcoming, in that some people actually rushed to forge the Jordan River to assist in David's crossing. Among them was Shimei, the Benjamite who had initially cursed and stoned David on the road to Bahurim (2 Samuel 16:5–6). Shimei now displayed a change of heart. There was also Ziba, who had started his career many years earlier with King Saul, but now had become a loyal servant to David. He, his family, and household met David at the river. There were a thousand Benjamites, as well as members of the tribe of Judah, who joined in the joyous welcome home (Ecclesiastes 3:5b). A ferryboat was also provided for David and his possessions. Nothing less than royal treatment for their beloved king.

A Time for Reacquaintance (2 Samuel 19:19–39)

It was time for David to now take inventory of his followers and assess whether they would be useful in his new administration (Ecclesiastes 3:6). This required David to extend forgiveness and repair relationships with former acquaintances.

- Shimei was the first man to reacquaint himself to David. In a previous encounter with David, he had been very angry with him and even attempted to kill him. David's men wanted to punish Shimei at the time, but David would not agree to this action (2 Samuel 16:9, 11). Shimei had lived with his guilt and was now ready to ask for forgiveness. He said, "Do not hold this against me and try to forget what I have done." True forgiveness always includes an effort to forget the past offense. Against Abishai's recommendation to punish Shimei, David promised Shimei that he would not die. David was even offended by Abishai's advice, because with the re-establishment of his new government, David wanted to forget the past and move on to the future. It was natural for David to forgive, because of his experiences with God's forgiveness to him (Psalm 86:5).

- Mephibosheth, Jonathan's son whom David had received into his household at one time, came out to meet David. He experienced such angst at David's loss of his throne, that he had ignored his own personal hygiene. Mephibosheth had not been able to follow after David because of his physical disability and difficulty with travel. He also admitted that he did not have any right to ask for favors from the king. Mephibosheth now humbly reminded David of the false accusations that Ziba, his servant had previously made. Ziba had come into David's life during his abdication. He supplied David with food and donkeys at a time when Mephibosheth could not accompany him. The supplies from Mephibosheth were a welcome gift. Ziba also brought untruthful news that Mephibosheth was planning to take over the throne with the encouragement of Saul's loyal supporters. Because of David's momentary sense of gratitude for the warning and the supplies he decided to transfer Mephibosheth's wealth to Ziba. Now, as Mephibosheth stood before David, he confided to David that Ziba had lied and slandered him. David understood the difficulties this man had experienced in his life. He recalled his earlier promises to Mephibosheth (2 Samuel 9:6–11) and that he had given all of Saul's land to him. Ziba was to only farm the land, as we read in 2 Samuel 16:1–4. Now that Ziba's actions could be carefully scrutinized, according 2 Samuel 19:24-30, David clearly seemed to want closure with the ongoing drama between Mephibosheth and Ziba. So, he said to Mephibosheth, "Why are you coming to me? Just divide the land with Ziba and be done with it." Mephibosheth responded by saying, "Then Ziba can have all of it." David's apparent desire was to bring peaceful relationship between the two men and himself despite a somewhat fragile domestic dynamic (Ecclesiastes 3:7).

- Barzillai, the wealthy and now very old man from Gilead, made an appearance at the Jordan River to bid farewell to David. The king insisted that Barzillai return to Jerusalem so that he could repay him for his kindness. Barzillai was touched, but begged to return to his home. As an older man, he stated some very personal reasons for wanting to remain at his home.

  He admitted to not having the same mental awareness as when he was younger. His appetite and hearing were failing. And he preferred to live the rest of his days in a peaceful, quiet existence, surrounded by all that was familiar to him.

  David graciously accepted Barzillai's justification, and instead, took Barzillai's servant, Chinham, with him to Jerusalem.

- The men of Israel and the men of Judah came together to discuss their rights to the king. And David was caught in the middle. The men of Judah claimed their relationship to David and explained they would not take advantage of this privilege. The men of Israel defended the fact that they represented ten of the twelve tribes (Judah and Simeon were southern tribes). Thus were the lines drawn between the north and the south. The disagreement soon became confrontational and was to eventually lead to dissent and outright revolt.

A Time of Rebellion (2 Samuel 20:1–14)

From the men of Israel arose a rebel Benjamite named Sheba. There probably was still some residual loyalty to King Saul, after all this time. This contributed to the underlying hostility of his group. Sheba spoke for the men of Israel, and they repealed their allegiance to David. By the time David had returned to Jerusalem, Sheba had gathered his support and deserted the king. Upon return home, David reclaimed his ten concubines, only to provide for them in their remaining days. But he had no further intimacy with them since they had earlier been appropriated to Absalom. David wasted no time in addressing Sheba's revolt. He recognized the danger of this rebellion and directed Amasa to assemble the men of Judah within three days and report back to him.

Amasa delayed in reporting back to the king. So, David appointed Abaishi to gather Joab's remaining army, a few dissonant groups, and David's personal troops, the mighty men of valor. They set out to pursue Sheba and went to Gibeon, five miles north of Jerusalem. Whom should Amasa meet but Sheba and his men, including Joab. Remember that Joab had been replaced by Amasa, so there existed some contest between the two men. Joab approached Amasa, and it initially appeared that he was friendly; even asking about his health and extending a kiss. While Joab did this, however, he secretly held a dagger in his hand and stabbed Amasa once in the abdomen, causing a wound deep enough to expose his internal organs. He did not spare Amasa the agony of a painful, slow death. Instead, he moved him off the road and covered him as he writhed in pain, to prevent those passing by from gawking. It is especially abhorrent that Joab and Amasa were cousins; sons of David's half-sisters. These were men who probably started out life loving each other (Ecclesiastes 3:8a). Shortly thereafter, Joab realized he still had followers in David's army, and he took the lead to recruit still others from the tribes of Israel.

A Time for Retribution (2 Samuel 20:15–22)

Sheba was thought to be in Abel of Beth Maachah. David's troops, led by Joab, surrounded the city and attempted to break down the protective wall that encircled it. In fact, they quickly built a siege ramp. This was a ramp-like roadway that ran beside the city wall, allowing the invaders to destroy the wall at great heights. Suddenly, a woman's voice could be heard above the noise. She called to Joab and wished to speak with him. So, Joab gave her his attention. She first acknowledged that she was his maidservant, thus, immediately taking a submissive position. The woman is described as wise, and once she began to speak, it became evident that she, indeed, lived up to her reputation. She conveyed that her city was peaceable and honorable, saying that it was a "mother of Israel." Deborah, the Hebrew leader and prophetess who had lived several hundred years earlier, called herself "the mother of Israel" (Judges 5:7). The inference is one of strength. The woman wanted Joab to know that Beth Maachah was strong and prominent; an information center and a leader among cities. The woman delivered a wise message that the city should not be destroyed because it was an inheritance of the Lord, meaning that God had always sustained and protected it (Ecclesiastes 3:7b). Joab denied that his plan was to destroy the city and emphasized that his reason for being there was simply to find Sheba. He asked for Sheba to be delivered to him. The woman promised to search for him, and in addition, arranged for Sheba to be killed. This abruptly ended the invasion. After Sheba's death, the woman threw his head over the wall and Joab returned home in triumph, blowing his trumpet to announce Sheba's defeat.

A Time of Restoration (2 Samuel 21:1–14)

Israel had experienced three years of famine. So, David inquired of the Lord why he would allow this, when he knew God wanted to bless him and Israel. God was faithful to answer him. Unbeknownst to David, there was some unfinished business with the Gibeonites. Looking back to the Canaanite conquest, Joshua had made a covenant with the Gibeonites to provide protection from them (Joshua 9:9–11, 15). However, when Saul became king, he violated the covenant and in an action not recorded in the Bible, he killed some of the Gibeonites. Upon this revelation, David immediately prepared to restore the covenant. As David called the Gibeonites to him, he could see that they were a reasonable people. They stated that they wanted no payment of any kind. But they did request for Saul's ancestral line to be exterminated. The execution that followed was an unusual and unexpected procedure. Seven of Saul's sons and grandsons were delivered to the Gibeonites, who hanged them to death. This was not a simple punishment for murder. This was a symbolic display of God's displeasure, that the covenant had been broken and of the consequences that would follow (Ecclesiastes 3:2a).

Related to this, there is documentation of a grieving mother named Rizpah. This woman had been Saul's concubine, and she had now lost the two sons she had borne him. Her grief was so great, that she took sackcloth, which is a black cloth made from goat's hair. She laid the cloth on a ledge close to her son's bodies and sat on it. This would have been quite uncomfortable, for goat's hair is very course and not soft. The significance of the goat hair in bereavement was that the mourner should experience discomfort in order to identify with the loved one who has died. Rizpah guarded the bodies, as they hung there from April, the time of harvest, until at least late October, when the rainy season begins. As she sat there day after day, she protected the decaying bodies from carnivore birds. For to allow a body to be eaten by birds or animals was considered a disgrace. What was her real intent? It is thought that she may have realized the brevity of God's judgment in the end. The coming of October rains meant that his judgment had now ended and the land was cleansed. In any case, the Gibeonites were restored and their covenant with Joshua was preserved. Rizpah's actions most likely prompted David to bring proper closure to King Saul's dynasty. He gathered the bones of Saul and Jonathan and the bodies of the seven hanged men, and he respectfully buried them in the tomb of their forefather, Kish. Was God pleased with what had taken place? Verse 14 says that God heard the prayers of the land. Thus, we know that the land had been healed.

In closing this study, we have become acquainted with two unique and strong women. The wise woman of Beth Maachah showed remarkable courage by speaking on behalf of her city's safety. In the twenty-first century it is not uncommon for women to be outspoken. But this wise woman's intervention showed God's providence in sparing the city. The other unique woman was Rizpah. She did not fear public ridicule in response to her extreme actions. She conveyed a message of quiet strength and loyalty to her family name and is to be admired for that. But how can we be men and women of strong character, as the wise woman and Rizpah? James chapter 3 speaks to the qualities God wants us to have.

- James 3:2 refers to the control we may or may not have with our speech. Submission of mind and body to the Lord, including the tongue, are necessary. This happens through our prayer life, which should be a constant meditation that we say and do the right thing.
- James 3:10 teaches that we should honor God in all that we do and especially in all that we say. The dichotomy of blessing God one moment and cursing man the next, is not God-centered speech. Our speech should be consistent with respect for the basic premise that all men are made by the same creator and in the likeness of God. He loves each individual and so should we (Psalms 35:28).

In many life situations, we experience times of mourning, regrets, reconciliations, relocation, reacquaintances, rebellion, retribution, and restoration. It is comforting to know that no matter what we go through, God has a perfect order and plan of how it should go (Ecclesiastes 3:14–15). God's plan will endure forever and will not change. Our response should be one of reverence, acceptance, and obedience.

Personal Applications

1. We have observed that David had the godly ability to forgive. Why is it so difficult to forgive? How can we break down the barriers to forgiveness? Unforgiveness is related to a selfish desire to hold another accountable, even when this is not our right; it is God's right. But an unforgiving spirit can also rob us of a healthy relationship with God. Ephesians 4:32 explains that because Christ forgave us, we should in turn, forgive others.

2. How important are reacquaintances to you? Was there a time when you reached out to renew a friendship of the past? Is this something we should practice routinely?

3. Let us consider for a moment, the significance of a covenant with God. A covenant is a sacred agreement between God and a person or group. Have you ever promised God something in return for his help? An example might be a young couple who have dedicated their newborn baby to the Lord. They promise to raise the child in the ways of God in exchange for his guidance in child rearing. We may have made promises to him that need to be addressed and restored.

4. Have you ever waited for the news that you really did not want to hear? How did you feel? How did God help or how could he have helped you?
5. Sometimes, at the risk of hurting someone, the truth must be told. Has this happened to you?

A Time for Mourning and a Time of Healing
Chapter 15
References

Ecclesiastes 3:1 "There is an appointed time for everything. And there is a time for every event under heaven."

2 Samuel 18:1–33

Ecclesiastes 1:4 "A generation goes and a generation comes, but the earth remains forever."

2 Samuel 19:5–8

Ecclesiastes 3:3b "A time to tear down and a time to build up."

2 Samuel 19:9–14

Ecclesiastes 3:5b "A time to embrace and a time to shun embracing."

2 Samuel 19:15–18

2 Samuel 16:5–6 "When King David came to Bahurim, behold, there came out from there a man of the family of the house of Saul whose name was Shimei, the son of Gera; he came out cursing continually as he came. He threw stones at David and at all the servants of King David"

Ecclesiastes 3:5a "A time to throw stones and a time to gather stones."

Ecclesaistes 3:6 "A time to search and a time to give up as lost; a time to keep and a time to throw away."

2 Samuel 19:19–39

2 Samuel 16:9, 11 "Then Abishai the son of Zeruiah said to the king, 'Why should this dead dog curse my lord the king? Let me go over now and cut off his head.' Then David said to Abishai and to all his servants, 'Behold, my son who came out from me seeks my life; how much more now this Benjamite? Let him alone and let him curse, for the Lord has told him.'"

Psalm 86:5 "For You, Lord, are good, and ready to forgive, and abundant in loving-kindness to all who call upon You."

2 Samuel 9:6–11

2 Samuel 16:1–4

2 Samuel 19:24–30

Ecclesiastes 3:7 "A time to tear apart and a time to sew together; a time to be silent and a time to speak."

2 Samuel 20:1–14

Ecclesiastes 3:8a "A time to love and a time to hate."

2 Samuel 20:15–22

Judges 5:7 "The peasantry ceased, they ceased in Israel, until I, Deborah, arose, until I arose, a mother in Israel."

Ecclesiastes 3:7b "A time to be silent and a time to speak."

2 Samuel 21:1–14

Joshua 9:9–11, 5 "They said to him, 'Your servants have come from a very far country because of the fame of the LORD your God; for we have heard the report of Him and all that He did in Egypt, and all that He did to the two kings of the Amorites'…So our elders and all the inhabitants of our country spoke to us, saying, 'Take provisions in your hand for the journey, and go to meet them and say to them, 'We are your servants; now then, make a covenant with us.'" Joshua made peace with them and made a covenant with them, to let them live; and the leaders of the congregation swore an oath to them" (Joshua 9:9–11, 15).

Ecclesiastes 3:2a, "A time to give birth and a time to die."

James 3:2, "For we all stumble in many ways. If anyone does not stumble in what he says, he is a perfect man, able to bridle the whole body as well."

James 3:10 "From the same mouth come both blessing and cursing. My brethren, these things ought not to be this way."

Psalm 35:28 "And my tongue shall declare Your righteousness and Your praise all day long."

Ecclesiastes 3:14–15 "I know that everything God does will remain forever; there is nothing to add to it and there is nothing to take from it, for God has so worked that men should fear Him. That which is has been already and that which will be has already been, for God seeks what has passed by."

Ephesians 4:32 "Be kind to one another, tender-hearted, forgiving each other, just as God in Christ also has forgiven you."

David's Victory Prayer

*For You are my rock and my fortress; for Your name's sake You will
lead me and guide me*

—Psalm 31:3

As we approach the last chapters of 2 Samuel, we encounter an extraordinary literary work of poetry that is also transcribed in Psalm 18 (2 Samuel 22). The prayer is occasionally described as a psalm, which means song. The text (verse 1) clearly states that David spoke his words to God Jehovah as a prayer. David had the remarkable ability to analyze his personal and external experiences in a most intimate way when communicating with God. Many of the psalms reveal his literary skill in terms of self-evaluation and expression. In the prayer of 2 Samuel 22, David weaves his own reality with contrasting metaphors to describe God's sufficiency. The focus is nearly all about God's attributes and his personal deliverance. It is thought that the prayer was written while David was king, however, he surprisingly described himself as a servant of the Lord. This indicated his acknowledgement of God's kingship over him. The references to deliverance extend over many years; from King Saul's intent to destroy him to the final defeat of enemy peoples that had battled against him. The study of 2 Samuel 22 will also include a review of David's life and God's intervention as David realized it.

David's Resources (2 Samuel 22:2–7)

Verse 2. David referred to God as a Rock. The first recording of God as a Rock in the Old Testament is in the Song of Moses, where God's impenetrable strength and permanence are compared to an immovable stone structure (Deuteronomy 32:4). David had often taken refuge in the rocks for protection, as noted in 1 Samuel 23:25 and 24:2. Here, David gave God praise for divine safety in his Rock, the Lord.

Verse 3. Trust in the face of danger is the test of a true faith. Many years earlier God proved to be David's shield as he approached Goliath in the name of the Lord of hosts (1 Samuel 17:41, 45). Fighting the enemy under God's authority and power was the only shield he needed.

Personal application: Name one spiritual enemy and the authority God gives us.

Verse 4. David's dependency on God is described. He spontaneously went to the Lord, beginning with praise and worship. David had no doubt that his protection was secure in the Lord. We know that the results were directly associated with calling upon the Lord's name. When the Philistines attacked Israel in the Valley of Rephaim, David depended on God's direction and deliverance (2 Samuel 5:19).

Personal application: Describe a time when, as a first step, you prayed for help.

Verse 5. The image is of overflowing waters symbolic of distress or destruction. David often experienced fearful situations that certainly warranted death. One such experience occurred at night when David and Abishai entered Saul's camp of three thousand men (1 Samuel 26:12). The two men were dangerously at risk for the entire army waking up.

Personal application: Describe a dangerous situation you may have been in. Did you trust God, as David did?

Verse 6. David continues to describe an encounter with the certainty of death and that Sheol, or death, literally reached out for him. His perception was that the cords from the grave encircled him, pulling him into a downward spiral. A similar notation is found in Psalm 116:3.

Personal application: Have you ever experienced a near-death encounter?

Verse 7. David found himself at times in desperate circumstances, when all he could do was to cry out to the Lord, his deliverer. Samuel, in his grief, also cried out to the Lord for an entire night because of God's regret that he had made Saul king (1 Samuel 15:10–11). God heard Samuel's cries and provided an answer to prayer in the form of a message for Saul.

Personal application: Our appeals to the Lord are often spontaneous and brief. Is it realistic to pray all night over an urgent matter, or do you think the Lord understands and will answer if we have a continual prayer in our heart?

David's Recognition of Creation (2 Samuel 22:8–16)

Impressive imagery of the earth's grandeur is used to showcase God's justice. It may be that David encountered natural disasters in his time. He writes of environmental effects in verses 8–16.

Earthquakes (verse 8)	Forrest fires (verse 9)	Hailstones (verse 9)
Darkness (verse 10)	Windstorms (verse 11)	Thunderstorms (verses 12, 14)
Volcanic eruptions (verse 13)	Lightning (verse 15)	Rough seas (verse 16)

David compared these calamities to God's judgement. The underlying message is that all the earth's activities are controlled by the Lord. Pagan beliefs also incorporated the power of nature as metaphor in their philosophy. Baal, the Canaanite god, was known as "the rider of the clouds" (verse 11). However, God is magnified over all other gods in this passage and as the One who brings creation to submission at his feet. The vivid description of God's fury is indicative of several things.

- God's interaction with humans is often meant to show his power or displeasure.
- God clearly defines that he is just and holds humans accountable.
- God's anger is righteous, rooted in holiness, thereby guaranteeing that all his ways are perfect.
- God's creation is his to manipulate. In this context, it seems as if he could rearrange creation on David's behalf.

Personal application: Is it fair or unfair that we are at God's mercy to do what he pleases to us? Fairness means to treat all equally and God does this through his love and forgiveness. There is no one else who loves and forgives like he does.

David's Rescue (2 Samuel 22:17–28)

God's expansive outreach to David further emphasized the fact that David, like all others, was undeserving of God's great mercy. David had been in unsafe situations; times when God miraculously rescued him. David describes his actions.

- God reached down for him (verse 17)
- God took hold of him (verse 17)
- God drew him out of harm's way (verse 17)
- God retrieved him from powerful and consuming enemies (verse 18)
- God proved to be his mainstay (verse 19)
- God brought him out of distress (verse 20)
- God delivered him to himself (verse 20)

- God turned toward him with kindness (verse 26)
- God showed his holiness and justice to him (verse 27)
- God saved him in his affliction (verse 28)

In one of the fiercest battles between Israel and Judah, David risked losing his men and his future kingdom (2 Samuel 2:17). God finally gave him the victory after many years of war. He rescued him from the face of danger and affirmed His plan for David's kingdom (2 Samuel 3:1).

Personal application: Have you seen God's strategy at work in your life? He may have rescued you from perilous circumstances, but did you realize his motive? What did you learn from it? Did your relationship with God change as a result? Did your service to him mature as a result?

David's Response (2 Samuel 22:21–45)

David responded to God's rescue with a sincere and thankful heart. This is documented in the following ways.

- David is described as blameless or righteous (verse 21).
- David experienced victory (verse 21).
- David kept following the way of the Lord (verse 22).
- David was faithful to the Lord (verse 22).
- David lived by God's laws (verse 23).
- David's obedience kept him from sinning (verse 24).
- David's obedience led to a closer relationship with God (verse 25).
- David was able to completely destroy his enemies (verses 38, 39)
- David's strength and success in battle came from the Lord (verse 40).
- David, with God's help, claimed victory over hate (verse 41).
- David had the Lord on his side (verse 42).
- David's military defeats were destructive and complete (verse 43).
- David effectively governed his own contentious people (verse 44).
- David was feared and respected by foreign peoples (verse 45).
- David's captives submitted to his authority (verse 45).

What made David the greatest military king in Israel's history? There are examples in 2 Samuel 8:5 where David's army killed 22,000 Syrians in Damascus and in 2 Samuel 8:13 where David claimed defeat over 18,000 Syrians in the Valley of Salt. His military prowess and success was due to several advantages.

- David completely trusted God. In 2 Samuel 22, he claimed repeatedly that the Lord had delivered him and it was because of this trust. In most cases, his first action before every battle was to consult God.
- David had great military commanders and advisors. These were men like Abner and Joab.
- David was a born leader. In his early years of fleeing from King Saul, men were drawn to him. These were men who had defended and championed the same convictions that David had. In the account of David hiding in the cave of Adullam, four hundred men joined him and designated him as their captain (1 Samuel 22:1–2).

Personal application: Does God intend for you to be a spiritual leader? What do you think is required for this special role?

David's Redemption (2 Samuel 22:29–37)

Verses 29–37 describe God's blessing to David. As much as David was very beloved by his people, he was also hated by others. But God always offered a way of escape from his enemies or deliverance from his personal suffering. God, in his goodness, provided all that David needed, and more.

Verse 29. The metaphor of a lamp expresses hope. David was Israel's hope and promise of blessing during times of darkness and oppression.

Verse 30. Two seeming impossibilities required supernatural strength; running singlehanded towards an enemy, and climbing a great wall. However, the strength that David needed was more than physical stamina. He needed spiritual and mental boldness as recorded in Psalm 138:3.

Verse 31. God's characteristics include perfection, reliability, and trustworthiness. This was quite a contrast to the people that surrounded David. He was able to recognize that God's ways are always best. And he had God's word (his promises) for every aspect of his life.

Verse 32. David emphasized how very special God Jehovah is. There is no other like him. The prophet Isaiah wrote similar words about God (Isaiah 44:6, 8).

Verse 33. God's attributes could also be David's! One of God's promises was that David could be like Him. The word "excellence" refers to God's spotless integrity. God's power could also be dominant in David's life.

Verse 34. God was responsible for placing David in his exalted position as king. The metaphor of a female deer describes the ability to be light-footed and sure-footed as it traverses mountainous terrain. God would protect him from slipping and falling during life's challenges.

Verse 35. It was God, among others, who taught David the ways of war. He continued to use him to establish the Davidic kingdom. However, David wrote a contrasting description of God in Psalm 46:9; that he is also a God whose desire is for universal peace.

Verse 36. It was God who taught David humility, as expressed in the form of gentleness. David's worship experience on the Mount of Olives demonstrated a servant heart that surely characterized his greatness as king.

Verse 37. Who was it but God, who ensured that David's path to success and victory would be secure?

Personal application: How are God's attributes reflected in your life?

David's Resound (2 Samuel 22:47–51)

David further exclaimed his praise to God for his mighty attributes of salvation that afforded him protection. The word salvation in this text means deliverance and safety.

Verse 47. The "Rock of my salvation", also referenced in Psalm 89:26, speaks of David's intimate relationship with a living and present deity. A type of communal bond had always existed between God and David and it would continue to be solid as a rock.

Verse 48. David no doubt remembered God's hand of vengeance on Nabal, who lost his life because of his decision to withhold food and provisions for David and his men (1 Samuel 25:39). David now praised God for his intervention of justice.

Verse 49. David had often encountered men who could be described as violent. A more complete description of violent men is found in Psalm 140:1–5. They are characterized by evil scheming, warfare, gossiping, slander, wickedness, interest to cause David to fail, and proud hearts. The fact that God lifted up or exalted David over his enemies indicates an action of heaving. God physically caused this to happen, as in the account of David's invasion of Jerusalem and the scoffing Jebusites. David and his men accomplished what was thought to be the impossible, and scaled a fourteen-yard vertical shaft in the Warren tunnel system that provided water to the city (2 Samuel 5:7–8).

Verse 50. David once again offered his thanks and praise to the God of the Gentiles or nations; a statement of inclusivity. While God had avenged enemy nations for hundreds of years, David knew him to care for and be accessible to all people.

Verse 51. More personally, David closes with a statement that God has mercifully extended his salvation to him and his descendants. It is an everlasting covenant that God had established with David (2 Samuel 7:12–13).

In summary of the victorious prayer that David offered to God, we have realized how personal God was to him. David had resources available to him which were God-given. David had the ability to recognize and appreciate God's power in his creation. David experienced God's intervention in his life through many troubling times. And David's response was to turn to God, his source of salvation. David was able to place God at the center of his life by identifying God's attributes; all of which he could attain. Finally, David resounded with a joyous and personal thanksgiving to God that extended far beyond victories of the past. He knew that because of God's covenant with him, a future hope existed for the nation of Israel.

David's Victory Prayer
Chapter 16
References

2 Samuel 22

Psalm 18

Deuteronomy 32:4 "The Rock! His work is perfect, for all His ways are just; a God of faithfulness and without injustice, righteous and upright is He."

1 Samuel 23:25, 24:2 "When Saul and his men went to seek him, they told David, and he came down to the rock and stayed in the wilderness of Maon. Then Saul took three thousand chosen men from all Israel and went to seek David and his men in front of the Rocks of the Wild Goats."

1 Samuel 17:41, 45 "Then the Philistine came on and approached David, with the shield-bearer in front of him. Then David said to the Philistine, 'You come to me with a sword, a spear, and a javelin, but I come to you in the name of the LORD of hosts, the God of the armies of Israel, whom you have taunted.'"

2 Samuel 5:19 "Then David inquired of the LORD, saying, 'Shall I go up against the Philistines? Will You give them into my hand?' And the LORD said to David, 'Go up, for I will certainly give the Philistines into your hand.'"

1 Samuel 26:12 "So David took the spear and the jug of water from beside Saul's head, and they went away, but no one saw or knew it, nor did any awake, for they were all asleep, because a sound sleep from the LORD had fallen on them."

Psalm 116:3 "The cords of death encompassed me and the terrors of Sheol came upon me; I found distress and sorrow."

1 Samuel 15:10–11 "Then the word of the LORD came to Samuel, saying, 'I regret that I have made Saul king, for he has turned back from following Me and has not carried out My commands.' And Samuel was distressed and cried out to the LORD all night."

2 Samuel 2:17 "That day the battle was very severe, and Abner and the men of Israel were beaten before the servants of David."

2 Samuel 3:1 "Now there was a long war between the house of Saul and the house of David; and David grew steadily stronger, but the house of Saul grew weaker continually."

2 Samuel 8:5 "When the Arameans of Damascus came to help Hadadezer, king of Zobah, David killed 22,000 Arameans."

2 Samuel 8:13 "So David made a name for himself when he returned from killing 18,000 Arameans in the Valley of Salt."

1 Samuel 22:1–2 "So David departed from there and escaped to the cave of Adullam; and when his brothers and all his father's household heard of it, they went down there to him. Everyone who was in distress, and everyone who was in debt, and

everyone who was discontented gathered to him; and he became captain over them. Now there were about four hundred men with him."

Psalm 138:3 "On the day I called, You answered me; You made me bold with strength in my soul."

Isaiah 44:6, 8 "Thus says the Lord, the King of Israel and his Redeemer, the Lord of hosts: 'I am the first and I am the last, and there is no God besides Me. Do not tremble and do not be afraid; have I not long since announced it to you and declared it? And you are My witnesses. Is there any God besides Me, or is there any other Rock? I know of none.'"

Psalm 46:9 "He makes wars to cease to the end of the earth; He breaks the bow and cuts the spear in two; He burns the chariots with fire."

Psalm 89:26 "He will cry to Me, 'You are my Father, my God, and the rock of my salvation.'"

1 Samuel 25:39 "When David heard that Nabal was dead, he said, 'Blessed be the Lord, who has pleaded the cause of my reproach from the hand of Nabal and has kept back His servant from evil. The Lord has also returned the evildoing of Nabal on his own head.'"

Psalm 140:1–5 "Rescue me, O Lord, from evil men; preserve me from violent men who devise evil things in their hearts; they continually stir up wars. They sharpen their tongues as a serpent; poison of a viper is under their lips. Keep me, O lord, from the hands of the wicked; preserve me from violent men who have purposed to trip up my feet. The proud have hidden a trap for me, and cords; they have spread a net by the wayside; they have set snares for me."

2 Samuel 5:7–8 "Nevertheless, David captured the stronghold of Zion, that is the city of David. David said on that day, 'Whoever would strike the Jebusites, let him reach the lame and the blind, who are hated by David's soul, through the water tunnel.'"

2 Samuel 7:12–13 "When your days are complete and you lie down with your fathers, I will raise up your descendant after you, who will come forth from you, and I will establish his kingdom. He shall build a house for My name, and I will establish the throne of his kingdom forever."

17

David: God's Plan or Man's Plan?

I will instruct you and teach you in the way which you should go; I will counsel you with My eye upon you.

—Psalm 32:8

God had a perfect plan for David's life, as he does for our lives. We know that his ways, including his plans for us are always best (Jeremiah 29:11–14). God's plan was to give his people, Israel, hope and a future, expecting that they would turn to him. David had personally experienced the hope that accompanies God's plan (Psalm 119:49). Can we interpret this to mean that David always followed that plan? No, as we will learn in this study of David's mishandling of the census.

The Contentious Census (1 Samuel 24:1–9)

Toward the end of David's reign, where this account is placed, David prepared for his son, Solomon, to succeed him. The census could have been a logical rendering of this preparation. But more relevant is that an adversary caused David to take inventory of his military might. The adversary referred to in the text is Satan. As a result of allowing Satan to tempt him, David was compelled to assess the number of men in his army. The Hebrew definition of the action that Satan took was a pricking or a stimulation or a seduction that David felt he could not resist. He may have even known at the time, that this encouragement was not of the Lord. In God's eyes, David had sinned, revealing his pride. But there was another reason why David's action was sinful (Exodus 30:12). The law of the Torah required each man to make an offering for atonement in association with the census. This was intended to affirm their dedication to the Lord and to financially support the government services of that day. There is no indication that the atonement offering was conducted during David's census.

The Lord became angry against Israel. He was deeply disappointed with both the king and the people. His anger is described in the Hebrew as a flaring of nostrils. This was not some mild reaction from God. It was a holy response to the sinfulness of man. Because God's wrath is holy, it is necessary for us to trust that his actions and even his anger were justified.

The plan for a census was met with resistance and it came from none other than David's military commander, Joab. Joab had been reinstated to this position. He now questioned David's interest in taking the census, even stating that God had the ability to multiply the troops necessary for military might. But David prevailed and Joab set out to lead the expedition. It was an impressive effort, as every square mile in Israel and Judah were covered; or so David thought. First Chronicles 21:6 indicates that Joab did not completely follow through on David's order, for he purposefully omitted the tribes of Levi and Benjamin. Why these two tribes? The Levites, because of their role as priests, would have been exempt from a count used for combatant purposes. The tribe of Benjamin was thought to be "the least of the tribes" (Judges 21:1–23). Because we know that David's decision to conduct the census displeased Joab, he may not have valued the necessity of providing a thorough report. The census was completed in nine months and twenty days, and it verified that there were eight hundred thousand people (translated warriors) in Israel and five hundred thousand in Judah. Following the census, David reckoned that he had sinned.

David's Reckoning (2 Samuel 24:10)

David, whose heart was typically sensitive toward God, became guilt-stricken. He went to the Lord and made four acknowledgments.

- "I am your servant." David recognized his lowly position in comparison to God's sovereignty (Psalm 34:22).
- "I have behaved foolishly." This statement implies both intellectual and moral failure (Psalm 69:5).
- "My actions have been sinful." Sin had separated David from God and he deserved God's punishment (Psalm 51:3–4).
- "Remove this sin from me." David brought a request of forgiveness to God (Psalm 39:8).

David's reckoning can be a model prayer for us. As we approach God, we must recognize that our sin produces guilt. Our guilt should shame us, differentiating our inconsistencies from God's reliability. The lack of fellowship with him should capture our attention and cause us to be concerned. God is pleased with a heart that owns up to failures and turns away from that which causes us to stumble. Finally, our repentance should include the very important request for his forgiveness. When we take these steps, we avoid God's judgment and are able to allow his plan for our lives to evolve. His plan, not our plan, is best!

God's Judgment (2 Samuel 24:11–17)

During the night, God had been at work. His prophet, Gad, a contemporary of the prophet Nathan, arose and came to David with a message. God presented three choices of punishment for David.

- Seven years of famine for David and Israel
- Three months of persecution from enemy peoples with Israel on the defense
- Three days of plague

The famine, the sword, and the plague would certainly result in death for many. David later described God's judgment as "a great deep" (Psalm 36:6). The word picture of this judgment is a vast amount of water that totally engulfs. The pain, death, and grief that would follow would cause Israel to feel like they were swallowed up. David's response to God's punishment was one of great emotional distress. He understood God's judgment, but he could not appreciate man's judgment of him, as in the persecution from enemies. The Lord accepted David's sentiment and sent the three-day plague. This was probably the lesser of the three judgments because of the short endurance of time. However, the plague was devastating, causing seventy thousand deaths. Just as the angel of the Lord, who stood on Mount Moriah, was about to bring destruction upon Jerusalem, God intervened. Angels were often God's agents of judgment (Psalm 35:5–6). In our account, God allowed David to see the angel strike Israel. And as a good shepherd cares for his sheep, David, the shepherd-king, had compassion for his people. He and his family had not yet personally experienced the judgement. So, David asked God that he not punish the people, but instead, punish him.

A Sacrifice of Honor (2 Samuel 24:18–25)

Mount Moriah contained a threshing floor that was an ideal spot for David's sacrifice of atonement. A threshing floor was a flat surface; in this case, a ledge that was used for beating the grain husks to separate the chaff from the wheat. This particular threshing floor was owned by a citizen named Araunah. This man was eager to donate the field to David and even offered to provide the sacrificial animal and the wood for the fire. But David took his responsibility to God very seriously. He insisted that the sacrifice be one of honor; one which he had legally paid for. It is likely that he remembered Israel's history of Abraham's commitment to sacrifice Isaac on Mount Moriah (Genesis 22:2). Mount Moriah was a holy place and David recognized that his sacrifice must be above reproach. He paid Araunah fifty shekels for the threshing floor and oxen. First Chronicles 21:25 speaks of a different amount, referring to the entire lot of land surrounding the threshing floor. This, David bought for another six hundred shekels (fifteen pounds of gold). Once David made his purchase, he built an altar, offered the sacrifice, and prayed for forgiveness and for the land. He sought peace with God and peace for his people. And he found peace! In his goodness, the Lord heard David's prayers and withdrew the plague.

An Aging King (1 Kings 1:1–4)

The book of 1 Kings contains documentation of the end of David's reign in 970 BC and all of Solomon's reign from 970–930 BC. David had reached seventy years of age and was failing in health. He was confined to his quarters because of a circulatory disorder. David most likely had difficulty generating body heat. His loyal servants located a lovely young woman who was able to provide nursing care for David. A measure of her duties was to lie next to David in an effort to transfer warmth. Their relationship was limited to his physical care and was not intimate in nature. This way, the young woman could one day marry without breaking the law. And a proposal for her was soon to take place!

The Would-Be King (1 Kings 1:5–31)

David had another son whom we have not yet met. Adonijah was the son of Haggith, David's fifth wife (2 Samuel 3:4). Adonijah was born in Hebron while David's capitol was located there. Given that David was nearing retirement, Adonijah took advantage of his father's confinement and began to promote himself as the next king. He did not consult David and assumed that as the eldest living son, he was entitled to the royal position. What we know of Adonijah's character is that he resembled Absalom in many ways. He was handsome, boastful, spoiled, and used his family position to get what he wanted. His first strategy was to build an impressive entourage of horses, chariots, and fifty running men. This move might have brought suspicion to most fathers, but David appeared not to have questioned Adonijah's hawkish actions. Next, Adonijah obtained approval from a select group of David's closest advisors, including Joab and Abithar, the priest. Joab's fair-weather loyalty to David is further realized in this account. His record of faithful service to David had been accompanied by impetuous and violent behavior. Abithar had been one of David's most faithful supporters. But now both of these men had become infatuated with Adonijah, even when they knew of David's plan for Solomon to succeed the throne. However, others were not easily convinced—namely, Benaiah, Nathan, Shimei, Rei, and David's elite core of warriors; all loyal to his plan for Solomon to become king. Adonijah gave an extravagant feast, whereby his intentions would be announced in hopes that he would gain further support. The location of the feast is described as the Stone of Zaheleth. This steep, rocky hill was located south of Mount Zion, and it overlooked the Valley of Hinnom and the Kidron Valley, which held a large spring called En Rogel. The guests were a selective group that Adonijah felt comfortable with, such as family and supporters. However, certain key persons were missing from the affair—namely, Solomon, Nathan and Benaiah, David's mightiest warrior. Nathan immediately conveyed the information to Bathsheba, warning her that Solomon's life and possibly her life was in danger. Bathsheba had access to David, who would grant her every wish. Her message to David was well stated. She said:

- "You gave me your word that Solomon would reign after you."
- "Adonijah has, unbeknownst to you, become king."
- "He has given a celebration feast but has not invited Solomon."
- "All of Israel needs to hear from you as to who should be king."
- "After you are gone, Solomon and I will be treated as criminals!"

Meanwhile, Nathan grew impatient and just then gained entry to see the king. He paid his respect by bowing to the floor, and then sought confirmation as to whether David had truly crowned Adonijah king. Nathan questioned David as to why would he make such an important decision without informing him. Nathan's verbalization further substantiated Bathsheba's report. However, David dismissed him and requested Bathsheba's presence again because, as Solomon's mother, she had a lot to lose. David reaffirmed with an oath that Solomon would indeed, become king. In a remarkable statement of faith, he acknowledged the Lord's role in his life. David invoked a certainty of his promise, stating that his words were as reliable as God's very existence. A very relieved and thankful Bathsheba then expressed her desire that God would bless David by giving him many more years of life. Her words indicated that David had acted righteously and deserved God's blessings. God's plan was being fulfilled!

God's King (1 Kings 1:32–53)

David took immediate action to anoint Solomon as king. He summoned his faithful men—Zadok, Nathan, and Benaniah—to him and gave them instructions.

They were to place Solomon on David's mule and deliver him to the spring of Gihon, just outside the city wall. Zadok and Nathan, the men of God, were to anoint Solomon as king over all of Israel, blow the rams horn (schofar), and call, "Long live King Solomon!" Solomon's anointing symbolized God's presence with his chosen leader. The final instruction from David was that Solomon sit on the throne of the kingdom. So, as David had directed, his plans were carried out and Solomon became king. Benaiah, David's military captain, wholeheartedly agreed with the proceedings and then prayed to God that he be with Solomon and bless his kingly reign far more than David had been blessed. One might think, a good ending to a long story!

But in another Jerusalem neighborhood, only one half mile away, the celebrating turned to concern and then fear. It was Joab who first heard the horn and then inquired the reason for the noise in the city. And just then, a messenger arrived with news of the coronation. It was Jonathan, Abiathar's son, who explained that the whole city was rejoicing over their new king. At that moment, the guests became alarmed and fearful, and, one by one, all of Adonijah's guests quickly left the feast. This type of fear was so impactful that all who were present physically trembled. Adonijah, who was perhaps the most fearful, had good reason; for he would be considered a traitor in the new administration. The primary meaning of the fear that Adonijah felt is "to cut". He was suddenly cut out of the consideration to assume the throne. So, the emotion he felt was one of dismissal or abandonment. Adonijah found refuge at the tabernacle and specifically, the brazen alter horns. The horns were extensions of the bronze altar that contained the sacrifice. These horns held historical significance. God had given specific instructions for the original construction of the altar (Exodus 27:2). The altar was considered to be a place of sanctuary; and grasping the horns of the altar meant a person could find refuge there. David also referred to the horns of the altar in Psalm 118:27. It is God we should run to and it is he whom we will answer to. Adonijah's insincere attempt to get God's attention was ineffective. The text does not indicate that Adonijah called out to God for help, and he did not offer a sacrifice in repentance for his sin. Neither did Adonijah make his plea to Solomon, for he was fearful of him. So, we see that Solomon's first decision as king was a difficult one. What does one do with a brother who had attempted a takeover as king and who would possibly continue to be a threat to his kingship? Adonijah's future depended on whether he could be submissive to Solomon's rule, as is referred to in verse 51, or whether he be found a traitor in verse 52. Solomon asserted his authority with Adonijah, then abruptly dismissed him.

God's plan contrasted with man's plan causes us to be aware of God's greatness in comparison to man's inadequacy. David asked the question, "What is man, that you take knowledge of him?" (Psalm 144:3). God is keenly aware of our every thought, intention, and action. David wanted God's plan to materialize in every aspect of his life (Psalm 143:8). If viewed in this way, man's plan must become God's plan.

Personal Applications

1. Why does God allow Satan to tempt us? (2 Corinthians 12:7–10). God allows Satan certain liberties for the purpose of disciplining or refining us. It is never God's intent or plan to allow affliction to consume us, but in his eternal wisdom, he brings understanding, acceptance and strength to our minds so that we can better follow his plan and resist Satan.

2. Our impression might be that David went to extreme measures to please God. Why is this important? (Proverbs 16:7). Are there some who will not be able to please God? (Romans 8:8; Hebrews 11:6). We learn from these verses that faith is a prerequisite for pleasing God. And Jesus is the ultimate role model who brings God pleasure (John 8:29).

3. How do we find God's plan for us? We may never know all that he aspires for us, but there is one thing that we can be certain of. That he desires a relationship with us. Our lives should be centered on this relationship. When we walk with him, our day to day interests coincide with his.

4. What is God's plan for your life and is that plan becoming a reality for you?

David: God's Plan or Man's Plan?
Chapter 17
References

Jeremiah 29:11–14 "'For I know the plans that I have for you,' declares the LORD. 'Plans for welfare and not for calamity to give you a future and a hope. Then you will call upon Me and come and pray to Me, and I will listen to you. You will seek Me and find Me when you search for Me with all your heart. I will be found by you,' declares the LORD."

Psalm 119:49 "Remember the word to Your servant, in which You have made me hope"

1 Samuel 24:1–9

Exodus 30:12 "When you take a census of the sons of Israel to number them, then each one of them shall give a ransom for himself to the LORD, when you number them, so that there will be no plague among them when you number them."

1 Chronicles 21:6 "But he did not number Levi and Benjamin among them, for the king's command was abhorrent to Joab" ().

Judges 21:1–23

2 Samuel 24:10 "Now David's heart troubled him after he had numbered the people. So David said to the LORD, "I have sinned greatly in what I have done. But now, O LORD, please take away the iniquity of Your servant, for I have acted very foolishly."

Psalm 34:22 "The LORD redeems the soul of His servants, and none of those who take refuge in Him will be condemned."

Psalm 69:5 "O God, it is You who knows my folly, and my wrongs are not hidden from You."

Psalm 51:3–4 "For I know my transgressions, and my sin is ever before me. Against You, You only, I have sinned and done what is evil in Your sight, so that You are justified when You speak and blameless when You judge."

Psalm 39:8 "Deliver me from all my transgressions; make me not the reproach of the foolish."

2 Samuel 24:11–17

Psalm 36:6 "Your righteousness is like the mountains of God; Your judgments are like a great deep."

Psalm 35:5–6 "Let them be like chaff before the wind, with the angel of the LORD driving them on. Let their way be dark and slippery, with the angel of the LORD pursuing them."

2 Samuel 24:18–25

Genesis 22:20 "He said, 'Take now your son, your only son, whom you love, Isaac, and go to the land of Moriah, and offer him there as a burnt offering on one of the mountains of which I will tell you.'"

1 Chronicles 21:25 "So David gave Ornan 600 shekels of gold by weight for the site."

1 Kings 1:1–4

1 Kings 1:5–31

"And the fourth, Adonijah the son of Haggith; and the fifth, Shephatiah the son of Abital" (2 Samuel 3:4).

1 Kings 1:32–53

Exodus 27:2 "You shall make its horns on its four corners; its horns shall be of one piece with it, and you shall overlay it with bronze."

Psalm 118:27 "The LORD is God, and He has given us light; bind the festival sacrifice with cords to the horns of the altar."

1 Kings 1:51–52 "Now it was told Solomon, saying, "Behold, Adonijah is afraid of King Solomon, for behold, he has taken hold of the horns of the altar, saying, 'Let King Solomon swear to me today that he will not put his servant to death with the sword.' Solomon said, 'If he is a worthy man, not one of his hairs will fall to the ground; but if wickedness is found in him, he will die.'"

Psalm 144:3 "O LORD, what is man, that You take knowledge of him? Or the son of man, that You think of him?"

Psalm 143:8 "Let me hear Your lovingkindness in the morning; for I trust in You; teach me the way in which I should walk; for to You I lift up my soul."

2 Corinthians 12:7–10 "Because of the surpassing greatness of the revelations, for this reason, to keep me from exalting myself, there was given me a thorn in the flesh, a messenger of Satan to torment me—to keep me from exalting myself! Concerning this I implored the LORD three times that it might leave me. And He has said to me, 'My grace is sufficient for you, for power is perfected in weakness.' Most gladly, therefore, I will rather boast about my weaknesses, so that the power of Christ may dwell in me. Therefore, I am well content with weaknesses, with insults, with distresses, with persecutions, with difficulties, for Christ's sake; for when I am weak, then I am strong."

Proverbs 16:7 "When a man's ways are pleasing to the LORD, He makes even his enemies to be at peace with him."

Romans 8:8 "And those who are in the flesh cannot please God."

Hebrews 11:6 "And without faith it is impossible to please Him, for he who comes to God must believe that He is and that He is a rewarder of those who seek Him."

John 8:29 "And He who sent Me is with Me; He has not left Me alone, for I always do the things that are pleasing to Him."

18

The Way of All the Earth

For the king trusts in the LORD, and through the lovingkindness of
the Most High he will not be shaken.

—Psalm 21:7

The phrase "the way of all the earth" was used by David, referring to his imminent death (1 Kings 1:1–2). He had lived a long, satisfying, and successful life. His last mission was to admonish his son and successor, Solomon. This marked a transition of authority and a new era of leadership, even though David and Solomon probably shared the throne in these last years. The charge to Solomon began with an emphasis that Solomon be strong and prove himself as a man. David knew that the years ahead would not be easy for Solomon. His advice was to seize the opportunity and not be hesitant with his approach to leadership. It is not surprising that David was most attentive to Solomon's relationship with God. He had specific advice to him on this matter.

Solomon's Commission (1 Kings 1:3–4)

- That Solomon keep the charge of the Lord his God. This means that Solomon had a specific job to do for God and that God would be faithful in his direction for that job.
- That Solomon walk in God's ways. This would require him to be motivated; to intentionally communicate with God for guidance.
- That Solomon keep the Lord's rules and commandments of the Torah. Complete obedience would be the standard God required.
- That Solomon strive to be successful in every venture he pursued.
- That Solomon's future would be determined by wise living and his total reliance on God.

- That God's promises would be fulfilled regarding David's descendants.

Solomon Takes Charge

Solomon's success would require that he take disciplinary action toward David's enemies and those who might threaten his sovereignty.

1.   Joab, David's military commander (1 Kings 2:26–35)
     Joab was the first person that David recommended be eliminated. He had been responsible for mortally wounding Absalom and for the deaths of two innocent commanders, Abner and Amasa. His violent nature led to a condemnation of guilt. This means that Joab lived with a sense of guilt that was evident to those who knew him ("his belt and sandals were covered with blood"). Predictably, when Jaob heard that he would be held account-able to Solomon for his crimes, he imitated Adonijah. He went to the tabernacle and took hold of the horns of the altar, desperate that this could save him. Joab was found there by Benaiah. Benaiah had been assigned to find Joab and kill him. But Joab refused to leave the altar. In this case, Benaiah needed Solomon's special permission to strike him where he was in the tabernacle. After consulting with Solomon, he followed orders by strik-ing and killing Joab. As a reward, Benaiah was promoted to Joab's position as commander of the army. Joab went the way of all the earth.
2.   Adonijah, David's son (1 Kings 1:5–6, 28–34; 1 Kings 2:13–25)
     Adonijah was still up to his old tricks. He called on Bathsheba. Because she was skeptical of his visit, Bathsheba needed reassurance of her safety. Adonijah confirmed that he had, indeed, come in peace. His rheto-ric included the following.

- He still believed the kingdom belonged to him.
- He still believed that Israel wanted him for her king.
- He believed the kingdom had been unfairly taken from him.
- He believed that Solomon only gained the throne because of God; not because of his right as determined by David.

Adonijah's alarming message soon expanded into a more pointed con-versation. He wanted Abishag, the Shunamite, for his wife. There was a problem with this. For, to marry a woman from David's household would constitute a claim to the throne. Adonijah, probably feeling that he had been treated unfairly, used his annihilation as an excuse to remain a contender for the crown. Solomon, who had great respect for his mother, Bathsheba, gave her a place of honor at his right hand. She brought Adonijah's appeal to Solomon. But it seems that Adonijah's request was her request as well, for she petitioned to Solomon on his behalf. In previous situations like this, Solomon and David would have granted her every desire. But Solomon, in his wisdom, was keen to Adonijah's motive. He responded to Bathsheba with:

- Why would you advocate for Adonijah in this way?
- Since he is the oldest, just recommend that he take the kingdom.
- While you are at it, just hand over power to Abiathar and Joab, Adonijah's accomplices.
- Remember that my father, and God, himself, have placed me in my position as king.

With that, Solomon ordered that Adonijah be put to death. Solomon handily brought an end to the greatest threat of his new career. And Adonijah now went the way of all the earth.

3. Abiathar, high priest in David's administration (1 Kings 2:26–35)
    Abiathar was another opponent that Solomon would need to hold accountable. His role as priest had been inconsistent, according to God's commands. Many years earlier, in another account, God had instructed Eli, the priest, regarding his desire for him. The priesthood was both a duty and a privilege (1 Samuel 2:35). God desired that his priests be faithful. The requirement of faithfulness was that Abiathar should have fostered God's ways in all of his priestly practices. Hebrews 2:17 ascribes the quality of faithfulness to Jesus, our high priest. The word *faithful* means "to be trustworthy". Abiathar's career as David's godly and trustworthy priest had spanned many decades, beginning with his escape from Saul's murder of the eighty-five priests (1 Samuel 22:20–21). However, because Abiathar had now unwisely transferred his allegiance from David (including Solomon) to Adonijah, his faithfulness to God's work ended. This was viewed as a breech in service and Solomon then took the necessary action to discipline Abiathar. It is expected that Abiathar should be removed from service because of God's prophecy that Eli's line of priests, which included Abiathar, would be reduced in strength (1 Samuel 2:31). Solomon recognized Abiathar's role in carrying the ark of the covenant and for his loyalty to David. But Solomon more deeply valued God's direction in this difficult decision. So he removed him from his position and exiled him to his home in Anahoth. Thus ends the priestly line of Eli. God promised a future priest

who would be firmly established, fulfill his will, and be reliably faithful (1 Samuel 2:35).

Who would this faithful priest be? David knew of a coming person who would fulfill the role of both priest and king (Psalm 110:4). This would be someone who would hold the offices forever, as in comparison to the temporary dual role that Melchizedek occupied as an earthly king and priest. It was none other than Jesus Christ! (Hebrews 5:9–10 and 6:19–20). You see, there was need for a new priesthood; one that did not rely on man's performance (Hebrews 7:11–16 and 7:26–8:1). This new priesthood was consummated with the coming of Christ. It can be described in the following terms.

- It is a perfect priesthood; unlike the imperfect, weak Levitical priesthood which was plagued with disobedience to God's laws.
- A change in the priesthood meant a change in the legal system, upon which the Levitical priesthood was based.
- The new priesthood would arise from a different tribe, the tribe of Judah, which had no obligation to law giving, as the Levites had.
- The new and perfect high priest would be unperishable and everlasting.
- The new high priest would completely facilitate our intercession with God.
- The new high priest would be without sin; therefore qualified to represent us before God.
- The new high priest replaced the old sacrificial system with his one-time personal sacrifice.
- The perfect Son of God, Jesus Christ, has perfected the priesthood and it will last forever.
- Our great high priest, Jesus Christ, is now seated at God's right hand in heaven.
- The perfect priesthood of Jesus Christ equates to a profound solution for mankind's dilemma of sin.

  o It is a solution of simplicity; Jesus accomplished the work; our only action is faith in him.
  o It is a solution of salvation; we can be saved from ourselves.
  o It is a solution of eternal proportions.
  o It is a solution of promise and hope.

4. Shimei, an unpredictable acquaintance of David (1 Kings 2:36–46)

The next person that David advised Solomon to judge was Shimei. Shimei was the man who had cursed and stoned David during his exile while in route to Mahanaim. He had since displayed loyalty to David, but for Solomon, trusting him did not come easily. Solomon placed a confinement on him so that he could not leave his home in Jerusalem. The punishment of leaving would be certain death. Even though Shimei could not be trusted, Solomon gave him one last chance. Many years earlier, David had reluctantly promised to spare Shimei's life because of his repentance (2 Samuel 19:20, 23). Shimei heeded Solomon's warning for the next three years. But, one day, two of his slaves ran away to the Philistine city of Gath. And Shimei left the city of Jerusalem to capture and bring them home. Solomon immediately addressed Shimei's disregard for his authority.

- Solomon reminded Shimei that he made an oath to the Lord that he would not leave Jerusalem.
- Solomon reminded Shimei that the punishment would be death.
- Solomon reminded Shimei that he had agreed with the arrangement.
- Solomon inquired as to why Shimei did not keep the agreement.
- Solomon reminded Shimei of his past behavior towards David and how he had been a threat to the monarchy.
- Solomon emphasized that as king, he was commissioned to rule with God's authority.
- Solomon showed great respect for the continuing and eternal throne of David.

Shimei died when he was struck down by Benaniah and he went the way of all the earth. The culmination of Solomon's decisions was that his kingdom had been firmly established by the time he was coronated (1 Samuel 2:46). David's wisdom had been passed on to Solomon. The time came when David breathed his last and went the way of all the earth. He was buried in Jerusalem, where his ancestors were entombed. David was seventy years old when he died. No doubt, the prayer in his heart was the inscribed words of Psalm 100:4. "Enter into His gates with thanksgiving and into His courts with praise, be thankful to Him, and bless His name." David sang as he entered the gates of heaven and God's temple. And he died as he had lived; called, chosen, and faithful (Revelation 17:14).

Personal Applications

1. Capital punishment was a method Solomon used to secure safety for his future as king. Previous studies from the Old Testament supported the use of the death penalty. Does the Bible teach that this is appropriate action for today? We must remember that God instituted capital punishment (Genesis 9:6). We are also encouraged to respect the laws of the government that would enforce capital punishment. For it is God who has issued it as the necessary authority (Romans 13:1).

2. Since Jesus Christ is our high priest, does this eliminate the role of earthly priests or even pastors and ministers? No. The role of the minister or priest is to shepherd the flock, 1 Peter 5:2 but not to be an intercessor on our behalf. We can directly access God through Jesus Christ (Romans 8:34).

3. Who do you run to in time of trouble? It may not be the horns of the altar, but, are you drawn to the Lord in times like this? (Psalm 27:5)

4. May the Lord of lords and King of kings, who called and chose us, find us faithful as he found David. What is your record of faithfulness to him?

The Way of All the Earth
Chapter 18
References

1 Kings 1:1–2 "As David's time to die drew near, he charged Solomon his son, saying, 'I am going the way of all the earth. Be strong, therefore, and show yourself a man.'"

1 Kings 1:3–4 "Keep the charge of the LORD your God, to walk in His ways, to keep His statutes, His commandments, His ordinances, and His testimonies, according to what is written in the Law of Moses, that you may succeed in all that you do and wherever you turn, so that the LORD may carry out His promise which He spoke concerning me, saying, 'If your sons are careful of their way, to walk before Me in truth with all their heart and with all their soul, you shall not lack a man on the throne of Israel.'"

1 Kings 1:5–6, 28–34

1 Kings 2:13–25

1 Kings 2:26–35

1 Samuel 2:35 "But I will raise up for Myself a faithful priest who will do according to what is in My heart and in My soul; and I will build him an enduring house, and he will walk before My anointed always."

Hebrews 2:17 "Therefore, He had to be made like His brethren in all things, so that He might become a merciful and faithful high priest in things pertaining to God, to make propitiation for the sins of the people."

1 Samuel 22:20–21 "But one son of Ahimelech the son of Ahitub, named Abiathar, escaped and fled after David. Abiathar told David that Saul had killed the priests of the LORD."

1 Samuel 2:31 "Behold, the days are coming when I will break your strength and the strength of your father's house so that there will not be an old man in your house."

1 Samuel 2:35 "But I will raise up for Myself a faithful priest who will do according to what is in My heart and in My soul; and I will build him an enduring house, and he will walk before My anointed always."

Psalm 110:4 "The LORD has sworn and will not change His mind, You are a priest forever according to the order of Melchizedek."

Hebrews 5:9–10 and 6:19–20

Hebrews 7:11–16 and 7:26–8:1

1 Kings 2:36–46

2 Samuel 19:20, 23 "For your servant knows that I have sinned; therefore behold, I have come today, the first of all the house of Joseph to go down to meet my

lord the king. The king said to Shimei, 'You shall not die.' Thus the king swore to him."

1 Kings 2:46 "So the king commanded Benaiah the son of Jehoiada, and he went out and fell upon him so that he died. Thus, the kingdom was established in the hands of Solomon."

Psalm 100:4 "Enter His gates with thanksgiving and His courts with praise. Give thanks to Him, bless His name."

Revelation 17:14 "He is Lord of lords and King of kings, and those who are with Him are the called and chosen and faithful."

Genesis 9:6 "Whoever sheds man's blood, by man his blood shall be shed. For in the image of God He made man."

Romans 13:1 "Every person is to be in subjection to the governing authorities. For there is no authority except from God, and those which exist are established by God."

1 Peter 5:2 "Shepherd the flock of God among you, exercising oversight not under compulsion, but voluntarily, according to the will of God; and not for sordid gain, but with eagerness."

Romans 8:34 "Christ Jesus is He who died, yes, rather who was raised, who is at the right hand of God, who also intercedes for us."

Psalm 27:5 "For in the day of trouble He will conceal me in His tabernacle; in the secret place of His tent He will hide me; He will lift me up on a rock."

David's Crowning Glory: The Messiah

"For You meet him with the blessings of good things; You set a crown of fine gold on his head."

— Psalm 21:3

The crowning glory of David's life, according to the book of Psalms, is that he was a predecessor of the Messiah. David received inspiration from God as he wrote and God manifested to David a revelation of himself. This revelation foretold of the Messiah through prophetic typology or symbolism. David's revelations concerning the Messiah point to a future time of fulfillment, called an antitype. Evidence of the fulfillment would be recorded and is found in the New Testament. As the Messiah's earthly and eternal reign is culminated, he will be blessed with a victorious crown worthy of a heavenly king.

Messiah: The Righteous Seed

The Messiah, as described in Rabbinical Judaism, is called Messiah Ben David, or the son of David. David knew that through his seed, his dynasty would reign forever. Many kings from his linage would rule Israel; but most significant would be a heavenly kingdom where Messiah would rule. Psalm 89 further details the righteous seed that would arise as a result of covenantal promises. These were promises from God that David knew he could rely on and trust in. He knew that God's words were absolute. Psalm 132:11 Psalm 89:29 states that the seed of David would extend to an eternal kingdom. Righteousness would dominate (verse 14). The covenant that would stand forever would be as faithful as the creation which promises a rising sun (verse 36–37). The fulfillment of David's seed is Jesus Christ. Romans 1:2–4 One day following His resurrection, Jesus opened the scriptures to His disciples. Luke 24:44 His encouragement to them was that the Messianic writings of the Psalms would be fulfilled. In fact, Psalm 40:7 states that one must come, a future presentation, of which it is foretold in the scriptures. Matthew's genealogy also traces the linage of Christ back to King David. Matthew 1:1 David spoke of a branch of righteousness who would originate from his seed. Who was this descendent of David's who would come? It would be a royal branch of righteousness, the Messiah. Jeremiah 23:5–6.

Messiah: Son of God

The coming Messiah was portrayed in the Old Testament as the begotten Son of God (Psalm 2:7). We should not misinterpret the meaning of "begotten", as a father bearing a son; but it is more in the sense of a relationship. The descriptive words in this verse state that God's Son is the one and only Son. Their relationship is as a father and a son. And as in human relationships, the father delegates authority to his son and the son represents him. Further clarification is provided in 1 John 1:1–3. God the Father and God the Son have existed as one from the beginning of time. Mary, the mother of Jesus, received a message from an angel (Luke 1:31–33). Her son would be called Jesus; He would be great; he would rule the nation of Israel as her king; His kingdom would never end; and most importantly, his identity would be Son of the highest, or Son of God. As an adult, Jesus received public approval from God as He was being baptized by John the Baptist. An audible voice from heaven proclaimed Jesus the son of God, whom He pleased (Matthew 3:16–17). David's royal line also produced a Messiah who would be king of the Jews.

Messiah: King

David's words prepared for the coming king. This king would be referred to as the king of glory (Psalm 24:7–10). The text describes a celebration of the king of glory who will bring deliverance. The proclamation of Jesus as king was also voiced in Jerusalem by the crowds who welcomed him as their king (John 12:12–13). At times, the Messiah is referred to as King David, or the greater David, because the Messiah would come from King David (Mark 10:47). At the end of time, the Messiah will be identified as a King who rules over all kings and a Lord of all lords (Revelations 19:16). We know that David will reign with Jesus in the Millennium, as will all saints (Daniel 7:27).

Messiah: Lord

The one who would come, the Messiah, was David's Lord (Psalm 118:26). A more complete description of David's Lord is found in Psalm 110:1. David stated that "the Lord" (Hebrew = Jehovah) "said to my Lord" (Hebrew = Adoni). David's lord was Adoni, or Jesus. There is a New Testament reference to this verse in Matthew 22:41–45. Jesus quoted God's words and asked the question, "How could David simultaneously call the coming Messiah his son and his lord?" Jesus's point was that the Messiah was much more than a descendant to David. He emphasized that the Messiah was David's supreme authority. This is important, because humans place great value on family heritage. However, Jesus taught that all humanity is subject to his lordship. David's lord is given a place at the right hand of God (Yahweh). This person is the Messiah, or Jesus Christ, who is the king over all the earth, unlike King David. Revelation 3:21 indicates that this position at God's right hand has been filled; Father and Son sit and reign together (Psalm 80:17 Acts 5:31). Thus, the Son of Man is a Messianic title referring to the God-man, Jesus Christ.

Messiah: The Creator

David acknowledged his Messiah, Jesus, as the creator. Genesis 1:1 says that God created the world. The Hebrew for the word God is pleural, meaning more than one God. Later, the inspired words in Colossians 1:16 give better clarification that God created the world through Jesus Christ. Christ, the Son of God, is the exact representation of God the Father. Christ, then, is God's agent of creation (Hebrews 1:1–3; Psalm 8:5–9). He rules over God's works and holds authority over all things (Hebrews 2:5–8).

Messiah: Suffering Christ

A much different reception awaited the Messiah, as he made appearances in the holy land of Israel. Psalm 22 vividly expresses the suffering that Jesus endured.

- Messiah would cry out to God; be forsaken by God. Verses 1–2 (Mark 15:34; Matthew 26:38–39).
- Messiah was despised and rejected by his own people. Verse 6 (Luke 23:21)
- Messiah was made a mockery. Verse 7 (Matthew 27:39)
- Messiah was challenged by men to ask God to deliver him. Verse 8 (Matthew 27:41–43)

- Messiah would be abandoned by his own followers and the disciples. Verse 11 (Mark 14:50)
- Messiah would experience loss of blood. Verse 14a (John 19:34)
- Messiah would experience thirst as he died. Verse 15a (John 19:28)
- Messiah's onlookers at his death would be identified as both Jews and Gentiles. Verse 16 (Matthew 27:41–43)
- Messiah's hands and feet would be pierced. Verse 16 (John 20:25)
- Messiah would be a spectacle. Verse 17 (Luke 23:35)
- Messiah's garments would be bartered. Verse 18 (John 19:23–24)

There are still other prophetic psalms that describe the Messiah's persecution.

- Messiah would be falsely accused. Psalm 35:11 (Mark 14:55–59)
- Messiah would be hated unjustly. Psalm 35:19 (John 15:24–25)
- Messiah would not rebuke his accusers. Psalm 38:13–14 (Matthew 26:62–63)
- Messiah would be betrayed by one of his disciples. Psalm 41:9 (Mark 14:17–18)
- Messiah would be rejected and hated. Psalm 64:4 (Luke 23:13–22)
- Messiah would be condemned for God's sake. Psalm 69:7 (Matthew 26:65–67)
- Messiah would be rejected by his brothers and his own people. Psalm 69:8 (John 1:11)
- Messiah would be offered vinegar while dying. Psalm 69:21 (Matthew 27:34)
- Messiah would give up his spirit. Psalm 31:5 (Luke 23:46)
- Messiah would pay the ultimate sacrifice for mankind. Psalm 40:6–8 (Hebrews 10:10–13)
- M essiah would forgive His enemies. Psalm 86:5 (Luke 23:34)

Messiah: Resurrected

The bodily resurrection of the Messiah from the grave secured his position as the Son of God (Mark 16:6). Jesus Christ overcame the strongest opposition and punishment a man could endure. However, we know that he was not just a man, but his divinity ensured his defeat over death. The bondage of corruption referred to in Romans 8:21 had not conquered him. David wrote of Messiah's resurrection in Psalm 16:9–10. Jesus Christ, the Messiah, would not remain dead for long (Acts 2:23–24).

Messiah: Our Eternal Hope

The announcement of the Messiah to the world by David and other prophets was a foretelling of future events. These prophecies were fulfilled through the seed of David, down through the generations to the birth of Jesus Christ, the God-man. God publicly recognized him as his Son even as Jesus proclaimed his deity to his immediate generation. David's earthly role as king held great authority, but one greater than he would rule as eternal king. God authenticated the Messiah as having been anointed for his kingly position. Messiah had always existed, and in fact, had created the world. The world would not accept him as the Son of God, Lord, anointed king, or creator. When God saw the world's rejection of his begotten Son, it was clear that mankind needed a savior who would make eternal hope possible (Psalm 89:27; Colossians 1:18; Revelations 1:5). As David wrote about the Messiah's enduring quality, he expressed knowledge of the eternal kingdom the Messiah would eventually bring. Psalm 145:13 David knew a futuristic kingdom of heaven would be far superior to any earthly kingdom, causing him to proclaim, "Praise the Lord! Praise the Lord, O my soul! I will praise the Lord as long as I live!" Psalm 146:1–2.

Personal Applications

1. Messiah's ancestry was very important. How should we view the study of genealogy? There are two New Testament references to genealogy—1 Timothy 1:4, Titus 3:9. Why would the Bible frown upon the study of genealogy, when we know there is historical value in its research, which is even documented in scripture? First Timothy speaks of the frequency of speculation and inaccuracies in genealogy. And in comparison, the truths and promises of God, through Jesus Christ, are sure. The Titus 3:9 context describes contentions regarding different genealogies that brought division. The message is that we should not seek after popular trends that would distract us from the depth of study that the Bible offers. David also advises that unity is important (Psalm 133:1).

2. What emotions did you experience when you thought about the suffering Messiah?

3. Have you accepted Jesus Christ as the Messiah, who came as an unassuming man but claimed to be the Son of God? The evidence of proof is overwhelming to the person with an open mind. Consider the Davidic prophecies and invite him to be your lord and king.

David's Crowning Glory: The Messiah
Chapter 19
References

Messiah: The Righteous Seed

Psalm 132:11 "The Lord has sworn to David a truth from which He will not turn back: 'Of the fruit of your body I will set upon your throne.'"

Psalm 89:29 "So I will establish his descendants forever and his throne as the days of heaven."

Psalm 89:36–37 "His descendants shall endure forever and his throne as the sun before Me. It shall be established forever like the moon, and the witness in the sky is faithful."

Romans 1:1–4 "Paul, a bond-servant of Christ Jesus, called *as* an apostle, set apart for the gospel of God, which He promised beforehand through His prophets in the holy Scripture. Concerning His Son, who was born of a descendant of David according to the flesh, who was declared the Son of God with power by the resurrection from the dead, according to the Spirit of holiness, Jesus Christ our Lord."

Luke 24:44 "Now He said to them, 'These are My words which I spoke to you while I was still with you, that all things which are written about Me in the Law of Moses and the Prophets and the Psalms must be fulfilled.'"

Psalm 40:7 "Then I said, "Behold, I come; in the scroll of the book it is written of me."

Matthew 1:1 "The record of the genealogy of Jesus the Messiah, the son of David, the son of Abraham."

Jeremiah 23:5–6 "'Behold, the days are coming,' declares the Lord, 'When I will raise up for David a righteous Branch; and He will reign as king and act wisely and do justice and righteousness in the land. In His days Judah will be saved, and Israel will dwell securely; and this is His name by which He will be called, the Lord our righteousness.'"

Messiah: Son of God

Psalm 2:7 "I will surely tell of the decree of the Lord: He said to Me, 'You are My Son, today I have begotten You."

1 John 1:1–3 "What was from the beginning, what we have heard, what we have seen with our eyes, what we have looked at and touched with our hands, concerning the word of life and the life was manifested, and we have seen and testify and proclaim to you the eternal life, which was with the Father and was manifested to us—what we have seen and heard we proclaim to you also, so that you too

may have fellowship with us; and indeed our fellowship is with the Father, and with His Son Jesus Christ."

Luke 1:31–33 "The angel said to her, 'Do not be afraid, Mary; for you have found favor with God. And behold, you will conceive in your womb and bear a son, and you shall name Him Jesus. He will be great and will be called the Son of the Most High; and the LORD God will give Him the throne of His father David; and He will reign over the house of Jacob forever, and His kingdom will have no end.'"

Matthew 3:16–17 "After being baptized, Jesus came up immediately from the water; and behold, the heavens were opened, and he saw the Spirit of God descending as a dove and lighting on Him, and behold, a voice out of the heavens said, 'This is My beloved Son, in whom I am well-pleased.'"

Messiah: King of Glory

Psalm 24:7–10 "Lift up your heads, O gates, and be lifted up, O ancient doors, that the King of glory may come in. Who is the King of glory? The LORD strong and mighty, the LORD mighty in battle. Lift up your heads, O gates, and lift them up, O ancient doors, that the King of glory may come in! Who is this King of glory? The LORD of hosts, He is the King of glory."

John 12:12–13 "On the next day the large crowd who had come to the feast, when they heard that Jesus was coming to Jerusalem, took the branches of the palm trees and went out to meet Him, and began to shout, 'Hosanna! Blessed is He who comes in the name of the Lord, even the King of Israel.'"

Mark 10:47 "When he heard that it was Jesus the Nazarene, he began to cry out and say, "Jesus, Son of David, have mercy on me!"

Revelations 19:16 "And on His robe and on His thigh, He has a name written, 'KING OF KINGS, AND LORD OF LORDS.'"

Daniel 7:27 "Then the sovereignty, the dominion and the greatness of all the kingdoms under the whole heaven will be given to the people of the saints of the Highest One; His kingdom will be an everlasting kingdom, and all the dominions will serve and obey Him."

Messiah: Lord

Psalm 118:26 "Blessed is the one who comes in the name of the LORD; we have blessed you from the house of the LORD."

Psalm 110:1 "The LORD says to my Lord: 'Sit at My right hand until I make Your enemies a footstool for Your feet.'"

Matthew 22:41–46 "Now while the Pharisees were gathered together, Jesus asked them a question, 'What do you think about the Christ, whose son is He?' They said to Him, 'The son of David.' He said to them, 'Then how does David in the Spirit call Him 'LORD,' saying, 'the LORD said to my LORD, 'SIT AT MY right hand, until I put Your enemies beneath Your feet?' 'If David then calls Him 'LORD,' how is He his son?' No one was able to answer Him a word, nor did anyone dare from that day on to ask Him another question."

Revelations 3:21 "He who overcomes, I will grant to him to sit down with Me on My throne, as I also overcame and sat down with My Father on His throne."

Psalm 80:17 "Let Your hand be upon the man of Your right hand, upon the son of man whom You made strong for Yourself"

Acts 5:31 "He is the one whom God exalted to His right hand as a Prince and a Savior, to grant repentance to Israel, and forgiveness of sins."

Messiah: Creator

Genesis 1:1 "In the beginning God created the heavens and the earth."

Colossians 1:16 "For by Him all things were created, both in the heavens and on earth, visible and invisible, whether thrones or dominions or rulers or authorities—all things have been created through Him and for Him."

Hebrew 1:1–3 "God, after He spoke long ago to the fathers in the prophets in many portions and in many ways, in these last days has spoken to us in His Son, whom He appointed heir of all things, through whom also He made the world. And He is the radiance of His glory and the exact representation of His nature, and upholds all things by the word of His power. When He had made purification of sins, He sat down at the right hand of the Majesty on high."

Psalm 8:5–9 "Yet You have made him a little lower than God, and You crown him with glory and majesty! You make him to rule over the works of Your hands; You have put all things under his feet, all sheep and oxen, and also the beasts of the field, the birds of the heavens and the fish of the sea, whatever passes through the paths of the seas. O LORD, our LORD, how majestic is Your name in all the earth!"

Hebrews 2:5–8 "For He did not subject to angels the world to come, concerning which we are speaking. But one has testified somewhere, saying, 'What is man, that You remember him? Or the Son of Man, that You are concerned about Him? You have made Him for a little while lower than the angels; You have crowned Him with glory and honor, and have appointed Him over the works of Your hands. You have put all things in subjection under His feet. For in subjecting all things to Him, He left nothing that is not subject to him. But now we do not yet see all things subjected to him."

Psalm 22: Suffering Messiah

Verses 1–2 "My God, My God, why have You forsaken Me? Why are You so far from helping Me, and from the words of My groaning. O My God, I cry in the daytime, but You do not hear; and in the night season, and am not silent."

Mark 15:34 "At the ninth hour Jesus cried out with a loud voice, 'Eloi, Eloi, Lama Sabachthani?' which is translated, 'My God, My God, why have you forsaken Me?'"

Matthew 26:38–39 "Then He said to them, 'My soul is deeply grieved, to the point of death; remain here and keep watch with Me.' And He went a little beyond them, and fell on His face and prayed, saying, 'My Father, if it is possible, let this cup pass from Me; yet not as I will, but as You will'"

Verse 6 "But I am a worm and not a man, a reproach of men and despised by the people"

Luke 23:21 "But they kept on calling out, saying, "Crucify, crucify Him!"

Verse 7 "All those who see Me ridicule Me; they shoot out the lip, they shake the head."

Matthew 27:39 "And those passing by were hurling abuse at Him, wagging their heads."

Verse 8 "He trusted in the Lord, let Him rescue Him."

Matthew 27:41–43 "In the same way the chief priests also, along with the scribes and elders, were mocking Him and saying, 'He saved others; He cannot save Himself. He is the King of Israel; let Him now come down from the cross, and we will believe in Him.' He trusts in God; let God rescue Him now, if He delights in Him; for He said, 'I am the Son of God.'"

Verse 11 "Be not far from me, for trouble is near; for there is none to help."

Mark 14:50 "And they all left Him and fled."

Verse 14 "I am poured out like water, and all My bones are out of joint."

John 19:34 "But one of the soldiers pierced His side with a spear, and immediately blood and water came out."

Verse 15 "My strength is dried up like a potsherd, and My tongue clings to My jaws. You have brought Me to the dust of death"

John 19:28 "After this, Jesus, knowing that all things had already been accomplished, to fulfill the Scripture, said, 'I am thirsty.'"

Verse 16 "For dogs have surrounded Me; the congregation of the wicked has enclosed Me. They pierced My hands and feet."

Verse 16 "They pierced My hands and feet."

John 20:25 "So the other disciples were saying to him, 'We have seen the Lord!' But he said to them, 'Unless I see in His hands the imprint of the nails, and put my finger into the place of the nails, and put my hand into His side, I will not believe.'"

Verse 17 "I can count all My bones; they look and stare at Me."

Luke 23:35 "And the people stood by, looking on. And even the rulers were sneering at Him, saying, 'He saved others; let Him save Himself if this is the Christ of God, His Chosen One.'"

Verse 18 "They divide My garments among them. And for My clothing they cast lots."

John 19:23–24 "Then the soldiers, when they had crucified Jesus, took His outer garments and made four parts, a part to every soldier and also the tunic; now the tunic was seamless, woven in one piece. So they said to one another, 'Let us not tear it, but cast lots for it, to decide whose it shall be.'"

Additional Psalms: Messiah's Crucifixion

Psalm 35:11 "Malicious witnesses rise up; they ask me of things that I do not know."

Mark 14:55–59 "Now the chief priests and the whole Council kept trying to obtain testimony against Jesus to put Him to death, and they were not finding any. For many were giving false testimony against Him, but their testimony was not consistent. Some stood up and began to give false testimony against Him, saying, We heard Him say, 'I will destroy this temple made with hands, and in three days I will build another made without hands.' Not even in this respect was their testimony consistent."

Psalm 35:19 "For they do not speak peace, but they devise deceitful words against those who are quiet in the land."

John 15:24–25 "If I had not done among them the works which no one else did, they would not have sin; but now they have both seen and hated Me and My Father as well. But they have done this to fulfill the word that is written in their Law, 'They hated Me without a cause.'"

Psalm 38:13–14 "But I, like a deaf man, do not hear; and I am like a mute man who does not open his mouth. Yes, I am like a man who does not hear, and in whose mouth are no arguments."

"Matthew 26:62–63 The high priest stood up and said to Him, 'Do You not answer? What is it that these men are testifying against You?' But Jesus kept silent. And the high priest said to Him, 'I adjure You by the living God, that You tell us whether You are the Christ, the Son of God.'"

Psalm 41:9 "Even my close friend in whom I trusted, who ate my bread, has lifted up his heel against me."

Mark 14:17–18 "When it was evening He came with the twelve. As they were reclining at the table and eating, Jesus said, 'Truly I say to you that one of you will betray Me—one who is eating with Me.'"

Psalm 64:4 "To shoot from concealment at the blameless; suddenly they shoot at him, and do not fear."

Luke 23:13–22

Psalm 69:7 "Because for Your sake I have borne reproach; dishonor has covered my face."

Matthew 26:65–67 "Then the high priest tore his robes and said, 'He has blasphemed! What further need do we have of witnesses? Behold, you have now heard the blasphemy; what do you think?' They answered, 'He deserves death!' Then they spat in His face and beat Him with their fists; and others slapped Him, and said, 'Prophesy to us, You Christ; who is the one who hit You?'"

Psalm 69:8 "I have become estranged from my brothers and an alien to my mother's sons."

John 1:11 "He came to His own, and those who were His own did not receive Him."

Psalm 69:21 "They also gave me gall for my food and for my thirst they gave me vinegar to drink."

Matthew 27:34 "They gave Him wine to drink mixed with gall; and after tasting it, He was unwilling to drink."

Psalm 31:5 "Into Your hand I commit my spirit; You have ransomed me, O Lord, God of truth."

Luke 23:46 "And Jesus, crying out with a loud voice, said, 'Father, into Your hands I commit My spirit.' Having said this, He breathed His last."

Psalm 40:6–8 "Sacrifice and meal offering You have not desired; My ears You have opened; burnt offering and sin offering You have not required. Then I said, 'Behold, I come; in the scroll of the book it is written of me. I delight to do Your will, O my God; Your Law is within my heart.'"

Hebrews 10:10–13 "By this will we have been sanctified through the offering of the body of Jesus Christ once for all. Every priest stands daily ministering and offering time after time the same sacrifices, which can never take away sins; but He, having offered one sacrifice for sins for all time, sat down at the right hand of God, waiting from that time onward until His enemies be made a footstool for His feet."

Psalm 86:5 "For You, Lord, are good, and ready to forgive, and abundant in lovingkindness to all who call upon You."

Luke 23:34 "But Jesus was saying, "Father, forgive them; for they do not know what they are doing.""

Messiah: Resurrected

Mark 16:6 "And he said to them, 'Do not be amazed; you are looking for Jesus the Nazarene, who has been crucified. He has risen; He is not here; behold, here is the place where they laid Him.'"

Romans 8:21 "That the creation itself also will be set free from its slavery to corruption into the freedom of the glory of the children of God."

Psalm 16:9–10 "Therefore my heart is glad and my glory rejoices; my flesh also will dwell securely. For You will not abandon my soul to Sheol; nor will You allow Your Holy One to undergo decay."

Acts 2:23–24 "This Man, delivered over by the predetermined plan and foreknowledge of God, you nailed to a cross by the hands of godless men and put Him to death. But God raised Him up again, putting an end to the agony of death, since it was impossible for Him to be held in its power."

Messiah: Our Eternal Hope

Psalm 89:27 "I also shall make him My firstborn, the highest of the kings of the earth."

Colossians 1:18 "He is also head of the body, the church; and He is the beginning, the firstborn from the dead, so that He Himself will come to have first place in everything."

Revelations 1:5 "From Jesus Christ, the faithful witness, the firstborn of the dead, and the ruler of the kings of the earth. To Him who loves us and released us from our sins by His blood."

Psalm 145:13 "Your kingdom is an everlasting kingdom, and Your dominion endures throughout all generations."

1 Timothy 1:3–4 "As I urged you upon my departure for Macedonia, remain on at Ephesus so that you may instruct certain men not to teach strange doctrines, nor to pay attention to myths and endless genealogies, which give rise to mere speculation rather than furthering the administration of God which is by faith."

Titus 3:9 "But avoid foolish controversies and genealogies and strife and disputes about the Law, for they are unprofitable and worthless."

Psalm 133:1 "Behold, how good and how pleasant it is for brothers to dwell together in unity!"

Appendix

Meet the Characters

Abiathar – son of Ahimelech
Abigail – wife of Nabal and David's second wife
Abinadab – a man of Kirjath Jearim in whose house the ark was kept for twenty years
Abishag – Shummanite woman who cared for David while ill
Abishai – brother to Joab and Asahel
Abner – son of Ner, commander of David's army
Absalom – David's third son
Achish – King of Gath
Adonijah – David's fourth son
Ahimelech – high priest, whose grandfather was Eli, the priest
Ahinoam – Jezreelite who was David's third wife
Ahithophel – David's counselor
Amalekites – Canaanites originally in the promised land
Amasa – David's nephew who became a military commander
Amnon – David's firstborn son
Araunah – owner of the threshing floor
Asahel – brother to Joab and Abishai, killed by Abner
Barzilli – David's wealthy supporter in Gilead
Bathsheba – wife of Uriah, wife of David
Cushite – Egyptian currier
David – youngest son of Jesse and second king of Israel
Doeg – an Edomite who was Saul's chief herdsman
Eliab – Jesse's eldest son
Gad – God's prophet who foretold a famine
Gibeonites – covenant-protected Canaanite people
Goliath – giant from Gath who served in the Philistine army
Hiram – King of Tyre
Hushai – David's friend
Ishbosheth – Saul's son

Jesse – grandson of Boaz and father of David
Joab – commander of David's army
Jonadab – David's nephew
Jonathan – Saul's son who befriended David
Medium Woman – consulted by Saul at En Dor
Men of Israel – the army of men from 10 tribes of Israel
Mephibosheth – Jonathan's lame son
Merab – Saul's eldest daughter whom he chose to be David's wife
Michal – Saul's daughter who became David's first wife
Moabites – descendants of Lot who occupied territory east of the Dead Sea
Nabal – wealthy farmer who lived in Maon
Nathan – God's prophet who followed in Samuel's footsteps
Obed-Edom – Gittite who housed the ark for three months
Philistines – war-like Canaanites who were descendants of Ham
Rizpah – Saul's concubine
Rizpah – Saul's concubine
Samuel – God's prophet and contemporary of Saul and David
Saul – first king of Israel, from the tribe of Israel
Sheba – rebal Benjamite
Shimei – madman and kinsman of Saul
Solomon – son of David and third king of Israel
Talmi – King of Geshur
Tamar – Absalom's sister, whom Amnon loved
Uriah – the Hittite and devoted warrior to David
Uzah – died after he touched the ark
Woman in Abel of Beth Maachah – God used her to preserve her city
Woman of Tekoa – a wise woman used by Joab to manipulate David's sympathy for
    Absalom
Ziba – Saul's servant
Zadok – priest in David's court

Guide for the Group Leader

These suggestions are useful for initiating discussion.

Chapter 1

1. Provide an introduction to the study of David. Describe how he made a difference in history, who he was as a person, and his relationship with God.
2. Briefly describe why Israel wanted a king and why God allowed it.
3. Provide a description of what David's family home life might have been like.
4. Introduce the scene of Samuel's visit to David's home and address the dynamics between family members.
5. Discuss what it is like to be chosen for something special. How does it make us feel?
6. Ask what it means to have a heart like God's heart. Even though the study gives a description of this, some answers will be personal and unique.

Chapter 2

1. Initiate a discussion about sheep, sheepherders and farmers; responsibilities, risks and rewards.
2. Ask the group to recall a serene place where the water is completely still and the grass is lush.
3. Describe a time when you were spiritually parched and in need of revitalization.
4. A path, a trail, a walkway all describe points of origination and destination. Ask for experiences the group has encountered on narrow paths and wide paths, obstacles in reaching their destination or delights they experienced while in route.
5. Tell of a frightening experience you have had and how the good shepherd alleviated your fears.
6. Research the use of oils with medicinal treatment and present findings.

7. A cup is a measure that provides a required amount or just satisfactorily meets the need. Ask how this compares to the promises of an overflowing cup.

8. Discuss the length of one's life and what percentage of it has been spent on appreciating God's goodness and mercy.

9. Ask the group about worship. Do we have restrictions with worship? Does worship only mean church attendance? How can we better worship God?

Chapter 3

1. Special procedures and rituals accompany the coronation of a king or the swearing in of a president. Discuss these procedures and or rituals, their significance and those that follow historical tradition.

2. When God wants to work in our life, he will make a way. Ask for testimonials where God's work went forward despite resistance, obstacles or disobedience.

3. Discuss the role of the Holy Spirit. How do we know his prompting? Is his presence in our lives temporary or permanent, personal or distant, satisfying or convicting, helpful or elusive?

4. Discuss the presence of evil spirits in our world.

5. Music therapy has become a popular treatment in healthcare. However, it historically dates back to David and Saul! Ask for examples of the benefits of music.

Chapter 4

1. Provide a photo of the Valley of Elah, where this account took place.

2. The account of David and Goliath has been considered by some to be a fable. Ask the group if they believe the account to be factual and why.

3. Special operations soldiers such as the Army Rangers and the Navy Seals show the same courage on the battlefront as David. Ask what are other similarities they may share.

4. Discuss sibling rivalry. Was it present in David and Eliab's relationship? Or were their other extenuating factors that led to family disharmony?

5. Open a discussion on the presence and influence of clergy in the military. Has their influence been reduced in recent years and do you think it makes a difference with the psychological trauma that war brings and methods of therapy and recovery?

6.   Marrying inside one's "class" or into a "good family" is still important in some circles. Saul demonstrated this line of thinking. Discuss trends and traditions within families.

Chapter 5

1.   Open the discussion with a description of friendship and ask the group to think about the best friend they ever had. As the lesson progresses, continue to compare their best friendship with David and Jonathan's.
2.   Present a difficult question but do not require answers, as this could be a sensitive topic: Have you ever been physically abused? David was mentally and physically abused. Yet, as the account shows, he was resilient and seemed to almost be unaffected by the mistreatment from King Saul. What is the reason for this?
3.   Ask "How have you been able to encourage a friend?"
4.   A sign of true friendship is generosity. Ask whether this is a virtue that we find in friendships today.

Chapter 6

1.   Discuss the problem of legalism in religious circles today. What is the group's understanding of laboring as compared to resting on the Sabbath?
2.   Ask the group for successful strategies that have been used to deal with the proud and self-assured. A strategy could be something as simple as expressing humility or as complex as challenging the truth.
3.   Play a video clip of military miracles. One suggestion would be God's Hand in the Six Day War https://www.youtube.com/watch?v=7wMIq6X4zi4 YouTube
4.   Discuss qualities or weaknesses of contemporary military commanders. Are these same characteristics observed in the conflicts between David and Saul?

Chapter 7

1.   When jealousy rears its ugly head, its impact can be devastating to relationships. Start a conversation on examples where this has happened. Emphasize solutions for jealousy such as
     •   Recognize that jealousy is rooted in selfish, vain and insecure emotions

- • Determine to love the person (I Corinthians 13:4)
- • Find contentment in the Lord's strength.

2. "Unequally yoked" marriages refer to the union of a believer with a non-believer. Ask for testimonials that speak to the importance of this biblical requirement.

3. Prepare the group's mindset for the account of David's joyful return to Jerusalem. Quote together Psalm 100.

4. Ask suggestions on how to best live with a spouse who is successful in life but does not acknowledge God.

5. In many ways, Abigail exhibited characteristics of the Proverbs 31 woman. Introduce these qualities so that as the group studies the account of Abigail, they will see the similarities.
   - • Earns respect and trust from her husband
   - • Unafraid of hard work
   - • Industrious and creative
   - • Shows care and concern for others, including her household
   - • Careful and skilled money manager
   - • Sensitive and responsive to the needy
   - • Makes her family her priority
   - • Supports her husband publicly
   - • Speaks words of wisdom
   - • Makes practical decisions
   - • Finds joy and strength in the Lord
   - • Praised by her husband and children
   - • Inner beauty dominates her appearance
   - • Provides an example of reverence for God

Chapter 8

1. Share stories of how obscure individuals became great leaders and compare to Saul's beginning.
   - • Benjamin Franklin, the son of a common candlemaker
   - • Frederick Douglas, former slave
   - • Thomas Edison, hearing disability and only 3 months of formal education
   - • Clarence Thomas, homeless as a child and abandoned by his father
   - • Others

2. Share stories of how power, privilege, and lack of ethics possessed and destroyed famous leaders.

- Alexander the Great (his arrogance resulted in failure to prepare for a successor)
- Napoleon (his ambition led to denial and non-acceptance of defeat)
- Nicholas II (unprepared and incompetent ruler who could not relate to his people)

3. Ask the group whether suicide is ever justifiable. It has been an exit strategy for some, but what better options might there be for the troubled individual?

Chapter 9

1. Elected officials have occasionally experienced difficult transitions to their new position, just as did David. Ask the group for a list of obstacles they have noticed in recent times with presidential incumbents (avoid a political discussion).

2. We often have close associates or family who are difficult to work with or who cause conflict. Begin a discussion describing characteristics of these people. (untrustworthy, self-serving, dishonest, contentious, scheming).

3. There are several accounts of murder in this study. Give the definition of murder.

   To kill deliberately or by premeditation in association with another crime (1st degree)

   To kill with intent but without deliberation or premeditation (2nd degree)

   Ask the group to consider these definitions as they read and discuss the study.

4. Provide a description of the Warren Shaft Tunnel System. http://www.jewishvirtuallibrary.org/biblical-water-systems-in-jerusalem Jewish Virtual Library

Chapter 10

1. Encourage the group, as they read the account of the Philistine battle, to assess what their response might be in a situation like this. Read aloud and discuss the situational application.

2. Mystery enshrouds the final destination of the ark of the covenant. One theory, among many, is that the ark is located under the temple mount in Jerusalem. The group may have interest to watch a 3-minute video https://

www.israelvideonetwork.com/the-ark-of-the-covenant-may-be-hidden-under-the-temple-mount-in-jerusalem/ by John Ankerberg

3. Ask for testimonials on a time when the group members may have put God first. What was the result, the reward or the lesson learned?

Chapter 11

1. We can be easily tempted by many things in life. Before we claim victory over temptations, we must first acknowledge what those temptations are. Ask the group to privately write a list of their own personal temptations. Each person can thoughtfully refer to the list during the study and apply the scriptures as needed.

2. Discuss the deceptions of Satan; especially the deception that Satan does not exist or that he holds no power over us.

3. We have the same temptations, desires, and weaknesses as David had. But we can also overcome the lure of sin by being strong in the Lord. Say this covenant prayer with the group.

> Lord, help me to always be alert and of sober mind. I Peter 5:8
>
> Lord, may I avoid temptation by being watchful and spending time in prayer. Luke 22:40
>
> Lord, teach me to rightly discern between my flesh and the Spirit. Galatians 5:17
>
> Lord, may I always be aware of your faithfulness to me. 1 Corinthians 10:13
>
> Lord, give me confidence that I can overcome with your strength. Philippians 4:13
>
> Lord, remove my fear of failure and replace it with trust in you. John 14:1
>
> Lord, you are all that I need and I promise to stay true to you. I John 4:4

Chapter 12

1. The consequences of sin always lead to sorrow; possibly not immediately, but at some point in time. Ask the group to recall one particular sin that affected them or their family. Evaluate
   - What pleasure or benefits did the sin bring?
   - Was it long-lasting or temporary?
   - Who did it effect and did the sin cause sorrow or suffering?

- Was it worth it?

2. Begin a prayer to confess unforgiven sin. Give the group a few silent moments to communicate with the Lord.

3. Read Psalm 30 together.

4. Resolve that you as a group will cling to the promises of Psalm 30
   - Beseech the Lord for healing.
   - Express thanks to the Lord for his forgiveness and favor.
   - Recognize that internal suffering need only be associated with unforgiveness.
   - Accept God's mercy as precious proof of forgiveness.

Chapter 13

1. Create a somber and virtuous atmosphere in preparation for the account of Amnon and Tamar. Pray for the group, that all conversation about the characters and situation might be respected and that all thoughts would be God honoring. Recite together Psalm 19:14.

2. The emotion of hate is prevalent in this chapter. Give the definition of hate. Intense dislike that results in hostility towards someone. Discuss the kinds of hate that we encounter today.
   Jealous, covetous, resentful, aggressive, passive, ect.

3. Study Romans 14:10

Chapter 14

1. Alfred Edersheim, in his article The Upbringing of Hebrew Children quotes, "Rabbi Jehudah, the son of Tema, says: "At five years of age, reading of the Bible; at ten years, learning the Mishnah; at thirteen years, bound to the commandments; at fifteen years, the study of the Talmud; at eighteen years, marriage; at twenty, the pursuit of trade or business;". More information is available at Bible Hub. Use this knowledge to better understand what Absalom's role and responsibility should have been.

2. Prior to studying Absalom's power grab, review the account of Jesus's disciples' attempts to receive power in his future kingdom. (Matthew 20:20-28) Focus on the importance of servant leadership in Christ's kingdom and compare to Absalom's interest in a forceful kingdom take-over.

3. David will travel across the Jordan River to escape Absalom in this study. Discuss the dangers and difficulties that David may have encountered on this trip. Consider his circumstances:

- Large entourage because of his position
- Enemies lying in wait
- Unpredictability of the Jordan River
- Other

4. Show a picture of a Terebinth Tree.

Chapter 15

1. Elizabeth Kubler-Ross's theory of grief claims that there are five stages which a grieving person experiences. They are denial, anger, bargaining, depression and acceptance. Place the five stages on a 11x7 poster for view by the group. Analyze David's grief together and determine if it was typical of the theory. Discuss the reasons. Also refer to Chapter 12.

2. God gave David discernment with choosing or losing friends and followers. Review the following verses that describe how God protected David from harmful relationships.
   - Psalm 3:1 (It was the godless who rose up against David, causing trouble for him)
   - Psalm 5:9 (Speech and flattery reveal his true friends)
   - Psalm 18:47 (God put men in subjection under David)
   - Psalm 28:3 (Acquaintances who lived pretentious lives)
   - Psalm 38:11 (Family and friends hesitated to help David in his hour of need)
   - Psalm 41:9 (Untrustworthy friends)
   - Psalm 55:12-13 (Friends who betrayed David)

3. Hebrew women were considered to be an intricate part of home activities, however, they seldom played visible roles as community leaders or organizers. Ask the group for a few examples of women in biblical history who were outspoken or who took a strong stand.

Chapter 16

1. David writes that God was a material and non-material resource for him. Begin a discussion regarding the resources God has been or provided to the group.

2. Discuss how God's power is seen through his creation.

3. Inquire whether God has rescued group members from danger. What were the circumstances?

4. As the group studies David's successes, remind them that they can be just as successful!
5. Ask the group if they are experiencing God's attributes in their lives.
6. Close the study with a group prayer where members participate with parts of David's prayer.

Chapter 17

1. The first biblical census is described in Numbers 1:1-3. Read these verses before moving into the study.
2. Provide a description of the plague. According to Wikipedia, plague is "an infectious disease caused by the bacterium Yersinia pestis. Symptoms include fever, weakness, and headache. Usually this begins one to seven days after exposure. In the bubonic form there is also swelling of lymph nodes, while in the septicemic form tissues may turn black and die, and in the pneumonic form shortness of breath, cough, and chest pain may occur. Bubonic and septicemic plague is generally spread by flea bites or handling an infected animal. The pneumonitis form is generally spread between people through the air via infectious droplets." Other than prevention, the only treatment is antibiotics. Large numbers of people died because of its contagious transmission and that treatment was unavailable.
3. Google pictures of threshing floors and display for the group.
4. The rightful succession of Solomon to the throne met with resistance from a sibling. This has been a common occurrence throughout history. Get a consensus of whether the group thinks Solomon has a right to the throne or whether it should be Adonijah.

Chapter 18

1. Fathers often pass down to their son valuable life lessons. Some examples would be:
    *   How to treat people
    *   How to manage money
    *   How to be a good husband
    *   How to take care of a home

    Ask the group to share examples of their own father's advice and role modeling. Include examples of spiritual leadership.
2. Solomon needed great insight to make some very difficult decisions. Ask the group, where do you think his wisdom came from?

Chapter 19

1. Review the meaning of the word Messiah with the group. It means anointed one who has a special, God-ordained purpose. The divine purpose was that Messiah would redeem his people from their sin through his death and resurrection.
2. Challenge the group to personally confess Jesus Christ as the Messiah as Peter confessed in Matthew 16:16 and Martha confessed in John 11:25-27.
3. Pray this closing prayer with the group. Dear God. I know that I am a sinner, and I ask you to forgive me. I believe that Jesus Christ is your son. I believe that he died for my sin and that you raised him to life. I want to trust him as my savior and follow him as Lord, from this day forward. Guide my life as I try to follow you and help me to do your will. I pray this in the name of Jesus Christ. Amen.

Notes

Notes

Notes

Notes

Notes

Notes

CPSIA information can be obtained
at www.ICGtesting.com
Printed in the USA
FSHW020045210319
56481FS